Why Are We Like This?

Stories of Transformation

Rowan Murphy and George Hightower

Copyright © 2025 by Rowan Murphy and George Hightower

All rights reserved.

No portion of this book may be reproduced in any form without written permission from the authors, except as permitted by U.S. copyright law.

This book is neither authorised nor approved by Netflix Studios LLC or Alice Oseman. Heartstopper® is a registered trademark of Netflix Studios, LLC.

Book Cover by Lenny DiChiara

First Edition November 2025

This book is dedicated to Alice Oseman, who has ignited a beacon of hope which helped us see that we are all worthy of joy and love. Thank you for helping us find and live our inner truth.

Rainbow Railroad, a global not-for-profit organisation, is the light at the end of the tunnel for many escaping persecution. A portion of the proceeds from this book will be donated to support their indispensable work.

Contents

1. An Advisement for Self-Care to Readers — 1
2. How a Sparkle Became a Beacon — 2
3. A Rainbow of Heart-Shaped Stories — 26
4. Rowan's Story — 46
5. George's Story — 56
6. The Power of a Positive Bisexual Portrayal — 65
7. Courtney-Jai Niner's Story — 74
8. NYMinTX's Story — 77
9. Laura's Story — 80
10. B's Story — 83
11. Michelle's Story — 86
12. Claudine's Story — 91
13. Heather's Story — 93
14. Suzie Davidson's Story — 95
15. Stephanie Archer's Story — 98
16. Lisa's Story — 100
17. The Gift of Asexual Representation — 103
18. Jackie Ross-Lavender's Story — 112
19. MP's Story — 116

20.	A. Murray's Story	120
21.	Caecilia's Story	123
22.	Iris' Story	126
23.	Sophie Grudin's Story	129
24.	Jae's Story	132
25.	Gender Journeys	134
26.	Rose's Story	141
27.	Sammy's Story	143
28.	Sunny's Story	145
29.	Zack's Story	148
30.	Jordyn Lenz's Story	152
31.	Marieke's Story	154
32.	A Message of Hope for Viewers with Mental Health Conditions	157
33.	Ruth K's Story	167
34.	Harry's Story	171
35.	Luke Adams' Story	175
36.	Heather's Story	180
37.	Izzy's Story	183
38.	C's Story	187
39.	Kayla P's Story	190
40.	Michaell K Herrera's Story	193
41.	Bellerine's Story	196
42.	From Surviving to Thriving	199
43.	Ann-Marie's Story	206

44.	Narnia's Story	212
45.	Joanne's story	215
46.	Rebecca P's Story	218
47.	Rhyn's Story	222
48.	Molly Robins' Story	224
49.	Bob's Story	227
50.	Claire's Story	230
51.	Brandon Ford's Story	233
52.	Community and Meaningful Human Connections	235
53.	Ashley Hullett's Story	243
54.	ZH's Story	246
55.	Harrison Taylor's Story	254
56.	AJ's Story	257
57.	Michelle W's Story	261
58.	A. Fletcher's Story	263
59.	PF's Story	267
60.	Lety's Story	272
61.	Kermit's Story	276
62.	Final Thoughts	280
63.	THE END?	283
	Acknowledgements	285
	Glossary	286
	Organisations supporting the LGBTQIA+ Community	298
	Mental Health and Crisis Resources	303
	Participant Demographics	306

About the authors

An Advisement for Self-Care to Readers

We couldn't publish this book without making readers aware ahead of time that some of its contents may elicit strong emotional responses.

Within these pages are many deeply personal and moving stories, some of which touch on trauma the writers experienced in their lives. While none of these narratives include graphic descriptions or explicit content, many of them have sensitive details that could be upsetting to readers.

Please be kind to yourself. If you need help, we have included resources for individuals in crisis or those in need of support for their mental health, to be found towards the end of the book (page 303).

All of these stories speak to the transformative effect *Heartstopper* has had on many lives, and they are a testament to the fact that hope prevails above all and that it is never too late to pursue a happier, more fulfilled life.

We sincerely hope that these stories leave you feeling seen and validated.

How a Sparkle Became a Beacon
By Rowan Murphy

Why write this book?

I was 50 years old when I first saw the Netflix show *Heartstopper* in May of 2022. It was pure coincidence that led me to watch it; I was staying with a friend, and I wasn't in a good place mentally or physically, so I had been looking for some light entertainment. Never in my wildest dreams did I expect to stumble upon a show that would become the catalyst for a seismic shift in my life, as you will see when you read my story.

Social media quickly revealed a growing fan base, which I joined. Through a particularly amazing Facebook group, I met hundreds of other fans online, and a few of them in person as well. Over time, I heard many stories and was both astounded and immensely relieved at seeing so many profound reactions to the show firsthand. Astounded, because some of the stories were not only incredibly powerful, but also spanned across a wide range of demographics. Relieved, because it proved I wasn't somehow unhinged, or that my reaction was disproportionate.

For the past three years, I have been wondering: What is it about this particular show that evokes such a strong and emotional reaction in so many folks from all walks of life? How did a sweet, LGBTQIA+ teenage love story become a phenomenon, causing such complex and far-reaching impacts across every imaginable population? How did it become the impetus for major, positive life changes?

After hearing so many truly inspiring and moving stories, I felt strongly that they needed to be shared with the world. Living in the political and social climate of the US in 2025 further reinforced my belief that we really need these stories of hope, courage, self-discovery, and resilience right now.

What is *Heartstopper*?

Most individuals picking up this book probably know everything there is to know about *Heartstopper*, but one should never assume, so here's a quick introduction.

Heartstopper is a coming-of-age romantic comedy/drama series based on Alice Oseman's webcomic and graphic novel by the same name. It revolves around Charlie, a somewhat anxious gay student at an all-boys grammar school in the UK, who strikes up an unlikely friendship with Nick, a popular, sporty, seemingly straight lad in the year above. If you've seen it, you know what happens; if you haven't, we will do our best not to spoil it for you entirely (but you should watch it as soon as possible!).

The show was produced by See-Saw Films, the makers of *Ammonite* and *Slow Horses* (and many other fantastic creations). Streaming rights were acquired by Netflix, where Season 1 was first released on April 22, 2022, with eight episodes lasting less than 30 minutes each.

Heartstopper was produced with a clear target audience in mind. Alice Oseman explained their goals for the show in early interviews: "There's a lot on TV now that has queer content, but it's definitely for adults," [...] and even now, "a lot of queer stories are still very serious or focused on trauma."[1] Netflix Kids & Family Content director Alexi Wheeler felt similarly, stating that the story "deserves to be told" due to its relatability among the young demographic.[2] The intent was to reach young LGBTQIA+ viewers, and special care was taken to have age-appropriate TV ratings to enable this reach.

Unexpected triumph and vast viewership.

What happened after the show was released came as a surprise to everyone involved in its production: Viewers of all ages (including those not part of the LGBTQIA+ community) were captivated, and the show became an overnight sensation. The existing fandom garnered by the webcomic and graphic novels was already quite large. The webcomic alone, which was updated weekly, had accrued over 124 million views,[3] yet the fan base grew exponentially when the show was released (as of July 2025, it reached 740 million views between Webtoon and Tapas, not counting Tumblr or Patreon).

"We definitely didn't think it would blow up to the extent that it has done. It's so mainstream now, like it's huge. I never imagined it could be that big," Alice Oseman stated in a radio interview. "I never imagined that so many people of all different ages and life experiences would be able to find something in *Heartstopper*, but they have, and that's really special."[4] Critical acclaim further

---

1. Lydia Wang, "For Writer Alice Oseman, 'Heartstopper' Fulfills a Years-Long Crush", Netflix Tudum, 22 April 2022

2. Alexi Wheeler, "Netflix UK Commissions 'Heartstopper,' a New 8-Part Live Action Series From See-Saw Film", Netflix Announcement, 20 January 2021

3. Alice Oseman's, "The History of Heartstopper", http://aliceoseman.com

4. Podcast with Tommy DiDario, Alice Oseman, and Patrick Walters on http://iheart.com, 21 October 2024

highlighted just how special and important the series was. At the inaugural Children's & Family Emmy Awards in 2022, Season 1 received 9 nominations and won 5 awards, including Emmys for Outstanding Young Teen Series and Outstanding Writing for a Young Teen Program.

The LGBTQIA+ representation at the heart of this series was unprecedented as recognised through multiple awards from LGBT+ organisations. For instance, Season 1 received the GLAAD Media Award for Outstanding Kids and Family Programming (an achievement that was repeated with Seasons 2 and 3), the Dorian Award for Best LGBTQ Show, Gay Times Honours in the category "On Screen Trailblazer", and an Attitude TV award (Attitude is a best-selling British LGBTQ+ lifestyle magazine).

The inclusion of a token gay, lesbian, bisexual, or trans character in a TV show wasn't new at the time. It wasn't exactly uncommon either. However, seeing all of these identities together, featured as the main characters, all in a single show? LGBTQIA+ characters that weren't there for comic relief, hyper-sexualised storylines, brutal trauma, death, or other sinister plot twists victimising them? That was certainly extraordinary. More remarkably, these characters' stories were centred around love, romance, joy, and hope, even while going through some admittedly painful plot points. Their struggles felt realistic, but they weren't the primary focus of the show.

> "It was so groundbreaking, the ordinariness of queer existence that it portrayed."
>
> Benwvatt

Most refreshing was the trans representation, which started with Elle in the first season and included more characters under the trans umbrella in subsequent seasons. This was quickly recognised in media coverage: "Elle, played by internet sensation Yasmin Finney, is a huge step forward in trans representation done right. [...] At a time where transphobia and openly transphobic stances are on the rise in the world, [...] it is refreshing and reassuring to see such a positive trans storyline."[5]

In an award acceptance speech, Yasmin Finney succinctly described what most of us felt: "I think I speak for 99% of the room when I say we all needed a *Heartstopper* growing up. And I am just so happy that we get to be that representation for the new generation to come. And they get to finally have the happy, positive, natural representation that they deserve. The queer TV magic isn't stopping there; it's only the beginning."[6]

Fan responses were immediate and overwhelmingly positive. *Heartstopper* became one of the top ten most-watched Netflix shows in the UK just two days after its release. Within a month, it had reached Netflix's Top Ten list in 54 countries, reaching the number one spot in many of them.[7] It launched with a remarkable 100% rating on Rotten Tomatoes (a feat it was able to replicate with both subsequent seasons).

The sweet innocence of first love and coming of age were portrayed beautifully; the cast had fantastic on-screen chemistry, and it was clear how much care and consideration every department involved in the production had taken. At its core, *Heartstopper* is a teen romance, the story of a somewhat unlikely match that

---

5. Elie Breton des Loÿs, "Heartstopper: Understanding The Phenomenon And Why It Matters So Much", *Unibathtime,* 10 June 2022

6. Natalie Clarkson, "Highlights from the 2022 Virgin Atlantic Attitude Awards – Michelle Visage, Heartstopper and More", http://virgin.com, 13 October 2022

7. Amber Dowling, "'Heartstopper' Sets New Trending TV Record as 'She-Hulk' Storms In", http://variety.com, 23 May 2022

blossoms into a tender relationship, showcasing all the joy and insecurity and hope that comes with the territory. Those qualities broadened the appeal of the show beyond the LGBTQIA+ community.

Oseman freely admitted they relied on tried-and-true romance tropes to reinforce the rom-com feel of the show, which has been likened to a warm hug or a cosy blanket. In an interview for Netflix Tudum, they stated, "I always think a trope is a trope for a reason. Tropes can feel overused. But when it's featuring marginalised characters, you probably haven't seen that as much as you think you have."[8]

This was the key point, exactly: because the tropes were applied to LGBTQIA+ characters, viewers were enchanted. Opposites attract, secrets, forced proximity (in the vertical form setting, where Charlie and Nick are made to sit together), happily ever after; these are all familiar themes in television shows, but not in this context. On top of that, we got to see Charlie – a bullied, young, gay teen – have a staunch defender in his best friend Tao, whose witty repartee entertained me to no end. We witnessed Charlie being gallantly rescued, by the captain of the rugby team, no less. Some of us who experienced bullying and/or physical assault in our younger years would have loved even a fraction of this kind of support. *Heartstopper* portrayed reciprocation of unconditional love and encouragement, something we don't often see for LGBTQIA+ roles. We watched emotionally intelligent characters modelling mature, healthy communication. Warm hug, indeed.

---

8. Lydia Wang, "For Writer Alice Oseman, 'Heartstopper' Fulfills a Years-Long Crush", Netflix Tudum, 22 April 2022

> "*Heartstopper* didn't just give me representation. It gave me hope, self-acceptance, and the belief that love, real, soft, meaningful love, is possible for me too."
>
> Braeden

More than a sweet LGBTQIA+ romcom

Beyond the positive viewer reception one might expect from a well-executed, sweet rom-com, the intense response from so many viewers indicated that something much deeper was happening. It wasn't quite the reaction one would expect from a sweet little show featuring 14- to 16-year-old teens with diverse identities. That in and of itself wouldn't cause such a multitude of diverse people to examine their own lives and make fundamental changes.

Many articles have been written in an attempt to explain the astonishing response to this show, which some have coined "*Heartstopper* syndrome". Terms like "phantom nostalgia"[9] have emerged as a description for older viewers' reactions, who expressed sadness about not having had similar programming and representation when they were younger. Add to that the wish that we, as LGBTQIA+ people, could have experienced a romance like Nick and Charlie's during our own school years, rather than facing the choice between bullying or hiding in the closet, and there's reason enough for nostalgia.

It's easy to forget how recent the legalisation of homosexuality was. Granted, capital punishment for being convicted of homo-

---

[9]. Manual Betancourt, "The Phantom Nostalgia of Heartstopper", http://vulture.com, 2 June 2022

sexual behaviour ended in the UK and the US in the 19th century, with the last executions taking place in 1835 and 1873, respectively. But other draconian measures still applied, including fines, jail time, and castration, and those remained in effect for another century (think Alan Turing). Gay and bisexual men and women continued to be arrested until the 1990s for public displays of affection with a member of the same sex.[10] That's not even 40 years ago.

Same sex marriage has only been legal for little over ten years in both the UK and the US, and hate crimes committed against members of the LGBTQIA+ community based on sexual orientation or gender identity didn't become punishable by federal law in the US until 2009.

Between the legal landscape and religious condemnation, along with the witch hunts of the McCarthy era, it comes as no surprise that the general public was largely homophobic, and these beliefs were passed on to new generations. Propaganda resulting from the AIDS crisis in the 1980s further fuelled the anti-gay sentiment and hateful rhetoric. To this day, society still embraces heteronormativity (the expectation of heterosexual relationships being the norm), which is deeply ingrained in our culture.

> "But the heteronormative society I've grown up in made sure I had never questioned my sexuality once."
> Claudine

When I see headlines about recent surveys finding that the proportion of LGBTQIA+ individuals is suddenly growing at an aston-

---

10. Peter Tatchell, "Don't fall for the myth that it's 50 years since we decriminalised homosexuality", http://theguardian.com, 23 May 2014

ishing rate, it seems disingenuous to assume that the numbers should be taken at face value, and that the youth of today has a higher rate of LGBTQIA+ members. I flinch when I read assertions that "Adults in these younger generations are far more likely than those in older generations to identify as LGBTQ+,"[11] because it seems obvious to me that there is so much more to these trends.

Growing up in a society whose moral code deems homosexuality to be shameful, unnatural, or even criminal, invariably affects a person's belief system, causing internalised homophobia and repression. I believe that Gen Z and Millennials are simply more willing to explore and understand their gender and sexual identity, and less likely to remain closeted, because they haven't experienced the same levels of judgment or hate. Lack of public persecution and easier access to information due to technological advancement play a big part in this, as does representation in print and broadcast media, which, until recently, didn't include many happy, positive storylines for LGBTQIA+ characters.

Media representation is an important component that shapes our self-perception. If all you ever see is that people "like you" are traumatised or ostracised, it influences your expectations in life – even if only subconsciously.

It is, therefore, not surprising to see a deeply emotional response to a show like *Heartstopper* from not only young viewers but also older generations, who experience a wistfulness induced by watching a beautiful love story that wouldn't have been remotely possible in our younger years. But for many, the impact goes far beyond just that contemplative melancholy. *Heartstopper* is much more than just a simple LGBTQIA+ teen rom-com. This television

---

11. C Mandler "The number of U.S. adults who identify as LGBTQ+ doubled in 12 years, new poll shows", http://npr.org, 13 March 2024

series has sparked introspection and self-discovery, and it has motivated people to actively pursue happiness and fulfilment.

> "More than anything, it said to me, 'Want more!', 'Don't settle!', and 'You are valid!'"
>
> Joanne

After sharing my thoughts and feelings with a very good friend of mine, we decided to explore this further. We made it our mission to find and share inspirational stories from fans of the show to illustrate the true impact of *Heartstopper*, and to demonstrate why a show like this is so very important, especially in the current social and political climate. We talked to lots of fans to find out what specifically resonated and how their lives have been irrevocably changed for the better.

Beyond the innocent romance of it all, this show touches on real issues that permeate the lives of the LGBTQIA+ community: discovering one's identity; the forced conformity imposed by society, and breaking free from it by owning who we are; the journey of coming out – including the violation of being outed against our will – and dealing with homophobia and bullying.

Seasons 2 and 3 also touch on serious mental health issues, body image, gender dysphoria, and eating disorders. These topics are handled with extreme care, and somehow, even through the painful journeys, *Heartstopper* manages to maintain its hopeful tone.

Themes that particularly resonated with fans were love, friendship, self-discovery, authenticity, LGBTQIA+ joy, resilience, and compassion. While these themes aren't necessarily new or revolutionary in their own right, they were absolutely groundbreaking in the context of a diverse group of LGBTQIA+ characters.

Every show has its critics

All in all, *Heartstopper* had an overwhelmingly positive response. "I like to think [the lack of negativity] is because *Heartstopper* is so positive and joyful and full of love, so it's hard to actively hate without seeming like a horrible person," said Oseman. "But that's not how bigots work, so I'm not sure how it's avoided that. But I'm glad that it has."[12]

Yet the hopeful tone and joyful ending, particularly after the first season, drew some mild criticism. Some called the show "unrealistic", "cringe", and "puritanical" (due to its lack of sex). This is a sad testament to how warped societal views still are around the rainbow community, especially as portrayed on screen.

Why do audiences still expect LGBTQIA+ characters in movies or TV shows to be either promiscuous, victimised, or stereotyped for comedic value? Despite the legal and societal improvements we have seen over the past 10-15 years, this still seems to be the general expectation – sometimes even within the community. Don't get me wrong, there is a time and place for camp, and for drama, but we need to be able to see ourselves portrayed as normal people, too.

> "If we were portrayed at all, we were either killer deviants or sissies in frocks; something to be laughed at ... and not in the Modern Family way. I often refer

---

12. Dan Seddon, "Heartstopper creator Alice Oseman shares surprise at reaction to season 1", http://digitalspy.com, 19 November 2022

> to *Heartstopper* as the After School Special we never had."
>
> Anthony David

I've looked at the main points raised by critics. One claim was that the show is unrealistic because "everyone's gay". That's actually a false statement. Yes, the **featured** characters are part of the LGBTQIA+ community. However, the majority of pupils at both schools are straight: We witness the bullying and toxic masculinity at the all-boys school, we hear disparaging comments and discussions about lesbians at the all-girls school; these represent the majority of the student body in both schools.

Teenagers are known to flock together based on shared interests or other commonalities. The friend groups featured in *Heartstopper* consist mostly of LGBTQIA+ characters, although they include some cis-het[13] individuals as well (prime example: Tao, the "token straight friend"). What we have here are minority individuals banding together and supporting each other in a relatively hostile environment. As Tao describes their little group, they are borderline outcasts, but their bond and mutual support are all the stronger for it.

As to the unrealistic nature of the blossoming relationship, let's be honest: A romance like Nick and Charlie's isn't the norm, whether you're gay or straight. But somehow, audiences have no issue with starry-eyed, fanciful romances and tropes when the characters are cis-het. After all, Hallmark has generated millions with its straight-laced, family-oriented, cheesy romance programming.

---

13. Cishet is a term blending the words cisgender and heterosexual. It is used to refer to a person whose gender identity aligns with their sex assigned at birth, and who is sexually attracted to members of the opposite sex.

Some viewers called *Heartstopper* the "purest, cleanest, most wholesome show"[14] ever. As mentioned earlier, some even called it puritanical. Strange, given the depiction of sexual assault in the very first episode, along with themes of bullying and homophobia, as well as the mental health issues that are hinted at in Season 1, which are further explored in subsequent seasons. Maybe it's become so normalised for LGBTQIA+ characters to go through these types of traumatic experiences that audiences are entirely desensitised to it. Also, this was a show designed for young teens – how graphic did folks expect it to get?

The rather innocent and optimistic tone of this show has also helped to protect it from censorship. Despite anti-LBGTQIA+ sentiments rising globally, *Heartstopper* is still accessible on Netflix in most countries, and the book has not been removed from many shelves – although it has faced temporary removal from some school libraries in Florida, Missouri, and Oregon. *Heartstopper* does not present the best target for right-wing partisans as it lacks the typical elements of LGBTQIA+ shows; there is no graphic violence, very little crude language, no explicit sexual scenes, and not much content that could be politicised.

The lack of sexual interaction between Nick and Charlie was another element of the show that critics referred to as unrealistic. One thing to keep in mind is that the age of consent in the UK is 16; at the start of the show, Charlie is only 14 years old. The decision to maintain a certain level of innocence was clearly deliberate, given the target audience, and it's no coincidence that the protagonists do not approach the realm of sexual interaction until Season 3, when Charlie is 16.

---

14. Dan Seddon, "Heartstopper creator Alice Oseman shares surprise at reaction to season 1", http://digitalspy.com, 19 November 2022

Aside from that, not everyone engages in sexual activity at 14 or 15. Does it happen? Absolutely! And there's certainly enough peer pressure to do so. According to a study by the NHS, while individual cases vary widely, the average age of first sexual interaction in the UK is 16-17 years.[15] A key consideration with *Heartstopper* is that in Season 1, Nick has just discovered a new facet to his identity, and he's still processing all of it. He's not likely to act on his physical attraction to Charlie immediately, especially considering he had no prior experience with intimacy. Both boys have reasons to take it slow; Nick is only just discovering his bisexuality and understanding what it means, and Charlie's experience with bullying and with a toxic ex-boyfriend has left him struggling mentally.

These emotional journeys are portrayed brilliantly by Joe Locke (Charlie) and Kit Connor (Nick), whose stellar performances brought their characters to life with such nuance and authenticity that they captivated audiences all around the world. As a result, they both shot to overnight fame, their social media following growing literally by millions.

The double-edged sword of rising to fame

The young cast of *Heartstopper* was relatively unknown; while some had prior screen experience (Kit Connor and Sebastian Croft, for example), they hadn't quite risen to international fame just yet, and many of the actors had never appeared on screen at all. The casting team discovered some extremely talented, intuitive people who brought the graphic novel to life with obvious care and passion, even though they never expected the show to achieve such levels of popularity. For some, *Heartstopper* became

---

15. "Sexual activity and the under-sixteens", https://www.nhsborders.scot.nhs.uk > patients and visitors > our services > general services > underage sexual activity interagency guidance

a launching pad into promising acting careers; Kit Connor and Joe Locke have both worked on several highly successful projects since then.

Kit and Joe each had critically acclaimed Broadway debuts in 2024. Joe also appeared in the Marvel series *Agatha All Along*, where he proved he could hold his own among a cast of powerhouse female actors (Kathryn Hahn, Aubrey Plaza, and Patti LuPone are certainly forces to be reckoned with). He was nominated for the Independent Spirit Award for Best Breakthrough Performance as Billy Kaplan in this series. Kit delivered a beautiful and heartfelt voiceover performance in *The Wild Robot*, which earned him an Annie Awards nomination for Outstanding Achievement in Voice Acting in an Animated Feature.

Both have been recognised for their commitment to LGBTQIA+ causes, not only for contributions to positive LGBTQIA+ visibility in the media, but also for using their platforms to raise awareness of the issues faced by our community. Among several awards and nominations, Joe received the Human Rights Campaign (HRC) Impact Award in 2025 for his role in *Heartstopper* and his wider work in bringing authentic LGBTQIA+ narratives to a global audience. His acceptance speech was astoundingly eloquent and mature, ending with the statement, "I promise to continue to use the platform that I've been given to do the right thing, not the easy thing." Similarly, Kit has received several LGBT-focused nominations and awards, including the British LGBT Awards in 2023, and made the top 20 on the UK Pride Power List for three consecutive years. He also won the first-ever Children's and Family Emmy Award for Outstanding Lead Performance in *Heartstopper*.

Unfortunately, their experiences haven't been solely positive. Like most active fan spaces, the *Heartstopper* community includes a small minority that harbours an unhealthy obsession with members of the cast. Overzealous fans are nothing new, and while parasocial relationships are fairly common in this day and age, they can reach an unhealthy intensity level. Sometimes, the lines between the actor and the role become blurred, and a fan is no longer able to separate the character from the real person.

In some cases, one-sided connections to celebrities can be enjoyable and enrich a person's life: fans bonding over a shared passion can make for wonderful friendships. Relating to characters who are positive role models can enable viewers to see themselves in a positive light and believe in their own worth and strength in ways they never have before. The cast have said in interviews that they enjoy the small tokens of appreciation they receive from fans and feel touched to know they're making such an impact on people's lives. But when fans become obsessive, they can have a detrimental effect.

The fascination is understandable, to an extent. Nick Nelson, for instance, is a lovable character: Not only is he good-looking and popular, he is also kind, compassionate, easy-going, intuitive, emotionally intelligent, and quite mature for his age. Kit Connor's rendering of Nick's self-discovery arc was incredible; he really brought emotional depth to his performance. The raw vulnerability that is portrayed as Nick goes through his sexuality crisis makes him relatable on so many levels, and even though he makes mistakes along the way, he owns up to them and apologises, trying to set things right. And he's completely besotted with Charlie, ready to take on the world for him, which makes it easy to forgive any minor missteps.

Many fans have expressed the wish to find their "own Nick Nelson", citing this character as the gold standard for a romantic partner. On the surface, there's not too much wrong with this, especially when it becomes a catalyst for people to realise that they deserve unconditional love and that it is okay to want a relationship based on mutual respect and support. Still, it becomes problematic when fans are so invested that any hint of a romantic or even close platonic relationship in the actor's life causes them to spiral.

Kit Connor, early on, appeared to be the target of unhealthy fan fixation. He was harassed online with accusations of "queerbaiting" (a misuse of the word) over a photo of him holding hands with a female actor he was working with at the time. To my horror, which was shared by almost everyone in the fandom, the cyberbullying led to him capitulating and unwillingly coming out as bisexual on Twitter:[16] "I'm bi. Congrats for forcing an 18-year-old to out himself. I think some of you missed the point of the show. Bye." (Kit's Twitter post on 31/10/2022)

How people could call themselves fans of this particular show and then engage in this type of behaviour is beyond me. As Alice stated in a response to Kit's tweet: "I truly don't understand how people can watch *Heartstopper* and then gleefully spend their time speculating about sexualities and judging based on stereotypes [...]." One of the main points of the show and graphic novel is that no matter how a person presents, you should never speculate about their sexuality, and they do not owe anyone that information. In fact, viewers felt a sense of release from this message, expressing that the pressure of finding a label to describe oneself can be quite limiting.

> "It made me feel like I could breathe, just a little. Like I didn't have to be all the way out, or all the way certain, to be real."
>
> A. Fletcher

---

16. Emma Saunders, "Heartstopper's Kit Connor says he was 'forced' to come out as bisexual", http://bbc.com, 1 November 2022

> "I've been a lot happier not identifying with a label and just loving whoever I want."
>
> Kenadie Benales

The outpouring of support for Kit from the vast majority of the fandom showed that, no matter how vocal the toxic few, their voices will continue to be drowned out by waves of positivity.

Joe Locke also experienced the downsides of being in the public eye, and addressed the common issue of privacy violation in the lives of celebrities in an interview with Teen Vogue:[17] "There's an idea that it's part of the job to lose your privacy, that you lose your right to having privacy. That's something I hope the next generation of people in the public eye can change…. I think people are understanding that privacy is a non-negotiable." […] Locke is also considerate of the sacrifices made by his friends and family. "It's a weird guilt I sometimes feel that, by association, their lives are affected by choices in my life," he says. […] "It's a mutual thing. I need to learn my boundaries, and people need to learn their boundaries. Most attention comes from a really good place, and I hope I always appreciate that."

Anyone who has been involved in a fandom at some point in their life will know that these experiences, unfortunately, are quite common. However, they feel particularly jarring and out of place in the *Heartstopper* community, which is founded on love, compassion, and mutual respect. I have found that within our circle of fans, the response to any issues is to refer back to the ethos of the show and graphic novels. Most of the fans I've encountered are exceedingly kind, accepting, and supportive of each other; the

---

17. K-Ci Williams, "Kit Connor and Joe Locke's Friendship Is Heartstopper's Unsung Love Story", Teen Vogue, 7 August 2023

primary fan group in which I still actively participate today quickly nipped unkind or problematic interactions in the bud at the very beginning and established a true safe space for any fan of the show, regardless of demographic.

I admire these young actors for handling their sudden rise to fame with such poise and maturity. For his part, Joe's performance as Charlie Spring was brilliant. Considering that this was his first on-screen acting gig, his achievement is all the more impressive. From the first episode, Charlie's character had me spellbound. I was able to identify with his story on so many levels, and it was portrayed with obvious care and authenticity. I didn't know at the time that Joe Locke had no prior screen credits, and I would never have guessed it.

Charlie is a character that most LGBTQIA+ individuals can relate to, at least to some degree. Many of his challenges and trials are part of the fabric that makes up our community: Bullying, homophobia, and mental health issues – these are quite common for us. But underneath it all, he shows enormous strength and fortitude. He knows who he is, and he won't compromise that. He cares deeply for those who are close to him, and his quiet confidence is seriously inspiring, even when he can't see it himself. Alice wrote this character in a way that deeply resonated with me, as I'm sure it has with many others.

As the story continued in Seasons 2 and 3, Joe's acting talent became even more obvious. He and Kit were a powerful duo, navigating the complex and serious topics of eating disorders, self-harm, and the feelings of helplessness and emotional anguish a person can experience while supporting a loved one who is struggling. The roles became more demanding, but these two young men really rose to the challenge, delivering powerful and memorable performances.

Life-changing impact for some

When fans started sharing the transformative impact *Heartstopper* had on them after the first season, there were many narratives about late-in-life discovery, including a newfound freedom to re-evaluate sexual orientation without shame. So many stories were shared about journeys of self-realisation and/or coming out: People who realised they had repressed a part of themselves felt liberated in acknowledging their bi- or pansexuality; many felt safer in acknowledging facets of their identity, and some even used the show to come out to family and friends. Older LGBT+ folks shared their feelings of sadness and how it was a healing balm, alongside happiness that younger generations would not be saddled with the same amount of shame or fear.

Unsurprisingly, the asexual representation on the show, particularly in Season 2, helped quite a few people realise that they weren't alone in their lack of sexual and/or romantic attraction. Asexuality is one of the identities the general public is probably least aware of, and it is woefully underrepresented in all forms of media. Witnessing Isaac's journey of discovering that he's aromantic and asexual (aro/ace), which is at odds with what he had always believed about himself, was a revelation to many.

Self-actualisation has no age limit, nor does the healing of old wounds, as many older fans will attest. Authentic representation can have an enormously powerful impact. Seeing something within yourself reflected in another person, fictional or real, is a huge relief when you've always felt out of step, like you were different or didn't fit in.

Belonging (the feeling of acceptance, security, and connection within a group) is widely recognised as one of the fundamental needs of human beings. I could write pages on this, but I will spare readers that particular soapbox. The reason this is important here is that an existence outside of "societal norms", whatever those may be, can be a cause of alienation, rejection, and isolation. There were ages when our very survival depended on being part of a tribe or community, and even in modern times, we will go to great lengths to avoid marginalisation. This becomes tricky, however, when the essence of who we are is at odds with established norms. Conformity offers a certain sense of security, as we "fit in" with general societal expectations, yet it requires those of us who are inherently "different" to abandon our true selves. That degree of inner conflict is detrimental to both our mental and physical health.

The level of positive representation and normalisation of LGBTQIA+ identities in *Heartstopper* was momentous to fans of all ages, ranging from under 15 to 75 and beyond. While ageism was definitely an issue in the fandom early on, due to younger fans not understanding the fascination the show had for older people, which led to some disparaging comments, it gradually diminished – especially as the community grew and older fans discovered they weren't a small minority. Many of the larger social media groups also have admin teams to ensure mutual respect and resolve conflict when it arises; in my favourite group, there is zero tolerance for any form of bullying or phobia.

Our elder LGBT+ members deserve our admiration; without them fighting for equal rights, a show like *Heartstopper* would never have been possible. (Side note: Out of respect for our elders, George and I are avoiding use of the word "queer" in our writing, though it will still appear in fan stories or direct quotes. Many older fans have voiced a strong dislike due to the originally derogatory meaning of the word, even though younger generations feel like they have reclaimed it.)

There are a lot of possible explanations as to why so many people from all walks of life connected so intensely with this show, and I have my own thoughts on this. Many of the fans who wrote about figuring out facets of themselves that place them in the LGBTQIA+ community have wondered why this show, as opposed to any other LGBT+ show they had seen in the past, reached something inside of them that others failed to do, and led them to self-discovery. I was in the same boat, so I pondered this at length.

I believe that the way LGBTQIA+ characters have historically been portrayed has allowed people, particularly those of us who lived a mostly heteronormative life, to maintain some level of emotional distance. While there certainly have been relatable stories, many of which made me emotional, the characters were written in such a way that they maintained some level of stereotyping or stigma, such as rampant promiscuity, exaggerated camp, or dealing with HIV. Their plotlines were usually related to trauma that is specific to the community, so I was never able to fully immerse myself in these characters, not having been part of that world.

Heartstopper, on the other hand, presents fairly typical teenage experiences that include elements which practically everyone can relate to, while sexuality and gender identity didn't take centre stage the whole time (especially in Season 1). We've all been teenagers once, and we remember what it was like to grow up and come of age. By showing a shared experience with likeable characters and normalising the LGBTQIA+-specific elements, it limits our ability to maintain that internal distance and invites us in to make that emotional connection. For many of us, this has led to more openness to explore our own identity and examine our lives.

Surprising levels of participation

When we first asked fans to share their stories, we had no idea what to expect. After all, these journeys are deeply personal and would require a willingness to be vulnerable, even if sharing them anonymously. Neither of us is an influencer, nor do we have a large following on social media, so there was no guarantee that people would be interested or ready to share.

We were delighted to not only receive many responses, but also to hear from other fans how much they liked our idea and supported this endeavour. Within four months, we had more stories than we could possibly print, so we reviewed every entry and made a preliminary selection of about 75 stories which contained common experiences within the fandom and were heartfelt. After editing these, I worked directly with each of the storytellers; most of them met with me in video or audio calls to review and finalise their submissions together, and the stories of those who needed to protect their privacy and anonymity were collaboratively edited via email. Sharing vulnerable and emotional pieces of yourself is never easy, and I applaud the courage of every single person who submitted their story. We included 50 stories in this book that represent the majority of experiences shared with us; it wasn't easy to choose, but we tried to pick the most compelling and meaningful experiences, the stories that made us feel the strongest emotional connection. We also wanted to incorporate the most poignant statements from the unpublished stories, which you will see scattered throughout the introductory sections we wrote for this book.

Truly profound life changes have been brought on by *Heartstopper*. Most stories involved forms of self-discovery, some unrelated to gender and sexual identity. Fans examined their lives from various angles and began seeking happiness in so many different ways. Some were compelled to leave abusive relationships, aim for more fulfilling careers or creative endeavours, form deep and lasting friendships, start therapy to deal with trauma, or even use insights from the show as teaching tools. It's really incredible what amazing things this show has motivated people to do. Not only that, but it literally saved lives, including mine and George's.

These are the stories we felt duty-bound to share because they are genuinely captivating. They are stories of strength, resilience, courage, and hope. Finding the capacity to love oneself and being willing to take risks in order to actively pursue love, fulfilment and joy – what is more inspiring than that?

> "I am finally awake and happier and more in love with life and myself than before."
>
> Kayla P.

A Rainbow of Heart-Shaped Stories

By George Hightower

You are holding a rainbow of heart-shaped stories in your hands. Each page that you turn is a page of someone's heart. Notice the watermark of love on each page.

The fans who courageously shared their innermost thoughts and feelings did so for the benefit of readers in the hope that it would validate, empower, and assist them in healing the fragmented parts of themselves that hurt. For some, the process of putting their deeply emotional experiences to paper was cathartic and healing; for others, it was painful and difficult. Some shared their stories at great risk to life and limb since they are surviving in regions where even the suspicion of being LGBTQIA+ could lead to dire consequences for themselves and their loved ones.

All credit goes to those who contributed their stories, whether they were included in this book or not, for they brought us closer, and offered greater clarity, to answering the multifaceted question: why are we like this? Without their participation, this book would not exist. I hope readers will feel supported and uplifted by these stories.

The life-changing impact that *Heartstopper* had on my life is what first planted the seed in me, in 2024, to write a book about its profound effect. After discussing it with my friend Rowan, we decided to write it together because we had both heard many stories from fans about how the show profoundly changed their lives for the better. I could not remain quiet in the face of so much collective pain and growth. The least I could do was bear witness and honor the commonality of experiences that bind us together in the same safety net of love.

Many of the contributors to this book have expressed their appreciation to Alice for the life-changing impact her work has on their lives. As a way of honoring their wishes, we've chosen to dedicate this book to her. *Why Are We Like This?* exists as an acknowledgement of the profound ways in which Alice and the cast members infused their characters with their hearts to transform ours. The overwhelming number of submissions we received serves as a testament to how much their cherished work and personal sacrifices have forever changed the course of more lives than can fit in any book. I firmly believe there is no higher art form than that which alleviates the suffering of others and inspires them to make their own world and thus the wider world a better place.

Timestopper

Thoughtful consideration was given when creating this book to ensure its message would be right for posterity and not just for now. In two hundred years, a viewer may look at *Heartstopper* as a love letter not only to the past, but to future generations, and as a time capsule that captured the best of the LGBTQIA+ community during a time of challenge and struggle. Perhaps they will look upon the program with awe for showing them a glimpse of what our community was and aspired to be. Conceivably, they may regard this fandom with the same reverence and gratitude as we regard our community's elders, upon whose shoulders we stand.

> "It will forever be a part of history as the *Heartstopper* cast tells this heart-stopping story that will live rent-free in our minds, souls and hearts FOREVER."
>
> Lisa Dimmitt

For many fans, we remember the exact moment in time when our hearts stopped, missed a beat, and reset with a renewed resolute rhythm, in sync with *Heartstopper's* heartbeat. Whether that moment was when Nick rescued Charlie from Ben, Nick and Charlie's epic first kiss, Nick's coming out to his mother, or the long-awaited "I love you", the result was universal: we were no longer the same. Some viewers have said that a certain scene "broke" them. It is understood that they meant it broke their heart. However, given the subsequent magnitude of transformation, one might conclude that what they really experienced was a **breakthrough**.

Some of us have marked that watershed moment like Neil Armstrong did when he first walked on the moon, and the whole earth looked different. *Heartstopper* allows us to warp time by enabling us to look back at past clouds from a higher perspective while also shifting into the future to envision a sky with brilliant rays of hope.

> "I saw hope that even in my struggles, I could find my way through. I felt at home."
>
> Art

The timing of the Netflix series is crucial; the world needs its message of unconditional love and acceptance now, more than ever, because of increasing violence and LGBTphobic encroachments on our rights in many countries. It functions as an antidote to the rising tide of hatred and is a balm to the heart. It synchronizes hearts all over the world, dissolving distance to a single point in time. When it was released, we were still in the wake of isolation due to the pandemic. This afforded some viewers more time for introspection, connecting through online forums, and carefully analyzing episodes. It enabled their hearts to sometimes heal at a subtle and slower pace, allowing for incremental shifts that, over time, coalesced into a monumental transformation.

> "*Heartstopper* helped me so much to take my time to figure things out and even embrace the uncertainty in the journey, where I could just be questioning."
>
> Pauli

Heartstopper's approach is cumulative. A simple smile or furtive glance may seem slight, but repeated over time, it can become a grammar of love that fans internalize. The same applies to intimacy and tenderness, which are built in a series of moments that invite multiple viewings and slow attention.

For some, it is bittersweet to consider the years of healing and happiness that could have been experienced sooner had *Heartstopper* existed when they were younger. "Time makes us sentimental. Perhaps, in the end, it is because of time that we suffer".[1] The show has reset the clock for some older fans by rewinding them and allowing them to dream and heal in reverse.

> "I'm just relieved that future generations of queer kids will have stories like Nick and Charlie's to read and watch to help them on their journey."
>
> Oli

---

1. André Aciman, Call Me By Your Name

Liberating the inner child

Heartstopper appeals to many different demographic groups because it connects with a universal common denominator: the inner child. The show unlocked a memory cage to reveal hidden pathways to self-understanding, which led to transformation. By engaging our inner child, Alice narrowed the gap between our physical age and our inner child's age, thereby shortening the time to unite and heal the two at once. That is why age does not determine the magnitude of transformation, or relatability to *Heartstopper*, which resonates with the ageless part of us.

For those who were bullied or ostracized as children, an invisible minefield of memories and unresolved trauma can remain. *Heartstopper* sheds light on the trip wires, so we can slowly tiptoe to a safe place where we can process surfacing emotions gently, and at our own speed.

> "*Heartstopper* made me realise that several wounds of my past are still affecting me today, and, in a way, it has helped me repair some of them. I didn't understand it right away, but the fact that I had to watch it over and over was a clue."
>
> Adele

It is difficult to care for a wound that one is unaware of. *Heartstopper* reveals our wounds and shows us that there is a better way to heal. Its characters model how to navigate through life with perseverance, communication, and compassion. Perhaps more importantly, it teaches us that *how to deal with an issue is the issue*. For example, Nick followed the advice he received from his aunt about how to best help Charlie. He also started journaling as a way to deal with his own concerns. More importantly, it was the honest and gentle way he supported Charlie through his mental health issues that made it easier for Charlie to heal.

The fact that so many of us experienced such powerful memories, thoughts, and feelings after watching the show is not a coincidence. We were ready to tackle what came up, even if we thought we weren't prepared at the time. That powerful awareness can enable our inner child and adult to move mountains together going forward, even if we feel that we are not ready. That may be one reason why many of the story contributors report moving through blocks that previously held them back. Seeing how the characters navigate through similar challenges empowers us to follow in their footsteps.

> "*Heartstopper* has given me a way to heal those old wounds; I hadn't understood that they were not fully healed until I realized that's the reason why I love [the show] so much."
>
> Mark A. Barnhouse

Emotional Quotient and Intelligence Quotient

LGBTQIA+ characters have often been portrayed in the media as having a lower emotional quotient (EQ), also known as emotional intelligence, than intelligence quotient (IQ). They have been depicted as unstable, impulsive, emotional, irresponsible, and self-destructive. Many of the *Heartstopper* characters demonstrate high EQ, such as Nick, who is understanding and communicative even though he's still just a teenager. Tao responds in a patient and mature fashion when Elle confides that she is experiencing gender dysphoria. Tori consistently demonstrates an intuitive connection to Charlie and senses when there is something wrong, to the point of asking Nick when he is going to return from vacation out of her concern for him. Even Issac quickly dispenses with being upset and shifts towards compassion after finding out that Charlie lied to him when he told him that he was okay, even though he really wasn't [S3 E2]. The show offers viewers a blueprint for higher emotional literacy by demonstrating qualities such as forgiveness, apology, and support for one another. This pedagogical model can shape young minds and old memories to a higher standard. Many of the contributors to this book show a strong correlation between the qualities they observed in *Heartstopper* and what they are striving to have more of in their lives.

> "The friendships and relationships in the series have modeled the types of people I want to surround myself with."
>
> Winston

Come out, come out, wherever you are

Many of the stories we received involved people coming out to others, including to their parents. Some did not come out to their parents until much later in life, if at all. A few of the contributors who are parents said that, because of what they learned from *"Heartstopper* University", they would educate their kids earlier about diversity so that they would feel safe growing up to be their authentic selves.

In this section, by "coming out", I am referring to parents coming out to their children with a welcome mat of unconditional love at an early age. To directly communicate to them first that no matter who they are or will become, they will always be loved and embraced. The burden for a young person to come out first is counterintuitive and demonstrates the danger of preprogrammed assumptions that their child is or will grow up to be straight. The degree of a parent's willingness to adhere to that assumption can equal the amount of unnecessary fear and anxiety that their kid may experience during their coming out process or their decision not to. By releasing that assumption, parents can grease the skids for their children to have their coming-out experience be angst-free and loving.

> "I took my almost-7-year-old son to London to the Alice Oseman pop-up, and he came to Pride too; and just knowing that I am showing him that it is absolutely fine to be whoever you are (and love whoever you want to) makes me so happy."
>
> Kayleigh Clarke

The Sword and Shield

For many viewers, Nick Nelson appears as the archetype of the knight in shining armor; however, beneath his glistening breastplate, there's a vulnerability that is actually a source of strength. As you delve into these stories, look for the hidden shining knight; he is there within you.

> "I realized after some reflection that what touched me most is that the characters were loved for all of their strengths and needs, and were beautifully strong in their vulnerabilities, and beautifully vulnerable in their strengths."
>
> Melanie Pearl

In contrast to so many other popular male characters, Nick is a shield for Charlie, and sometimes for himself. He is strong, resilient and has the tender heart of a lover, not a fighter (except for that time in the cinema). He is full of kindness, which tramples the toxic trope that "real" men are tough and unkind – a mentality that can fuel bullying. Society teaches boys and men that to be vulnerable or kind is to be weak and less of a man (more like a woman), which underscores the inherent misogyny that is a root of homophobia. Nick redefines what it means to be a man liberated from societal expectations. Some of us who have been shaped by society have unwittingly surrendered our personal power. Nick shows us how we can reclaim it by being true to our authentic selves. Many of the stories in this book involve the reclamation of personal power.

The knight archetype involves the protection of the innocent and the courage to fight valiantly for what is right. Some of us who had been bullied many years ago were incapable of dreaming of even the possibility of someone who could rescue us. For those fans, seeing Charlie rescued by Nick in so many ways fulfills an unconscious wish. What makes the dynamic between Nick and Charlie interesting is that Charlie is also protective of Nick and helps him come to terms with his awakening by giving him courage. This bidirectional mirroring reflects a more realistic relationship because, like most people, Nick has his issues, too.

It is important to see a bisexual character represented as loving and nurturing. Detractors have labeled Nick as an unattainable figment of fantasy, too perfect to be real. I perceive the opposite. Nick presents a wonderful opportunity to raise our standards for what we want in a loving relationship. Why can't we aim to have a partner in our life who embodies Nick's positive traits, and is simultaneously allowed to be vulnerable and imperfect? To not only be loved, but to be loved exceptionally well, and show that same love to our partners.

> "I kept telling my daughter that when she looks for a boyfriend/girlfriend, to accept nothing less than a Nick Nelson, as that's what she deserves. Bad experiences made me realise I deserve a Nick Nelson, and I deserve to be happy within myself. I thought for so long I didn't deserve happiness."
>
> Amy Williams

It may be an oversimplification to regard the lower standards some have settled for as a manifestation of internalized homophobia; however, being bombarded with negative messaging from society, religion, and government can make some feel like they are unworthy of better. We can reclaim our power, pursue our highest aspirations, and in the process, demonstrate to ourselves and others that we are worthy of a seat at the table as much as anyone else. We are worthy of a feast of love.

In contrast, it might be easy to misperceive Charlie as a victim archetype; however, that would be inaccurate. The fortitude he possesses to face his outer bullies and inner struggles, day after day, in a difficult environment, demonstrates resilience and an inner strength, like a sword in a stone. It is the degree of challenge that tempers the sword he needs for the hard work to address his mental health issues. He becomes worthy of wielding that sword through his journey, which he couldn't have done without Nick fiercely protecting and loving him. That sword becomes a shield, enabling him to always come to Nick's defense when Nick needs him.

Those of us who have been bullied and had legitimate reasons to feel victimized may benefit by connecting with our inner knight, who brought us this far. Perhaps we are stronger than we were led to believe, and it is the bully who is weak. Some of the stories in this book reflect how people discovered their strength because Nick and Charlie handed them the sword of truth to reveal their true potential and purpose.

Better Together

There has been much discussion about why female fans, regardless of their orientation, have fallen so deeply in love with Nick and Charlie and their relationship. 59% of the stories that we received were from cisgender women, most of whom are bisexual. I can only speculate about the reasons for this. My attempt to shed some light on it is admittedly imperfect in that it may represent simplified suppositions. For every stereotypical example present-ed, there are even more exceptions. As a gay man, I could write a book about this topic alone.

Throughout history, unique friendship dynamics have existed between many gay and bisexual men and women. In a world where women and gay men have been historically oppressed and treated inferiorly, it is easy to see what they have in common. Both groups know what discrimination and marginalization feel like. They share an understanding of the grammar of repression, toxic masculinity, and privileged patriarchy. Because of their commonality, they may trust each other more easily. Where there is trust, there is bound to be deeper communication and the sharing of secrets, which offers a powerful bonding experience. We received some stories from women who reported that they did not feel safe confiding in their partners. In contrast, I know of several women who knowingly married gay men and had happy marriages where each was the other's confidant. It is therefore understandable how the friendships in *Heartstopper* provide a model for how gay or bisexual men and women can relate to each other with affinity. Charlie's friendship with Elle is one example, and so is Nick and Tara's relationship.

Not only do gay men not pose a threat sexually, which allows women to feel safe enough to let their guard down, but women can connect emotionally to gay men in ways that they may be unable to with their straight male partners, who may not know how to be emotionally available or care to know. Conversely, some gay men may feel safer having an emotionally intimate friendship with a woman instead of a straight man. Generally, women pose little threat of violence to a gay man. Some gay men are more in touch with their feminine polarity than straight men and can enjoy common interests with women that historically have been limited to the feminine domain. So, the friendship between gay men and women is one of equals, where women do not have to fear being dominated, abused, or controlled.

Similarly, important qualities that many women want in a partner are emotional and mental intimacy. Nick's patience and listening skills make it easy to feel safe and communicate with him on an intimate level. In many ways, he is a poster boy embodying the qualities of a balanced Renaissance man. He is strong and gentle, mature and childlike. The conjoining of these contrasting opposites can be very alluring in its rarity and beauty, and so it is understandable how some women would be drawn to someone like that. They can dream of having a future partner like him, and a relationship like the one Nick and Charlie share.

To see Nick and Charlie care for each other as equals with tenderness, kindness, and respect for boundaries may be an epiphany to some women who might not have experienced this from a partner. Women who have been in dysfunctional relationships may look at what Nick and Charlie have as ideal. At the same time, they may miss not having that with their partners. To see these boys communicating feelings unreservedly, apologizing freely, and being loving toward each other can be a paradigm shift, representing hope for the future and sadness for the past. It also breaks with more common media tropes depicting men in conflict, competition, violence, trying to one-up each other, or mistreating women.

Some men who have close functional relationships with their mothers, like Nick, may find it easier to befriend women because that is what they are more accustomed to. When you factor this in with some women's propensity to be protective maternally, the mutual compatibility and attraction are understandable.

One size does not fit all

Some of the contributors referenced their struggle with mental health issues and decided to seek professional help. Contending with the challenges of being LGBTQIA+ in a sometimes less-than-welcoming world can be, in and of itself, a direct cause of being unsteady, and the double stigmatization only compounds the problem. Some psychological professionals who are not members of the LGBTQIA+ community, despite their best intentions, do not fully understand the LGBTQIA+ experience and take a one-size-fits-all approach to treatment, which can lead to ineffective results or worse. This can be true when it comes to addictions, anxiety, depression, and eating disorders in particular, which are highly complex to treat and may involve adjunct abandonment issues that a straight eye can't perceive.

Is it any wonder that so many beleaguered members of the LGBTQIA+ community suffer from mental health issues, given the fact that our very right to exist is under increasing threat? We live under many forms of societal pressure, yet when our backs break, society says, "Oh look, a sick camel!" while ignoring the mountain of straws at our feet.

A number of the stories in this book include some degree of bullying or the fear of being bullied. This is a common experience in our community, one that many of us are still processing. To have survived bullying is an indirect act of defiance, even if it was not realized at the time. It takes great power and resilience to endure suffering. Perhaps that power and courage are what bullies subconsciously seek, because they themselves lack it. Our collective light can illuminate the dark spaces for those who are still suffering, while casting shadows on bullies like Harry and Ben, who think they convey strength when they only demonstrate cowardice in camouflage.

By the end of season 2, watching Charlie, we see that the trauma he endured at the hands of bullies has not yet healed. However, self-awareness, community, and compassion, including professional support, can facilitate the healing of similar scars in us, just as they eventually did for Charlie. The *Heartstopper* community has played a crucial part in that process, in part by sharing their stories in online forums and in this book. We hope the stories here will help you, or help you help others who have been the victims of bullying. If each of us is like an injured phoenix, then our only hope of soaring is if we embrace one another.

The tender way *Heartstopper* portrayed mental health and treatment was accurate and dispelled some of the misinformation about what the therapeutic process involves. Asking for help was rightly shown as a sign of strength and courage. Charlie's sexual orientation was relevant and not ignored but treated in a normal and ordinary way. One key area that is often overlooked in the portrayal of those with mental health issues is the suffering of their loved ones and the helplessness and deep despair that they feel. The show did an exemplary job of showing the effect of Charlie's mental issues on Nick and his friends and family.

Heartstopper's life lessons are powerful: It can take more than one person to help another. Sometimes we need to step back and let the professionals lead the way; sometimes we require a different path. And most of all, having the intention to help someone is more important than knowing exactly how to initially help them. *The intention will produce the method.* At first, Nick did not know how to help Charlie, but in time, the path forward was revealed. It required fortitude on both Nick's and Charlie's parts. *Heartstopper* induces courage and powerful intention, which you will see reflected in contributors' stories, where they did not initially know how they were going to change, except that they realized that not changing was no longer acceptable. That is one metric of the power of *Heartstopper*.

What we see, we become

Why Are We Like This? poses tangential questions, among them why viewers have had such powerful emotional and cognitive experiences both during and after watching *Heartstopper*.

There is a plethora of psychological research and theories to explain how, when watching an immersive work of art such as a television show or film, the brain enables the willful suspension of disbelief, allowing viewers to accept a fictional story as real. "It isn't that we stop disbelieving—it's that we believe two inconsistent things. We accept that we are sitting and reading or watching a movie. We also believe or, more accurately, feel that what we are reading or viewing is happening."[2] *Heartstopper* fans are keenly aware of how **real** the show feels, and how effortlessly the boundary between ourselves and the story dissolves. It's as if we are in the story, sharing the same experiences with the characters in real time.

Because of its catalytic power, the *Heartstopper* phenomenon goes way beyond merely affording viewers a vicarious experience to piggyback on. There is a part of the brain that, when activated, can result in mental, emotional, physical, and behavioral responses identical to what would happen during a lived experience. Similar examples can be observed with the placebo effect, hypnosis, and creative visualization.

When watching the scene where Nick comes out to his mother, a viewer who has a strong emotional memory of a similar or opposite event may tend to have a stronger response than a viewer who has no prior personal reference point. The physiological response is not based on awareness of the difference between a real or fictional trigger; it is like an automatic reflex. That is why viewers have little control over the feelings that spontaneously emerge when they watch a scene which provokes a strong visceral connection. Theoretically speaking, if a viewer could have a do-over in real life of a prior actual event, like the scene with Nick, then their emotional response would be (respectively) identical or opposite to the one they had when they watched that scene in *Heartstopper*.

---

2. Michael Mueller, "What Brain Activity Can Explain Suspension of Disbelief?", *Scientific American*, 1 January 2014

> "There are emotions that you don't even know exist until you feel them."
>
> Daniella Mazzetti

For example, if someone came out to their mother and had a similar experience to Nick's coming out, then they would tend to experience positive emotions watching that scene. Conversely, if they had a negative experience, it might override their ability to have a positive response to watching it. Of course, there can be a combination of negative and positive emotional responses as well. There is an aspect of the subconscious mind that, under certain conditions, cannot differentiate between past and present, or real and imagined. This mind-body mechanism can be extremely powerful. In essence, the process of healing is overwriting your internal emotional memory. If you had a negative experience coming out to your mother, you have an option of releasing that painful memory and the negative emotions attached to it (catharsis), or identifying with how Nick felt (thankful, loved) after coming out to his mother in the scene. The most recent emotion can **replace** the original one as a way of finding closure with unresolved trauma or grief.

This is an abridged attempt to explain a healing construct that *Heartstopper* is uniquely well-equipped to evoke in viewers; however, I believe that *Heartstopper* also contains a magical element which cannot be entirely explained. Ultimately, there is nothing wrong with us for feeling the way that we do. If anything, our willingness to contemplate the question, "Why are we like this?" indicates a commendable degree of introspectiveness and intellectual curiosity.

The takeaway is to be gentle and patient with ourselves as we transition from new awareness to making changes in our lives.

We don't necessarily have to fully understand why we are like this; all we need is self-compassion, keeping our hearts and minds open, and being present in the moment so we can advance from stagnation to change, hurt to healing, and, ultimately, sadness to joy and freedom.

> "*Heartstopper* really helped me to see that I don't have to come out as anything, and I can just still find my identity. I can just be open to the people I love and let them be part of my journey and questioning without having to make a decision right now. *Heartstopper* showed me I don't have to have it figured out, I can just feel."
>
> Pauli

More than a word

Love!

That describes *Heartstopper* in a heartbeat.

When we envisioned this book, we wanted it to reflect the love that *Heartstopper* emanates. We spent countless hours on this project, our own labor of love, not only for the benefit of the readers, but for some of the story contributors who needed to share their truth publicly. This sea of *Heartstopper* love reminds us that each of us is our own wave, inextricable from the whole. For those fans who live in isolation or less-than-accepting places, *Heartstopper's* message is like a lighthouse beacon.

At its core, *Heartstopper* is a patient and positive portrayal of young LGBTQIA+ hearts learning how to love and be loved. It is a revelation of love in various forms, yet the essence of its message is formless. Even though sexual orientation and gender play significant roles in the story, on a deeper level, the characters' orientation and gender are immaterial (but not unimportant). *Heartstopper* demonstrates that labels can only go so far in identifying someone in that moment. The show's extraordinary emphasis on authenticity and kindness reframes "the love that dares not speak its name" as ordinary love. There is great power in ordinariness, especially for a community that has been stigmatized as other, strange, or deranged.

Alice's message is like a Trojan Unicorn carrying rainbow seeds of love. Once you have opened the gates of your heart to its enchanting spell, it's too late; the seeds have already sprouted in your consciousness and are bound to blossom in your life. This story has a way of sneaking past our defenses, forcing us to surrender to the love we are worthy of. The form of love does not matter; it could be love for yourself, a friend, or beauty.

In a world that often forgets how to love, who better than a marginalized class of outcasts to model what unconditional love looks like in myriad expressions? Members of the LGBTQIA+ community have an opportunity to love themselves more deeply and shine their rainbow light on the achromatic path of those whose hearts are eclipsed by hate, who have forgotten what they are made of: love. *Heartstopper* nudges their memory too.

There is a purity and innocence to Nick and Charlie's love. In watching the show, it's as if we are in a giant snow globe with them, our world shaken topsy-turvy as we witness these two snow angels falling head over heels. Like two unique snowflakes flurrying to the ground, the warmth of their love melts them into one, as our hearts melt too. And all becomes clear.

Perhaps that's what love is: Not that they are unaware of their flaws, but that they are making a conscious choice to embrace their uniqueness. This is an important lesson that challenges the trope that if one is flawed, then they are unlovable, and to be loved, one must hide their flaws. Nick and Charlie love each other, flaws and all. A perfect example occurs at the end of the second season when Charlie confides in Nick about self-harming, and Nick asks him to promise that if it ever gets bad again, he will tell him. In the final scene of Season 3, Episode 8, when they are about to make love and Nick removes Charlie's shirt, he stops and looks lovingly at him (including his scars) and tells him how hot he is. Their body language and tender chemistry communicate what words cannot convey. The way that Nick cradles Charlie's face in his hand, caresses his hair, and gently kisses his forehead is a masterclass in the expression of intimate love.

Their love for each other has changed them in positive ways, and they discover a new, transcendent love for themselves, for who they have become by being in love. Nick and Charlie are learning to see and celebrate the best in themselves because of the other. Although a love like theirs may be rare, it is not unachievable. And through loving them, we've learned to love ourselves.

While we are on this topic, there's just one more thing...

Love!

Rowan's Story

I remember it as if it were yesterday. May 22, 2022, was the day I first saw *Heartstopper*. I was visiting a friend in Dublin for several weeks, and I was alone at her flat for a few days. At the time, I was not in a good place, physically or mentally. I had a large, benign but painful uterine tumour for which I was awaiting surgery, and I was going through an identity crisis. On my own for the first time in 24 years, divorced, with kids who were pretty much grown up, I was at a crossroads. Not only was I trying to figure out who I actually was, but also what I wanted out of life. I had quit my corporate job after 20 years because it made me feel miserable and unsafe with its hostile and toxic environment, and I was working on a certification as a health and life coach. I knew that I wanted to leave the United States; it was something I had been thinking about for a couple of years by this point, because even after more than two decades living there, it still didn't feel like home. I missed Europe, and my longing to move back grew with every visit.

The coaching certification program was amazing, but it required a lot of self-analysis. It took me some time to fully comprehend that most of my life had revolved around the needs of others, and my primary survival mechanism had been to mould myself into the person they needed me to be. It was how I felt safe; when you're needed, you're less likely to be discarded – a fear that stemmed from being abandoned by my biological parents before I turned three. This was a strategy I successfully applied from a very young age and refined over the years; it aided me later in my career as well.

By the time I finally realised that many of my issues were rooted in a deep disconnect from myself, I had reached the ripe age of 50, and it was agonising. I felt utterly and completely lost. And so, as I was searching through Netflix for something light-hearted to distract myself from the physical and emotional pain of the moment, I stumbled across *Heartstopper*. Little did I know that this would become a pivotal moment in my life.

From the first episode, I was enthralled. I recognised pieces of myself in the protagonist, Charlie, right from the start. Existing on the fringes of the student body, somewhat shy unless he was with his friends, in a secret relationship with a boyfriend who took advantage of his vulnerability, tentative (yet hopeful) in accepting the friendship offered by the popular lad. Offers of friendship were very rare in my youth, and none lasted, but I saw what I had wished for very ardently in those days portrayed on screen. And I could definitely relate to the tentative and hopeful response from Charlie, as I have often reacted that way when new acquaintances developed into friendships.

By the second episode, I was a mess. Even though Charlie's experience of bullying was shown in a sensitive and mild manner, and only for a short moment, it still hit home. I endured years of bullying at school, from my very first day of primary school until the start of what is the German equivalent of A-levels. The episode ended with Nick, the other main character, starting the confusing and painful process of self-discovery. This obviously struck a chord, given my circumstances at the time, but so did the accompanying song that cracked me wide open: *Why Am I Like This*, by Orla Gartland. The lyrics were so poignant and felt personal in a way that was hard to explain; they reverberated in my soul like vibrations from a giant bell in close vicinity.

As I continued to watch the series, I felt shaken to the core and entirely overwhelmed. If anyone had asked me why, I could have offered no explanation. I simply wasn't prepared for the emotional gut punch when I innocently clicked on what looked like a cute, LGBTQIA+ inclusive teen show. By the end of the last episode, I was a sobbing mess.

The following weeks were a period of total confusion, along with an almost obsessive urge to rewatch the show, read the graphic novels it was based on, listen to the soundtrack, and finally, find a fan group on Facebook. My hyperfixation was rooted in a deep-seated need to understand what was happening to me. *Why Am I Like This* became a daily soundtrack, along with several other songs from the show (another unexpected benefit: I discovered a lot of new and amazing music), and while it baffled me, I simply could not shut down my almost obsessive preoccupation with everything *Heartstopper*-related.

I was 50 years old, for crying out loud! This was a TV show for teenagers, and LGBTQIA+ teens at that! I had read about parasocial relationships and post-series depression, and I knew that a slump or lull after finishing something exciting can leave you feeling empty and melancholic. I had previously experienced this after theatre performances, when the final curtain fell and something I had spent months preparing and rehearsing for had ended. But as a person who had lived, although uncomfortably, a cis-het white woman's existence for 50 years, this particular hyperfixation didn't make any sense at all.

However, the moment I described myself as a cis-het woman out loud to other fans, I felt oddly unsettled, almost queasy; the words felt inherently wrong. I was well aware that I had struggled with my gender from an early age. The concept of gender hadn't really entered my mind until one incident, which I remember vividly even though I was only six years old at the time. It was at the very beginning of year one at school. I always wore trousers and boyish clothes, often hand-me-downs from my older brothers, but it never bothered me. In fact, I felt quite comfortable in them, as I enjoyed playing rough and spent a lot of time outdoors. I was what some might have called a tomboy. My hair had been cut short due to an outbreak of lice at school; my mum didn't want to deal with pulling the individual nits out of my previously chin-length hair. Initially, I didn't care.

One day, maybe two or three weeks into the school year, some older boys started teasing me: "You look like a boy!" They seemed to think this was hilarious, but to me, it didn't really mean anything. Unfortunately, they took my lack of reaction as a sign that I didn't fully understand what they meant. So, they proceeded to drag me into the boys' toilets, pulled down my trousers and pants, and pointed out that I had "girl parts". It was horrifying, and I completely freaked out while they were holding me down. The next day, I begged my mum to buy me a dress. That was the beginning of a long and painful journey of suppressing anything boyish in my appearance and behaviour, and trying extremely hard to be what girls are expected to be.

No matter how hard I tried, I never felt comfortable in my body, and I hated every aspect of my female anatomy. Puberty was its own special brand of hell, and I never made peace with the changed body it left me to inhabit. Over the years, therapists tried to explain it all away with terms like "trauma response", "body dysmorphia", "cognitive bias" or "cognitive dissonance", but after thoroughly researching each of those, none of the descriptions ever made complete sense as an explanation for the disconnect with my biological sex.

Thinking back to my youth, I remembered so many suppressed thoughts and feelings, bending over backwards to fit in and feel like I belonged. My birth mother had left me in the care of a toxic family where I endured several forms of abuse and emotional neglect. Praise was scarce, criticism abundant. I was the only able-bodied child in the household, and so, despite being the youngest family member, I was heavily relied on to do most of the household chores and care for my disabled step-siblings, one of whom subjected me to the worst forms of abuse. I tried so hard to be good, to be who they wanted me to be, to earn the love and care I so desperately craved, but nothing I did seemed to be enough.

As I was ruminating on my past, suddenly, something registered: *Heartstopper* was a show where young people were living authentically, even in the face of adversity and harassment. They knew who they were, and they were unapologetic about it. And, more importantly, they had each other; kindred spirits banding together and refusing to let their environment alter their intrinsic nature.

Unlike me, most of the main characters didn't adapt to fit in. Despite their awareness of being socially sidelined, they were tenacious and resolute in living their truths and supported each other in doing so. There was one exception, Nick, and viewers became privy to his struggle to figure himself out. While he wasn't the character I related to the most overall, parts of his journey really affected me. And then, at the end of Episode 5, he asked Imogen if she ever felt like she was only doing things because it's what everyone does, scared to change or do something that might surprise others. He said he had been feeling like his real personality had been buried inside for a long time.

Those words felt like a physical blow. This was a popular, sporty lad, who on the surface seemed to have a lot of friends, and appeared to live a carefree existence – that is, until he met Charlie, and started to examine himself more closely. He had been masking and mirroring, at least to some extent, probably without noticing it, and now the façade was starting to crack. I recognised my modus operandi and saw myself reflected, since I was pretty much in the same boat, trying to dig up my real personality from its deep, dark grave.

Upon joining some Facebook groups, I found a lot of people who'd had similar, profound reactions to this show. Much to my surprise, the demographics spanned all ages, gender identities, and sexual orientations, everyone finding something in this series that struck a chord. What a relief it was to find I was not alone - I had worried about my excessive, maybe even unbalanced reaction, especially considering my age in relation to the clear target audience of this show. There were moments when I actually questioned my sanity, until I found these communities.

One Facebook group in particular seemed to include many kindred spirits, and in fact, I found some of my favourite people in that circle, whose friendships turned out to be more meaningful and unconditional than most. Within this fan group, I found a safe haven, an unusually kind and supportive online community. It was unlike any other fandom I had experienced up until that point, and remarkably, it has remained so for three years now.

It was within the safety of this community, and with the support of my friends, that I felt secure enough to explore my gender issues once again with a therapist, this time determined to find one who was experienced with gender-related issues. Unfortunately, most of the places and organisations I contacted in my vicinity only served teens and young adults, with their age cut-off anywhere between the ages of 21 and 35.

This was only the first of many obstacles I encountered, and the unwavering support from my new friends helped me through a lot of emotional turmoil. By the end of 2022, I finally found a local gender wellness practice without age restrictions, where my suspicions were confirmed with an official diagnosis of gender dysphoria.

By this point, the only remaining element of doubt was my attraction to men. Through a combination of deeply ingrained cis-heteronormativity[1] and lack of representation, I couldn't separate gender identity and sexual orientation. I had only ever seen or heard of *very* few trans men and never heard of a gay or bisexual one. Some twisted logic in my brain told me that I couldn't be a trans man if I was attracted to men. REPRESENTATION MATTERS! Once I searched for it, I found a couple of examples of gay trans men in the media, and it felt extremely validating.

Looking back at my life from this vantage point, a lot of things made much more sense. It felt like the last missing puzzle pieces were finally handed to me, and I was able to see myself clearly. It was liberating, not worrying about societal standards or twisting myself into someone I thought others might accept. I started my medical transition in early 2023, and it felt like a dense, poisonous fog was lifted. Suddenly, I was able to think clearly, I had energy, and my depression, which I had struggled with since my teen years, improved by leaps and bounds. The euphoria of letting go of expectations and norms, allowing myself to unfurl and let my true identity bloom, is beyond words. I realised just how much mental and physical energy had been taken up by forcing myself to be someone I wasn't, and keeping the pieces of me that didn't fit the "norm" imprisoned in a mental fortress.

The *Heartstopper* Facebook group was a crucial part of my journey; it was a safe place to voice my doubts, to share my fears, and to have a soft place to land. Everyone was incredibly supportive, empathetic and affirming. I felt, for the first time in my life, that I could just be myself, that my feelings were valid, and I didn't have

---

1. Cis-heteronormativity is the assumption of both cisgender identities (where a person's gender identity aligns with their sex assigned at birth) and heterosexual identities, which are perceived as the natural and default societal standard.

to put on an act any longer. Some people had to be cut out of my life, but it was largely a relief; they had been judgmental anyway and my views hadn't aligned with theirs for a long time, but I had found a new community.

While it might sound unrealistic, I honestly formed some lasting, meaningful friendships in this online environment. Some of the best friends I've ever made, I met through *Heartstopper*. When I travelled to London in the summer of 2023 for Pride and Trans Pride, one of these friends even invited me to stay with her, although we had never met in person. Yes, we had chatted online for months and even talked on video calls, but there's still inherent risk when inviting a virtual stranger into your home, for five weeks no less. But it was absolutely brilliant.

Over the past two years, I have met quite a few of these online friends in person; all of them lovely, authentic, kind, and supportive people. A handful of us have been in a group chat for three years now, and we still message each other every single day, although only a few of us have actually met in person due to geographical distance (US, Canada, Argentina, UK, Australia). We've had some video calls, and we cheer each other on all the time. I've called them my emotional support pocket group, as I'm literally carrying them around in my phone all day. They were the first people I came out to. It was utterly terrifying, and my heart was pounding, but I needn't have worried; everyone in the chat was cheering me on and offering me support. They suggested ways to celebrate milestones, they sent me flowers when I had top surgery (a procedure to remove breast tissue), and they always made sure I was okay. We all lift each other up, support whoever is having a low moment, and celebrate our victories together.

Two and a half years of hormone therapy, a legal name change, and three surgeries later (including the removal of the tumour), I feel absolutely amazing in my own skin. I don't dread the mirror anymore. I actually like my voice now. I walk down the street with confidence and pride, and I've stopped worrying about how other people perceive me. I'm just me, and it's incredibly empowering and liberating.

As I look back on these last three years, my intense reaction to the show makes total sense now. It wasn't that I identified with one main character or their journey, but several characters and topics that were touched on in the series. That didn't change with seasons two or three, either. So many of the themes are relatable, and the overall hopeful tone the show managed to maintain, even through difficult subject matter, was a tonic.

My extreme hyperfixation with *Heartstopper* has lessened a little over time, but I still firmly believe that this show steered me on a path that saved my life. The state I was in before I saw it was already precarious, my will to live hanging by a thread. And even though my initial reaction was deeply emotional and my inner pain was further amplified, it was the push I needed to figure myself out.

An acquaintance of mine once told me, "The seed has to crack for the tree to grow." This TV series cracked the seed, and not only have I grown, but I have thrived. The tree was always there, hidden, trapped, and now it is free to spread out and grow as many roots and branches as it wants. It can finally become what it always had the potential to be. Thinking about this analogy, I remember that when I was little, I always drew my trees without roots. The school psychologist brought this up to my parents as a concern that this pointed to some issues with my emotional well-being (I won't go into the details of why). I've thought about this over the years, and always figured people think of their roots as belonging to a place, or maybe a community. For me, at this point in my life, I feel like I'm rooted in myself – something that would never have occurred to me in the past.

The path here was treacherous, the journey often painful, but it led to acceptance. Not only can I fully accept my past pain and struggles and embrace the person I used to be, but I'm also able to feel thankful for the strength it has given me and appreciate the resilience I have now. I still carry it all with me, but it's no longer baggage.

To echo Nick's sentiment in the last episode of Season 1, that lovely scene when he pleaded with Charlie in the school corridor, my life is so much better because I found you, *Heartstopper*.

George's Story

In the fall of 2021, my mother, who was 99 years old, died at our home in New York City. To say that we had an unusually powerful and loving bond for 57 years would be an understatement. She lived with me, and I was her full-time caregiver from 2008 onward. She suffered for many years with Alzheimer's disease and poor health and spent the last three years of her life completely bedridden, aphasic, and reliant on life-sustaining devices.

After her death, I plummeted into a depression so severe that it progressed to full-blown PTSD and pseudo-dementia. I could not stop shaking for months. My health was deteriorating, and I was in agonizing emotional and physical pain. I was barely functional and incapable of living alone. Being single with no family did not help. I remember telling my therapist that I felt like a shattered Humpty Dumpty, on a life preserver emblazoned with "TITANIC", drifting on a sea of tears at night. I was unable to concentrate, and my memory was itself a mere memory. Despite having two psychology degrees and a life devoted to helping others, I couldn't help myself.

After several months, my friend Vikilaura List took me under her wing, opening her heart and home in Pennsylvania. I lived with her on and off for two and a half years until I gradually became more functional. It was there in May of 2022, while sinking in the quicksand of despair, that I turned on Netflix and saw a recommendation for *Heartstopper*. Even though I had never heard of the show, my finger automatically tapped the remote.

When Nick pulled Ben off Charlie at the end of the first episode, I was hopelessly and exquisitely hooked. In that moment, forever suspended in time, Nick also pulled something dark and heavy off me. In a heartbeat, a part of me resurrected from the dead and noticed something other than the pain of my broken heart. It was the first time in eight months that I peeked above the pit of grief. How I wished I'd had a Nick to protect me from the violent bullies who had attacked me in school.

Little did I realize then that *Heartstopper* would play a vital role in my road to recovery and ongoing healing process. It was like receiving a defibrillator shock that reset my faltering heartbeat to the rhythm of life. I kept binge-watching the first season, but I couldn't get enough. I developed an insatiable hunger for information about the show, story, characters, actors, and creator. I played the show's captivating music on a loop until the soundtrack of my life harmonized with it. I joined related Facebook groups and discovered thousands of others who shared my healthy obsession and validated my experience. I had found my tribe. If I was unbalanced, at least I had good company. I observed that most of the individuals in this fandom generally tended to be more emotionally available, supportive, and good-natured; qualities I resonate with.

Each night, my inner child would gingerly crawl into bed and watch the show as it took me gently by the hand, through the cloud cover, over the rainbow, and into a dream realm of sleep that had eluded me for many months. There, the portal between past and present, reality and illusion, hurt and healing opened in the curtain of time, enabling me to vicariously experience the heartbeat and breaths of the characters in sync with my own. I was Charlie, and I felt the tenuous pulse of a battered heart. Season one was my happy pill, mental floss, an emotional analgesic that soothed the parts of me that nothing else could reach.

Watching the series was not only an escape from the pain, but more importantly, it rolled out the welcome mat to thoughts, feelings, and memories that lay entombed for decades. This access would be the first step in the arduous process of emotional healing and reclaiming the disassociated parts of myself that had seemingly vanished. In Season 1, Episode 8, when I first heard Mr. Ajayi tell Charlie not to let anyone make him disappear, I realized I had slowly disappeared, little by little, with each passing day, and I had found comfort under a cloak of invisibility.

I strongly relate to Charlie. Growing up in the 1970s in New York City, I was relentlessly bullied from the ages of eight to sixteen. Although I loved learning, I dreaded going to school and trying to survive each day. The scenes where Harry bullied Charlie precipitated flashbacks of traumatic memories long repressed.

When I was in third grade, I had to eat my lunch sitting on the toilet in the last stall, with the door ajar and my feet up flanking the door so when the bullies came looking for me, my legs would not betray me. When I was in sixth grade, an older schoolmate held a switchblade to my back while I was in the bathroom. The word was out that it was open hunting season on the "queer faggot" who was outnumbered from the start. During dodgeball at school, the bullies would initially avoid targeting me, holding back until I was the last one left so they could line up to pummel me simultaneously. Once, when I made the mistake of fighting back, I ended up in a heap on the sidewalk, unable to get up. I quickly learned that fighting back only made it worse when it was one against many.

In eighth grade, we kept our lunchboxes in the cloakroom until lunchtime. By this point, I was no longer surprised when I frequently opened my lunchbox, bit into my peanut butter and jelly sandwich, and spit out the grit from the pink glitter that my classmates had added. I could not eat, nor could I stomach the ingredient of hatred directed at me. I could not understand why they wanted to hurt me. At the time, I thought perhaps I would be better off dead. So, when I watched Nick confront and punch Harry at the cinema [S2 E7], I felt as if Nick was defending me against those bullies from yesteryear. Although the scene was disturbing, it was also gratifying to see a white knight in golden armor knock the sneer off the face of a coward disguised as a bully.

Watching the other rugby lads idly stand by as Charlie was bullied reminded me of my classmates who did not come to my aid either. A passive student audience only added to my humiliation, and so my abandonment issues came to the forefront once again. While watching the show, I could see myself in the bullying scenes both as Charlie and as a detached observer who could perceive the pathology of the bully and not the asserted pathology of the one being bullied. I did not understand this as a child, when all I could think of was living long enough to escape the daymare at school, only to contend with the nightmare at home, where my physically abusive father bullied me as well. He was a violent alcoholic with a strong sadistic streak, who would have killed me if he knew I was gay. He came from a homophobic culture that equated any intimation of effeminacy with homosexuality, which would confer shame upon the family name. Seeing the way Charlie's father supported and stuck up for him was an awe-inspiring epiphany. Charlie was able to freely slumber under a roof of acceptance and safety. I slept with one eye open, wearing a straight mask under a blanket of fear.

Seeing Charlie struggle with the bullying, and hearing Nick tell him in Episode 7 of Season 1 that he shouldn't have to put up with it, brought me right back to my childhood, when I did have to put up with it because I had no choice, nor did I have an ally. Tears cascaded down my cheeks because Nick's truth spoke to the child I never got to be. I never felt free or truly safe back then.

Although I was not Catholic, I attended an all-boys Catholic high school. Conformity was key to fitting in, and my classmates quickly realized that I was "odd". It was not until the eleventh grade that the bullies began to back off as I had become part of a coterie of closeted classmates who had not come out, even to each other. I learned that strength in numbers offered some safety. I regret that we were not open with one another like the characters in *Heartstopper*, so that we could have supported one another more as we navigated the slippery slope of young adulthood. If *Heartstopper* had existed back then, perhaps we would have. At the time, coming out could have had dire consequences. I could never have dreamt of a story like *Heartstopper* and its normalized, unabashed depiction of love.

In July of 2022, two months after I first began watching *Heartstopper*, I went into the hospital for day surgery that promised to be uneventful. The next morning, a friend called for an ambulance when she found me unconscious on the floor in my apartment. I had suffered a massive internal hemorrhage. When I arrived at the hospital, I was rushed into the resuscitation room due to the imminent risk of my heart stopping. Transfusions and emergency surgery saved my life. After a week in the intensive care unit, I went back home and was bedridden for a few months. I was alone most of the time, hovering between a daze and depression. In all honesty, I was less than thrilled at having made it through alive. That is when *Heartstopper* saved my life a second time. It enabled my heart to attach jumper cables to its massive battery of energy and hope.

With each episode, I was transported across the Atlantic to a place where sparks of love abounded. I dreamt that one day when I got better, I would visit the filming locations. In the meantime, I looked forward to taking my medicine in episode form each day, which was the only thing that soothed my spirit. It took well over a year for my body to get back to normal. During that time, it gave me a safe harbor to retreat to where I could float on gentle waves of warm comfort.

In May of 2023, I could no longer resist the gravitational pull of London, so I made the trip. A new friend I met through the fandom gave me a tour of the most iconic *Heartstopper* scene locations. On the road there, a rainbow appeared ahead, and I wondered if I was hallucinating. It reminded me of the rainbow reflections rejoicing above Nick and Charlie's heads when they first kissed.

Visiting those places was a pilgrimage to an inner Mecca. It brought those scenes to life even more and blurred the boundary between reality and fantasy. And in that blurring, my feelings and memories became blurred too. Now, did I actually experience the bullying alone, or did I have "Nick" to defend and protect me? It certainly felt like I did. And if I felt like he defended me, then maybe that was all that was needed to heal my 8-year-old and 58-year-old selves at the same time.

Heartstopper not only allowed me to dream in reverse but to simultaneously heal retroactively. It was as if *Heartstopper's* positive movie print of healing imagery became superimposed over the negative movie print of my life.

After continuing to struggle with complicated grief for 22 months, I welcomed the debut of season two with bated breath. However, I was completely unprepared for its cratering emotional impact. It landed with a seismic thud, and I was lost in a mushroom cloud of trauma fallout. The final episode of season two broke me. Sanguine-stained shards of memory mirror lay at my feet, reflecting glimpses of self-inflicted childhood wounds and those inflicted on me by bullies. In that searing moment, I was Charlie crying in a Nick-less room. My tears became a torrent. I reached out for help in the online fandom. Hundreds offered their support, practical advice, and feedback. More than anything, I realized that I was not alone.

In an effort to assuage my grief, in the fall of 2023, I boarded a plane to London again, where, upon landing, I fell subject to the city's spell, and the depression became a little less intolerable. London has played a key role in my healing journey, and the fact that Alice Oseman, the cast, and filming locations are proximal to London has made my visits even sweeter and full of delightful surprises. During my prior trip, I went to see one of the cast members in a play. While waiting for the play to start, four *Heartstopper* cast members walked in and sat close by. While strolling through Covent Garden one evening, I serendipitously bumped into another cast member. It reminded me that one never knows what joy awaits around the corner. This helped bolster my sagging foundation of hope. I wonder if Alice ever envisioned that her magnum opus would lay the groundwork for a secure foundation for fans to rebuild their dream castles on. Alice can add "Architect of Hope" to her impressive resume.

Three weeks later, I returned home, dragging the depression in my suitcase. The upliftment that crested within me in London had found a transatlantic spillway, and I was floundering again. In the months afterward, I struggled like a salmon swimming upstream. *Heartstopper* was there throughout like a stalwart companion, not only to comfort me, but to keep me afloat.

In January 2024, I arranged for a group of *Heartstopper* fans to meet in New York. We were going to see Joe Locke on his auspicious opening night in *Sweeney Todd* on Broadway. At dinner, I met Rowan Murphy and others from around the country. Although my eyes could see Rowan clearly, there were aspects of him that were invisible to me. With time-trodden trust, the hidden pieces of his puzzle revealed a mosaic of a courageous man who is transmuting tears to triumph and helping others in their journey along the way. Who knew that in less than a year, we would embark on this collaborative literary endeavor to give *Heartstopper* fans an opportunity for greater understanding and self-compassion.

Because I could no longer shoulder the soul-crushing mantle of grief, I sought medical treatment. After a hellish period, I found help that significantly decreased my depression to the point that I could function. When Season 3 arrived in the summer of 2024, I was better prepared emotionally. I could relate to Charlie's struggle to regain his mental health. How quickly society can judge someone whose heart is hobbling on invisible crutches, yet disregards the strength and fortitude required to seek help and commit to getting better. Charlie is a hero in my eyes, and in his eyes, I caught a reflection of the hero in myself, too.

In September, a group of us went to see Kit Connor in *Romeo + Juliet* on Broadway. We were awed by his scintillating performance; however, the overwhelming fervor I witnessed on many a night when he came out to greet fans at the stage door left me concerned for his safety. Despite that, his remarkable poise made me realize that *Heartstopper* would never have been the same without the heart that he, Joe Locke, Alice, and every cast and crew member poured into it. Alice may have masterfully sculpted each character from the finest literary alabaster, but each gifted actor uniquely brought their character to life with their very breath and, in so doing, resuscitated generations of hearts that had stopped. For that, I am personally grateful, for it has made all the difference.

Soon thereafter, I spent five weeks in London. Upon arriving there, I realized that something profound had shifted inside me. My body felt lighter, and I could inhale more deeply. The remaining depression lifted and has not returned since. Even though I am still processing my grief that lurks below the surface, I hold a vision that one day I will meet my "Nick" and live happily in London.

After I returned to New York that November, I often waited for friends outside the theater who had come from overseas to see *Romeo + Juliet*. During those times, I listened as fans opened up to me about their personal stories of profound transformation because of *Heartstopper*. Some explained that the show had literally saved their lives. They shared stories of broken hearts and spirits that had lain buried for decades, only to come alive because the show compelled them to pursue their dreams and believe in the power of love. That is what inspired me to write. I wanted other fans to be inspired, too.

Shortly thereafter, Rowan and I discovered we had a strong mutual interest in creating a book to explore why *Heartstopper* is such a powerful catalyst for significant change in so many fans' lives around the world. It was clear to us that there was more to this story than met the eye. But not for *Heartstopper*, I would have been incapable of writing a book about it. What a poetic full-circle realization. *Heartstopper* is the rainbow in my clouds.

The Power of a Positive Bisexual Portrayal

By Rowan Murphy

Bisexuality is very underrepresented in mainstream media. The majority of LGBTQIA+ characters in TV shows and movies are either gay or lesbian, with the occasional transgender character in the mix. Thinking back to my youth, there's only one popular film I recall where a main character was fearlessly open in his bisexuality, and that was *The Rocky Horror Picture Show* (a minor obsession of mine in my uni years). On top of that, the few bisexual characters we got to see, mostly in supporting roles, were often reflecting common stereotypes and prejudices in society.

There has been improvement in the past decade or so; *Schitt's Creek* is a good example with one of the main characters, David Rose, whose pansexuality is just part of who he is, and not a vehicle for conflict. *Heartstopper* is recognised as one of the best examples of positive bisexual representation, and it made a huge impact, evidenced by the fact that the largest number of story submissions for this book came from bisexual individuals.

Bisexuality is not the only LGBTQIA+ identity that is attracted to more than one gender; others include pansexual, omnisexual, queer, and unlabelled, to name a few (for simplicity, I will refer to these groups as multisexual). Any representation of characters who are attracted to more than one gender will resonate and help those who aren't hetero- or homosexual. Bisexuality just happens to be the most common label used.

As part of my research, I looked at The Pride Study, one of the most comprehensive LGBTQIA+ surveys I know of. It has had over 33800 participants in the past year, making it a statistically relevant sample size in my opinion. It's a study run by Stanford University School of Medicine in partnership with the University of California, San Francisco. What I found was that the population of bisexual (24%) and pansexual (15%) participants was almost as large as the gay (26%) and lesbian participant pool (20%), and this is not counting other multisexual orientations. It stands to reason that there are likely more multisexual people than homosexual ones. Seeing how large this population is makes the shortage of representation even more glaring. Since Nick's character is bisexual, the focus of this text will be on bisexuality and its representation.

Bi erasure[1] is sadly very common, and it is an indicator of yet another binary that shapes societal perception: one is either homosexual or heterosexual, with no concept of anything in between. The fact that there is an entire spectrum of sexualities is lost on most people. The letter B, even though it has been part of the LGBTQ+ acronym since sometime around 1990, is the forgotten letter, the unacknowledged identity. I've often heard the LGBTQIA+ community collectively referred to as "the gays", either dismissively or just for "ease of reference", essentially reducing the entire rainbow of identities to just one.

A week after Season 2 of *Heartstopper* aired, the movie *Red, White & Royal Blue* was released, and it introduced another wonderful example of positive bi representation in one of the main characters, Alex Claremont-Diaz. His mother, Ellen Claremont, makes a powerful statement when he comes out to her: "You know, the B in LGBTQ is not a silent letter." That just about sums up the issue.

---

1. Bisexual erasure, also known as bi invisibility, is the denial or questioning of bisexuality's existence or legitimacy.

In addition to bi erasure, there are some common, biassed opinions which have serious impacts on people with multisexual identities, who often find their identity invalidated. If someone is in a hetero-presenting relationship, for instance, they may be told that their bisexuality "obviously isn't real," and they just "want to be interesting". And if they are in a relationship with a member of the same sex, well, then they're "clearly gay but afraid to admit it." This second stereotype is illustrated very well in *Heartstopper* through the interactions between Nick and his brother David, who, upon finding out his brother is dating Charlie, outright tells Nick to just admit that he's gay. These prejudices further complicate the already difficult process of self-discovery and coming out for anyone who falls between the two ends of the spectrum (straight or gay).

> "I have known I was bisexual since I was 15, but there I was at 36 – I've never formally come out to any of my people, I'd never claimed that title. I felt shame and unworthy of being a part of the community. [...] Every rewatch [of *Heartstopper*] brought down a little bit of my wall of internalised biphobia."
>
> Sarah

> "I had never explored the concept of queer identity before, just accepted bisexuality as part of me, feeling like it didn't really matter as long as I was in a heterosexual relationship."
>
> Skasi6

Some people assume that bisexuality is a 50/50 split, where people like both genders equally. As with most human experiences and characteristics, there are nuances, and individual preferences can vary. The outcome of Nick's online "am I gay" quiz, confusing as it may be for him, tells him he is 62% homosexual. While this might sound amusing, that result could be viewed as an indicator that he has a slight preference for men over women, but of course, these types of quizzes are highly unreliable and shouldn't be taken as fact.

> "I remember feeling I had to choose in order to have a supportive community, like I belonged neither in the LGBTQ+ nor in the cishet community. I chose to call myself gay and lesbian, but even today, I question my sexual preference."
>
> Janny

Coincidentally (or maybe it's serendipity), as I am working on this chapter, I am reading a *Heartstopper* fanfic which illustrates some of the challenges faced by bisexual individuals through Nick's inner thoughts:

> But he shoved it all into a corner of his mind. A dark place. A locked box filled with fear and discipline. Because no one said you could be both. No one gave that option. You were either straight. Or gay. Or confused. Or just attention-seeking. So he picked a side, because it was easier. More convenient. And tried to live whole with only half his body.
>
> It was a slow, awkward process, full of nameless guilt, fear of others' eyes, fear of being unwanted because he was too ambiguous. Fear of seeming like a fraud in any space. Too much for some, too little for others.

At 25, when he finally said "I'm bi" out loud to himself, the feeling wasn't just relief. It was anger. A silent, cold anger that crept into his bones as he remembered every time someone laughed, mocked, dismissed, doubted, confused him. Every time someone said, "Bisexual doesn't exist," "It's just a phase," "You want attention," "You just don't want to admit you're gay", – or the opposite, "You're forcing it to seem cool."
– *Honey in the Garden*

thesfps on AO3

This also speaks to a shared sentiment I've heard from many bi- and pansexual friends and acquaintances: They feel "too queer for some spaces, and not queer enough for others", and they never feel like they fully belong. They fear judgment in both communities, and this is especially true if they haven't experienced relationships and/or any kind of intimacy with members of more than one gender, as though some form of "proof" is required to substantiate one's sexual orientation.

> "I still find myself attracted to the same gender and others but wonder if I can really call myself bisexual or pan if I haven't had those experiences."
>
> Amy LB

> "I had definitely held back on coming out completely. I often felt like I didn't deserve to be a part of the queer community as someone in a straight-passing relationship."
>
> Chelsea K.

Sadly, these prejudices are pervasive even within the LGBTQIA+ community, sometimes to the extent that people don't feel the B belongs in the acronym. And then there's the warped idea that bisexual people are inherently promiscuous, that they just want to sleep with everyone. I've heard of gay people telling friends who are dating someone bisexual that they shouldn't bother, because they'll just end up being cheated on. Promiscuity is not, and never has been, a necessary or integral part of someone's sexual orientation, but unfortunately, media representation in the past has not helped in separating the two. The perception is made worse by the double standard that exists between the cis-het and LGBTQIA+ communities, particularly for men; straight men who have a lot of sexual partners don't receive nearly the same amount of criticism as those with a different sexual orientation. And in all communities, it's worse for women.

Given the stigma attached to the label, it comes as no surprise that many people suppress their bisexuality, especially if they are in a hetero-presenting relationship.

Within the stories that were submitted for this book, there were many accounts of internalised biphobia or feelings of imposter syndrome.[2] It may appear easier to ignore that part of oneself or stay closeted if one's life presents as heteronormative on the surface, but it comes at a price. No one should have to suppress part of themselves; research has shown that doing so has serious impacts on emotional health, including anxiety, depression, low self-esteem, emotional numbness, and relationship problems. Repressing part of yourself takes up a lot of mental and emotional energy.

---

2. Imposter syndrome is the fear of not belonging or being exposed as a fraud even when objective evidence contradicts this.

Nick Nelson is a refreshing change and a wonderful example of bisexual representation done right. He is a likeable, charming, good-natured boy-next-door type, universally liked because he doesn't have a mean bone in his body. His struggle with figuring himself out, realising how much he had been conforming in order to fit in and not rock the boat, and understanding how much of himself he had buried inside himself for a long time [S1 E5] is very relatable, as is his journey to coming out. The agonising fear of being rejected, judged, and possibly bullied is enough to make anyone have second thoughts about revealing that they aren't straight. Now, picture a popular boy in school who never had to worry about being a target, trying to navigate these treacherous waters, especially after only recently discovering how much torment his boyfriend had actually endured after being outed. Nick's anxiety over coming out is a realistic portrayal of what many of us have experienced firsthand.

As part of his journey, Nick does a lot of research (Googling is almost a character trait), and he finds a YouTuber (Courtney-Jai Niner) whose advice seems to really help him. In one of the videos, Nick hears him talk about how growing up bisexual means constantly second-guessing yourself, going from having a crush on a guy one day to having a crush on a girl the next, feeling forced to make a choice, and then finally realising that there is no choice, that it is a combination of the two, and that's okay. This struck a chord with a lot of viewers. There's a famous meme from Disney's *The Road To El Dorado*, where two characters are given a choice between two things, and they respond, "Both? Both. Both is good." This meme has been used for various situations involving a choice, and it started making a frequent reappearance in the context of bisexuality in *Heartstopper* fan groups, almost like an affirmation.

Season 2 brought us a female bisexual character, Sahar, who is another wonderful example of positive bi representation, especially as she owns it unapologetically and proudly when Imogen refers to her as an ally. Sahar's character is a winning combination of confidence and vulnerability. She is effortlessly cool as a member of her band and easily integrates with the "Paris Squad" friend group, and she is unafraid to confront Imogen when she feels like she's being used as an experiment. She really is a bi icon.

Heartstopper has helped many bisexual people (and those of other multisexual orientations) feel seen and validated. The fact that Nick was able to determine his identity and label it, even though he hadn't been physically intimate with both girls and boys, was a wonderful exemplification of the fact that you don't have to have experienced a same-sex relationship to be bisexual or any other non-heterosexual orientation. This was a very important message for many.

> "When Nick decided to identify as bisexual, even though he never tried to be intimate with anyone, something clicked for me. I realized that physical experiences weren't necessary for someone to decide their sexual orientation."
>
> Laura

> "I heard someone say that it's about attraction, not action, but I'm dealing with imposter syndrome most days."
>
> Chantal

Nick's journey demonstrates that no one should feel like a fraud or imposter just because of who they fell in love with. If that's someone of the opposite sex and you've lived a heterosexual experience, this doesn't negate who you are. What would you say to a young person who has never had intimate relations with anyone? You're not straight, or gay, or bi, or pan, or asexual, just because you haven't tried it out? We know what we feel, and we know what we like better than anyone else. No one should be trying to tell us who we are, and we don't owe anyone an explanation – that's one of the key messages *Heartstopper* conveyed, and it is so important for many to hear.

Courtney-Jai Niner's Story

My first reaction to *Heartstopper* was, "This is everything." It's hard to put into words, but it was a moment of euphoria, as though everything on my journey of being bisexual had finally come full circle. My first exposure to it was a script provided by Alice, and the production team invited me to record two short videos to share my experience of being bisexual. I recorded a few versions, and the one that was kept in the show was actually my real story. Throughout watching the show, I cried and laughed and fell in love with a story that was so beautiful and thought-provoking, one I wish I'd had during those difficult years of accepting myself. Seeing myself on screen was a cathartic experience and incredibly validating.

It's funny; the person I want to speak about most is my nan. She passed away from MS a few years ago, so she never got to watch *Heartstopper*. One thing she did, however, was watch every single one of my YouTube videos, no matter how cringy or bad. She's the woman who made me the man I am today; she was so supportive when I came out, and I know she would have sung the praises of *Heartstopper*.

Being part of the show and representing bisexuality is a great privilege that was given to me by Alice. I have never watched a show like this where the writer just understands every emotion, every small step; it felt like Alice just knew mine and every other queer person's struggles. The moment Nick looked up my

YouTube videos to research and understand bisexuality was a cathartic one, because I finally got to be what I never had. It was bittersweet because, on one hand, it would have been great to have this growing up, but it felt liberating to confidently represent bisexuality after being nervous and insecure about it for years when I was younger. Hearing other queer people telling you that you're wrong and that you're not part of the community was invalidating and affected my self-esteem.

I think the most incredible parts of the show have been watching not only the characters grow throughout the story, but also the actors who play them; they've made massive strides in the LGBTQ+ community. It's one thing to play a character, but to speak out for equality, and then to bravely come out in the face of horrible online harassment is another. Kit is the role model so many of us can look up to; he's inspired a whole generation of bisexuals to accept themselves.

I think the show has given me a lot of confidence. It has encouraged me to be myself, and it's pushed me to help others even more. One of the best things that happened after the first season came out was that I was getting messages from people I had helped in the past with their coming-out journeys. I got to hear their experiences of coming out with all the ups and downs, but most importantly, the stories of new loves found. There were also hundreds of new people asking for advice, which I was happy to give, and I love the idea that no one has to feel alone anymore, that there is something that we can all connect with.

I also made a very cool friend in Jackie Lavender, someone who's grown so much since the show came out. It has helped him realise he is asexual, after many years of being out as an openly gay man. In turn, this has helped me learn a lot about asexuality, too, and how misunderstood it actually is.

On the surface, my life hasn't really changed all that much. After the show aired, I was able to speak to a lot of people and made many new friends. I did some podcasts, being interviewed by fans and was generally able to do more creatively than before. I learnt a lot about the history of the queer community and how it has grown and evolved over time, and I made connections all over the world with people who were impacted by *Heartstopper*. I have a great community on YouTube, and I still have the passion to help others, which is all I've ever really wanted.

***

We also received a story from Desiree, who shared that watching Courtney-Jai's videos was an important component of her journey:

"When I started watching the *Heartstopper* YouTube reaction videos, I came across Courtney-Jai, who was in the show. He posted a lot of videos about being bisexual, which made me realize that I was. Up until that point, I had kind of ignored those feelings and called myself bi-curious, because I had never dated a girl. I erased my bisexuality because that's what I saw growing up, that it didn't actually exist; you had to choose one or the other. But through watching *Heartstopper* and his videos, I realized that I was valid; my feelings are valid, and I am bisexual. Since then, I've come out to a few people and have indirectly come out at work with a bisexual flag pin. I'm even more engaged in the community and feel more comfortable in my own skin."

NYMinTX's Story

After watching the first season of *Heartstopper* a few months after it came out, I thought it was cute. After bingeing the second season the day it was released, I was obsessed. I've always been a sucker for teen romance, and something about it – the casting, the dialogue, the story – just resonated with me in a way that very few things ever have.

I was 49 years old and had been married to my husband for 25 years when I discovered *Heartstopper*. I have a trans daughter and a gay son (and a straight, cisgender son), and even before I had kids, I considered myself a passionate ally (I remember having heated debates with my dad in the 80's about gay rights). But after watching the show more times than I can count, reading the books, interacting with other fans online and delving into the world of fan fiction, I've come to discover that I myself am bisexual and demisexual.

It's insane and a bit embarrassing that it took a young adult show to lead me to my queer awakening at the age of 50, but it's true. I started looking at same-sex friendships I'd had through the years, or actresses whose work I really admired, and realized that my feelings for them mirrored my feelings toward certain male friends or actors. Comphet (compulsory heterosexuality, which is the expectation of society that people are straight) had convinced me that when I had those thoughts toward guys, they were crushes, but when it was toward girls, it was just admiration.

Prior to *Heartstopper*, I had never heard of the asexual spectrum, and again, the *Heartstopper* community educated me on it and encouraged me to do my own research. I was learning a lot about asexuality by interacting with the fan community on Facebook and in the fanfiction groups (this was before Season 3 aired with Isaac's story arc). In doing so, I discovered that the way I feel attraction is not the "norm." I have never looked at another human and wanted to kiss them, have sex with them or see them naked. I usually don't develop a crush on someone until I get to know their personality, which I came to learn is called demisexual.

I have only shared my bisexuality with a couple of people – my daughter, a close friend and my lesbian cousin – and I haven't worked up the nerve to tell my husband yet. Sharing this was nerve-wracking, and it felt good at the same time, but I also felt guilty for not telling my husband. I don't think he will react poorly, but I don't want him to feel insecure about our relationship or my feelings for him. It's not like I plan to explore my attraction to women, so I guess it feels like a moot point. I may never divulge my demisexuality to anyone in real life. Honestly, having the label helps me know myself better, but it's not something I feel the need for others to know about me.

Seeing Nick go through the process of realizing that he had feelings for males before Charlie – for example, his crush on the rugby coach when he was twelve – was enlightening. My first reaction was that it was not realistic for him to have a crush without realizing it; it took a few viewings for it to sink in. The more I watched it, the more I started to feel like it was more realistic than I initially thought. I started to recognize myself; it was like someone shed a spotlight on my brain. Suddenly, I saw the admiration I had for people in my youth in a different context, realizing that they were crushes.

Heartstopper really helped me know myself better and also helped me to understand my kids more. It brought me a whole network of people who are like a sounding board for me; I can reach out when I have questions or struggle with anything. The world Alice has created gives me hope for the future.

Laura's Story

I kept seeing the trailer for the 3rd season of *Heartstopper* on my Netflix page, and it got me curious about the show. I binged all three seasons in October 2024 within two days and became completely obsessed. Over the next couple of weeks, I rewatched the show about seven or eight times. I told all of my friends to watch it, did a rewatch with my husband, bought and read the graphic novels, joined Tapas (one of the platforms where the *Heartstopper* comic is published online) and then later Patreon, and watched interviews with the cast and crew of the show.

My husband also thought it was a cute story, a beautiful piece of media. It made him happy to see stories of people being able to be their true selves. What further resonated with him was the mental health aspect. I have struggled with burnout multiple times in the last couple of years and suffer from seasonal depressive disorder in winter. People going through their struggles and the people who love them standing by them was portrayed beautifully.

From the beginning, it struck me how the show seemed to be crafted with such love and attention to detail, from the cast to the sets to the music. It spoke to me how there seemed to be little need for artificial drama other than the complex emotional situations the characters were going through, and how these situations were dealt with in such a loving and mature way. To this day, I can't properly put into words what exactly it was that charmed me so completely about *Heartstopper*. I simply got pulled into this cozy, heartwarming, life-affirming little universe and have not wanted to leave ever since. Not only the show, but the graphic novels, the fan community and Alice's interactions with us – all of it has felt very comforting, safe and joyful to me. It has taught me much about the LGBTQIA+ community as well as myself and I am forever grateful for that.

Nick's storyline had a huge impact on me. I started reflecting more on a time in my life when I was in love with a female friend of mine in my late teenage years. I had only been in relationships with men, and I thought most of my crushes had been boys or men. But as I kept thinking back, I realized there were more women that I had crushes on than I had previously realized. I had mostly ignored those, since they felt different - more romantic and less physical. I also thought it was simply a universal truth that women were more beautiful than men and everyone knew this?

When Nick decided to identify as bisexual even though he never tried to be intimate with anyone, something clicked for me. I realized that physical experiences weren't necessary for someone to decide their sexual orientation.

Mr. Farouk mentioning that he only realized he was gay in his late twenties, further encouraged me to reexamine and accept my romantic feelings towards women. I first came out as bi in a thread of the *Heartstopper* Patreon chat where people encouraged me and shared their own stories. That moment was both terrifying and exciting, and it acted as a catalyst for my being courageous. I then came out to my husband, and he reacted with so much love, pride, and acceptance. I have since come out to a handful of people that I trust and have been met with only love, empathy and curiosity.

I looked up local resources. Although the online community helped me feel much more comfortable in my identity, I felt I could benefit from meeting people in real life. I gathered all my courage to go to a meeting of the regional "Bi+" community and met accepting, friendly and interesting people. I have since then – with my husband's continued support, patience and understanding – started a relationship with a woman I met there. It has been a whirlwind of emotions and experiences I never thought I would be able to have. My husband and I have been together for ten years and have always had very open communication. It's always been us against the problem, not us against each other. There is a foundation of trust, kindness and security in our bond, which allows for exploration without judgment.

I am so happy and grateful that *Heartstopper* has helped to unlock this part of myself that I had not realized I had within me. This change has brought excitement, sadness, joy, fear, love, connection, and acceptance – none of which I would want to miss.

B's Story

Heartstopper made me feel hopeful. Perhaps I wasn't dead inside after all. Maybe there's still a chance to find real love – a love like Nick and Charlie's. This show stirred so many emotions within me, feelings I hadn't experienced in a very long time. It made me consider that I might not want to be alone forever, that I might be open to finding someone to share my life with, and that someone might not necessarily be the gender I'd almost always exclusively been with.

Perhaps I could find a true friend with whom I also share a spark. Such a rare combination, but if Nick and Charlie could find each other – even in beautifully written fiction – then maybe it's not impossible for me to do the same.

My heart truly cracked open with these boys and their love for each other.

The way they communicate also blew me away. I've always bottled up my feelings, but Nick and Charlie were so open with theirs, able to work through conflicts and express themselves deeply, creating a safe space for each other. The writing, acting, and magical score all contributed to what I feel is the most beautiful love story we've ever seen on our TV screens. It's perfection. And I will watch it over and over, feeling the exact same way I did the first time I devoured it in one sitting: pure joy and love for this beautiful story.

Heartstopper opened my eyes to many truths about myself.

Primarily, it made me realize that I didn't want to spend my life alone—and that it was okay to embrace and express my sexuality. After years in a heterosexual marriage where I never truly felt at ease, followed by many years of solitude driven by fear of entering another relationship, I began to understand why my past relationships hadn't worked out. I had been conforming to societal expectations, not forming genuine connections with the right people. I was also carrying emotional wounds, leading me to build walls and resign myself to the belief that meeting the right person was simply not in the cards for me.

Then, *Heartstopper* reopened my heart.

I developed a pretty intense crush on a friend whom I believed to be straight at the time... Disaster. Or so I thought. After weeks – maybe months – of uncertainty and nearly giving up, they revealed to me that they are also bisexual! I had always been too nervous to ask.

Well, I'd like to thank tequila for giving me the extra courage I needed to ask for a kiss (most likely inspired by Charlie's bravery), and they said yes! We've now been seeing each other for around five weeks. It's still early days, but in the words of Tao Xu, "It's been a whirlwind"[1] – for both of us.

None of this would have happened if it weren't for *Heartstopper*. It gave me the gentle push, encouragement, and courage to pursue something I've quite possibly been yearning for my whole life. I just didn't realize it until I encountered the sweetest love story of all time.

---

1. Quotation of dialogue from the Netflix series *Heartstopper*, based on the original book by Alice Oseman.

I'll always be grateful to Alice Oseman for writing such a beautiful, heartfelt story, and to the actors who brought it to life. The hope it instills in me and so many others to form healthy, loving connections is truly inspiring.

To quote the song *Charlie* by Mallrat: "I was really feeling nothing, now you got me feeling something."

Heartstopper got me feeling again.

Thanks for listening.

Michelle's Story

I think what surprised me most after my initial viewing of *Heartstopper* was just how MUCH I felt. It was near the end of February 2023, and I was lost in my various roles as mother, wife, and primary breadwinner. I spent my days working, my evenings chasing my toddler around, and my nights cleaning up to do it all over again. While I love my daughter dearly, I was going through the mundane motions of life. I stumbled upon this show, and it completely rocked me. I found myself sitting in the dark with tears streaming down my face, surrounded by books, toys, and other playthings. I had not actually felt anything like this in such a long time, the good, the sad, everything. I realized that in creating a family and building this prescribed life, I had somehow become numb. I had somehow lost myself.

My immediate reaction was surprise. Why was I so affected by what seemed to be a show made for people who were not me? I was, after all, straight, married, and much older than these characters. Why did I feel such a pull to watch it over and over again? There was something that I couldn't quite figure out that kept drawing me back, asking me to dig, to remember who I was, or to maybe find out for the first time.

At first, I felt comfortable saying I related to the parents in the series, wanting to raise a Nick and be a Sarah for my young child. But I knew that wasn't the whole truth. I saw myself in Charlie, too. The good parts, and the bad. I saw myself in Nick, as well. I even saw myself in Imogen and started to be more vocal about my allyship, dipping my toe in by quietly involving myself in local LGBTQ+ groups. But I hesitated, feeling the weight of imposter syndrome at every turn, since I wasn't actually part of the community, despite how strongly I felt about protecting it. It would take a long time, a lot of re-watches, Googling (of course), therapy sessions, self-reflection, and a beautifully unexpected connection to lead me to my truth.

After putting away the toys, wiping away the tears, and managing through a few more days of constantly watching the show, I finally realized I couldn't be the only one, so of course, I looked to the internet for answers. I ended up in a subreddit dedicated to something called *Heartstopper* Syndrome (different from imposter syndrome, though, as it turns out, I had both). I found so many posts and comments detailing the exact same feelings I was experiencing, and what a relief it was to know I was not alone. I was nearly a year behind the release of Season 1, so there were plenty of posts and comments, but not a lot of current activity.

Thankfully, I did manage to connect with someone who was the same age as me, with a similar story. We sent messages back and forth for a bit, and then somehow, I stumbled onto a Facebook group dedicated to the show and invited her to join me there, too. Compared to the subreddit, it was wildly alive with activity and thoughtful discussions, people sharing their stories, and thank goodness for that, because I was desperate to talk to anyone and everyone who would listen.

Between measured analysis of variable water content on denim shorts[1] and screenshots of text chains between fictional characters in the Facebook group, I felt a desire to have these deep discussions in real time, so I posted asking if anyone would be interested in a group chat. Quite a few folks responded, so it started large, but over time, as these things go, there were just a handful of regularly active people. Some of them I recognized from their activity in the group, and others I was less familiar with, but we were all there for the same reason: a shared love for this beautiful story. As time passed, this group solidified and became a fixture in my life. We all still talk almost daily, even now, two years later. We shared laughs and fears, our own stories of trauma and pain, all things *Heartstopper* and many things not. They became a support system I didn't even realize I needed.

In that group, in those early days, there was one person in particular who caught my attention. She and I always seemed to see things the same way. She was so funny, yet kind, and I was always excited to read her thoughts and ideas. I felt drawn to her in a way that was different to everyone else there; it was magnetic. We began chatting privately, and it was not long before I knew there was a connection between us that was undeniable. The feelings I was having for her were not just feelings of friendship; they were something much more. But of course, there were a host of reasons why I couldn't be feeling those things, the very least of which was that I had, up until that moment in my life, genuinely believed I was straight. I think, in some ways, *Heartstopper* gave me permission to understand what those feelings meant in a way I never could have before.

---

1. This is a reference to a continuity error in the last episode, when Nick and Charlie are at the beach together and Nick walks into the sea fully clothed and the bottom of his jean shorts get wet. The sequence of scenes shows inconsistent levels of wet denim.

Once it hits you, there it rolls, the footage of your life replaying in slow motion as you remember all the moments you ignored, pushed aside, or denied. Growing up in a world where the ultimate goal, as a woman, was to find a man who would want to marry you and be the father of your children, did not leave room for many other options. I started to question everything I knew about myself and who I was, the choices I'd made to get me here, and how much different my life would be if I knew then what I know now. It felt like the earth shifted under me; foundation unsteady. It was so overwhelming that I reached out to a therapist to try and help me unravel what this meant for me and for my life. It sounds dramatic to say, but it's quite unsettling when you find out you've been hiding yourself from yourself.

Through it all, she and I never stopped talking. I was working to understand and accept who I was, and she was there supporting me along the way, from across an ocean. Ours is a relationship and connection like none I've ever experienced, and despite all the reasons I couldn't be, I found myself in love with a woman and desperate to cross that ocean. And although I'd obviously been imagining how it might be to finally meet in person, I never really thought it would be possible. But it turns out, most of the time, if you want something bad enough, you'll find a way. And we did. Our time together now feels like a dream sometimes, though I know it did happen, and it was even more beautiful than I'd imagined.

I will be forever grateful for finding this story and for the color with which it's painted my life. It cracked open a part of me that lay dormant, shook me awake and reminded me what it feels like to experience being truly alive. It's the euphoria, the joy, the sparks, but also the fear, the self-doubt, the grief, and despair. The rainbow of human emotions that we are lucky enough to experience in this gift of life.

From an outsider's perspective, my life looks generally the same as it did before I watched *Heartstopper*. I am a few years older and still married to a man, living an outwardly completely heteronormative life. But to me, I am completely transformed. I now know who I am, even if I'm still working on how to share that with the world. I have a deep understanding of what it is to share unconditional love without expectations or fear. What it means to be truly vulnerable with another human being and feel totally seen and accepted. I now know why I care so much about protecting this beautiful community and why this story speaks to me so, so deeply. It's because this is where I belong; I am here because I am queer.

Claudine's Story

I found *Heartstopper* really joyful, and initially, it left me feeling warm and happy inside. This show was a breath of fresh air compared to other LGBTQ+ shows I'd seen, and my immediate reaction was to press play and watch it all over again.

After rewatching *Heartstopper* a number of times, I found myself seeking out any other LGBTQ+ content I could find. I'd always considered myself a straight ally, but something about this felt different. I started questioning why, and after a lot of soul searching and talking it through with a friend, I realised I wasn't as straight as I thought I was. I realised I was bisexual.

I'd never questioned my sexuality before, and at 45, it was very new to me. But the more I thought about it, the more I realised the female actor I "admired", for instance, was much more than that. And the things I'd said over the years throughout my life that I thought were normal, like "if I weren't straight, I'd fancy that (female) friend", weren't actually normal for straight people. But the heteronormative society I've grown up in made sure I had never questioned my sexuality once.

Now, I finally feel whole. I still get imposter syndrome, and my preference is still men, but I know I'm not straight, and that's thanks in a huge part to Nick Nelson and his own journey in the show, and consequently the books once I'd read them.

My life has changed in other ways, too. One example is in the friendships the show has brought into my life. Thanks to the Facebook fan group I joined, I have met people from all over the world, and some I have even met in person, and they have become more like family than just friends.

Some of them have had a very similar experience to mine with discovering/accepting their bisexuality because of *Heartstopper*, and it is life-changing to have people to talk things through with. We've had so many adventures together, both *Heartstopper*-related and unrelated, and they really support and understand me better than most other friends and family in my life.

I have also learned so much about the LGBTQ+ community, thanks to Alice and that Facebook fan group. I am by far a better and more complete person now, thanks to the world *Heartstopper* has opened up to me, and I will be forever thankful to have found it.

One thing the show did stir up in me, though, was a sense of grief and sadness. A grief for the life I could've had if things had been different. A grief for the lack of a supportive and genuine friendship group at school, like they have on the show. A grief for missing out on what could've been, and I sometimes struggle to cope with that, but again, that's something the Facebook group and my new friends help me to deal with, as so many other fans seem to feel the same.

Heather's Story

When I first watched *Heartstopper*, I thought it was captivating, and I needed to watch all of the first series in one sitting. Nick and Charlie have been a very important part of my life from that point onwards.

The books and the show have changed my life, and I couldn't be more thankful to Alice for creating this beautiful masterpiece that put me on a path where I could truly learn to be myself.

Before *Heartstopper*, I was a shell of the person I am now. I worried about people's perception of me and not being accepted. My confidence was low, but *Heartstopper* made me want to show the world who I really am. In 2022, I came out as bisexual after living with the fear that nobody could accept me. Of course, there were some people who had an unsavoury opinion, but for the most part, people were just welcoming me with open arms.

In my newfound determination to prove to myself that I can do more, that I need to reach out and do the scary things, I enrolled back into school to complete my GCSEs. I've completed an Access to Higher Education diploma and I'm going to university to study clinical psychology. *Heartstopper* was the key for me to open those doors within myself to take that leap. I was inspired by Charlie's determination never to give up, to seek help with my own battles, and to take chances. I loved Nick's bravery in taking a huge step in coming out to his mum, which inspired me to do the same, as well as coming out to people in my life. Without the beautiful show, I never would have had the confidence and courage to try and give life a go.

I wish I could say my journey has been easy, but there have been some challenges along the way. I did a lot of scary things and had to battle my anxieties, but I needed to grab life with both hands. Without the support of my best friend Michelle, this would have been a lot harder. She carried me throughout the particularly tough times when I needed a listening ear and a hug. She shares my love for *Heartstopper*, and we both have spent many hours watching the beautiful story of Nick and Charlie. I have no regrets. To quote Nick Nelson, "I like who I am. I like my life."[1]

I've met Alice in person, and I froze, but I did give her a letter with everything I wished I could say to her. She's changed my life and so many others; she's truly amazing! Watching Charlie's journey, coming out of his shell and letting his true personality shine, overcoming challenges with Nick's support, has been an inspiration to me to shine my own light and not be afraid of taking up space in the world.

---

1. Quotation of dialogue from the Netflix series *Heartstopper*, based on the original book by Alice Oseman.

Suzie Davidson's Story

I stumbled across *Heartstopper* after the first season was released on Netflix. I was instantly filled with a level of joy that I hadn't experienced before while watching TV. It felt incredible and a bit unbelievable to see queer representation in this format. I was transported back to my teenage years, literally feeling all the animated swirling leaves, electric shocks and butterflies right along with Nick and Charlie.

Heartstopper showed me how important representation is. The strength I found through the story of Nick and Charlie helped me come out to my teenage kids, paved the way to a deeper connection to my sister, helped our family process my nephew's OCD diagnosis, and has led me to an online community full of love, acceptance, music, and connection. In a period of my life that can feel dark, especially in the current political environment in the USA, *Heartstopper*, Alice, and the surrounding community bring in the light.

I am a bisexual woman in my mid-forties who has been happily married to a straight man (who has always known about my bisexuality) for nearly 20 years. We have two amazing teenage kids. When I came out as bisexual in my late teens, I never thought about the fact that I may one day have to come out to my kids. But, being in a hetero-presenting relationship, I came to realize that, while my kids understood my support and celebration of the queer community, they didn't see me as part of it. That was a heartbreaking realization, and I instantly felt like I was pushed back into the closet. Watching *Heartstopper* and reliving the fear, the relief, and ultimately the joy of coming out through Nick's story gave me the courage to start talking more freely about my sexuality with my kids. Thankfully, they are very open-minded, and although a little surprised, they had no issues.

My older sister and I have also bonded over our love of all things *Heartstopper*. She is a 52-year-old queer woman living with her wife and gender-exploring son on the other side of the country. We have always been close, even with the miles between us, but *Heartstopper* created a new level of connection. We both related to Nick's struggles and moments of discovery around his sexual identity, and Charlie's struggles with his eating disorder and OCD hit close to home. My sister discovered *Heartstopper* right after my nephew had been diagnosed with ARFID (Avoidant Restricted Food Intake Disorder) and OCD and was in a partial hospitalization treatment facility.

She had no idea that this beautiful coming-of-age gay romance story would also explore the very difficult and personal issues her family was currently facing. Charlie's Anorexia and OCD diagnoses allowed us to step into the journey of his character and process our overwhelm from there. It created a safe and relatable way for our family to discuss what was happening in our real lives. *Heartstopper* sparked a desire in both of us to be more honest and vulnerable with each other about the challenges and the beauty of our very different expressions of being queer in this world.

My love of *Heartstopper* grew to a new level after the 2024 US presidential election. I was devastated by the outcome, and as an act of resistance, I decided to find ways to support more queer artists. This brought me back to *Heartstopper*. I joined Alice's full-tier Patreon account and discovered the Osemanverse was so much more than the shows. I ended up buying and reading all of

Alice's books, following them and many of the cast on social media and finding an online community that gave me the courage to lean even further into my queerness.

I am so grateful to Alice and for this entire community. Thanks for providing a place for me to express that gratitude.

Stephanie Archer's Story

I thought *Heartstopper* was beautiful and heartwarming when I first watched it. It made me cry so much, I felt melancholy for something which I never had growing up in the 80s, amongst the fear of AIDS and systemic homophobia. I wish I'd had a group of friends like Charlie's, because my life would have been very different.

The scene where Nick comes out to his mum literally changed the course of my life. I was watching it on my own, and it felt like an explosion had gone off, and everything that I had tightly controlled since I was young came bursting out. It was very emotional and overwhelming; when I was a teenager, I didn't really have anyone I could talk to about things. Nick's character was so relatable, even though he is a boy, and seeing his journey portrayed in the way it was, it felt like it gave permission to people to come out as bi. I had never seen anyone on TV or in films come out as bisexual; I thought people just didn't. After watching this for three weeks, I had what can only be described as a mental health crisis. It totally floored me; I couldn't talk to anyone about how I felt, which culminated in me getting counselling.

I had known I was bi since I was 15 years old, but I didn't know the word for it. It wasn't until university that I heard the word from a friend who shared that he had kissed a boy. Even after a few short-term relationships with women at uni and after, I never came out. Very few people knew, and I kept it that way. Fundamentally, I was too scared – I believed that society thought being bisexual wasn't truly valid. I had a lot of internalised biphobia, with thoughts like *you are just kidding yourself, pick a side, just admit you are gay, you are obviously going to cheat,* etc. – things I heard from others that had stuck with me.

When I watched *Heartstopper* for the first time, I had been married for 17 years to a straight man. The counselling helped me to understand the effect that this coming-out scene had on me and why. Moreover, it led me to come out at 53 years old to my amazing, understanding husband and my closest friends.

In the 80s, there was no information and no one to ask about bisexuality. *Heartstopper* showed me how much things have changed for the better. Having this kind of representation is so very important, particularly for teenagers, and I am eternally grateful to this show for allowing me, at last, after so very long, to be able to be honest about who I am, and to be the real, authentic me, the person I wish I could have fully been for the last 38 years.

Lisa's Story

Married mom of 5 and newly minted bisexual, actually

Heartstopper made me smile from the first episode. The writing and the production design, the animation of the comic, the color choices and music, everything was done beautifully. The authenticity of the characters and their stories made me want to get to know them more. And when I did, I found myself getting very protective and attached to them. They became like another one of my kids. Picking a favorite? I can't. I love them all. I loved how they supported each other. I loved how they made mistakes and tried to do better the next time. And I loved how they cared. It was everything I wanted for my real-world kids. And it gave me hope that if *Heartstopper* could model a world where that existed, then the world was in better shape than I thought.

What surprised me is how much I ended up changed by this story. I saw my younger self in their struggles. And I felt their joy and pain. But I also felt their questions. The way Nick made his way towards his knowledge of being bisexual awakened questions in me, and at the age of 60, I realized I was also bisexual, actually. Nick talked about admiring his rugby camp coach. I admired the lead actress in a summer theater group I joined when I was in middle school. His eyes traveled between Kiera Knightley and Orlando Bloom when he watched *Pirates of the Caribbean*. I couldn't decide who I wanted to watch more – Emma Thompson or Alan Rickman in *Sense and Sensibility*. Or more recently, Yennifer and Geralt in *The Witcher* and Roy Kent and Rebecca Welton in *Ted Lasso*. I started to notice the pattern more and more. *Heartstopper* had given me the push I needed to free my mind of past limits. As Miguel and Julio said in *El Dorado*, "Both. Both is good."

My family was already a rainbow flag family. My oldest daughter is bisexual, the next daughter is aro/ace, as is my youngest daughter. My older son is what we laughingly call our token straight kid, and my younger son is gay. My husband is straight. Our journey as a queer family started out rocky, tethered by our upbringings, but my husband and I learned and worked through everything as best we could with love and acceptance as our guide. I learned even more from the *Heartstopper* characters and their stories. I have a better vocabulary and more insight when I talk to my kids. I understand more of the nuance of being aromantic and asexual because I was privy to Isaac and his friends as they navigated his blossoming understanding of himself. And like Sarah, I allow myself to just sit and listen without trying to fix things, and that has allowed me to enjoy watching my kids fly the nest, knowing I have prepared them as best I could.

My life has not changed on the surface. I'm still a wife and mother, pharmacist and friend. I'm still the lady who played piano for the kids' chorus at school and helped with scouts. When I shared my truth online while advocating for queer youth in our local schools, I was met with disbelief and an opportunity to educate my neighbors about the prevalence of LGBTQ people in the general (and local) community. But beneath the surface, my understanding of myself without the labels related to others has made me much more free. Alice has infused her characters with an emotional intelligence that elevates this story beyond most teen graphic novels. It's a love story. A beautiful love story. Not just between two boys, but also of themselves as individuals. They learn to love themselves in all their flawed glory.

There has always been something freeing in processing my emotions through art. Whether a play or a TV show, or a piece of music,

I find art is the language I need to unravel myself. Just like Nick and Charlie, through *Heartstopper*, I have made my own emotional journey. And the knowledge I gained of who I am has allowed me to express myself more clearly and fearlessly. This year was my first Pride as an out member of the community, and I spent it at World Pride in Washington, DC, purposefully alone to take it all in for myself. I ask for things I need, and I don't discount my own talents and treasures. I make better choices for myself and my family. And it has allowed me to navigate the road towards an empty nest with more grace.

For myself, *Heartstopper* became the story I went back to – for comfort, for understanding, for a soft place to land when the world was not what I envisioned. Finding new movies and shows through actor filmographies is even more rewarding now that I have a cast of talented young people to watch as their careers unfold. Experiencing Sam Gold's *Romeo and Juliet* on Broadway with Kit Connor and a cast of Broadway debuts was a revelation. As an amateur writer, I marvel at the story and character development of *Heartstopper*. I fangirl over the production details of color and music. It is beautiful, through and through. And even in adversity, with real-world problems intruding, I know "my" boys – Nick and Charlie – my kids, both real and wonderfully imagined by Alice Oseman and the creative minds of the *Heartstopper* team, will make it. They will make it and be OK.

Thank you, Alice, for letting us share your vision of what love and friendship can be. What a wonderful world.

The Gift of Asexual Representation

By Rowan Murphy

Asexuality, which is characterised by not experiencing sexual attraction, or not experiencing it the same way most people do, is probably one of the least well-known and understood sexual orientations, even within the community. As with bisexuality, there are those who resist including it as part of the LGBTQIA+ umbrella, in large part due to the lack of general awareness and understanding. Asexuality started to gain more recognition in the early 2010s, with the "A" becoming a fairly recent addition to the LGBTQIA+ acronym (around 2015). Aromanticism (not experiencing romantic attraction to others) is even less well known. People who fit into both categories often refer to themselves as aro/ace. In contrast, individuals who regularly experience sexual attraction towards others are referred to as allosexual (or "allo").

As a parent of an aro/ace child (who also contributed her story to this book), I have seen firsthand how many misconceptions and negative opinions exist about asexuality. I've watched the struggle my daughter had in making sense of an environment where romance and sex are deeply entrenched in most aspects of our lives.

Starting in middle school, when she was eleven, I heard my daughter wonder about her peers and how much they were talking about sex. She was utterly bewildered by it, but given her age at the time, I didn't think much of it. As she grew older and entered her teenage years, I remember watching TV shows and movies with her, and she would squirm uncomfortably in her seat or look away anytime more intimate scenes came on. She voiced her discomfort, like she felt squeamish when people were ostensibly having sex on screen (nothing explicit, obviously). Sometimes she would say how uncomfortable it must have been to film these scenes.

At first, I thought her reaction was due to her being embarrassed having a parent in the room when something like that was shown on TV, and that maybe it was just normal teenage awkwardness. But over time, it became clear that there was more to it. Seeing Isaac's story in *Heartstopper*, and later finding Alice's other book, *Loveless*, which also features an asexual character, were important moments for her.

Alice Oseman is open about being asexual and aromantic. "The world is obsessed with sex and romance. And if you don't have that, you feel like you haven't achieved something that's really important,"[1] Alice stated in an interview with The Guardian on 19 Nov. 2022. The importance of platonic relationships, as outlined in the article, is highlighted in all of their work and plays a significant role in the TV adaptation of *Heartstopper*. Acknowledging the lack of representation and general awareness, Oseman said that "we're never really going to see much cultural change in terms of awareness until a big celebrity comes out as being asexual."

Well, not to argue with a creative genius, but I would say that *Heartstopper* has made a huge difference, as proven by the sheer volume of story submissions that came in from people on the aro/ace spectrum, who made up the third largest group at 16% of our respondents. To put this number in context: According

---

1. Lucy Knight, "Heartstopper author Alice Oseman: 'If you don't have sex and romance, you feel like you haven't achieved'", http://www.theguardian.com, 19 November 2022

to asexuality.org, the estimate is that 1% of the total population identifies as asexual. Looking at the Pride Study (mentioned in the prior chapter), 8% of LGBTQIA+ participants identified as asexual. Visibility, information, and education are sorely needed so people don't feel alienated or like something is "wrong" with them.

> "I finally discovered that there's a name for how I'm attracted to people, and I'd never known it before, so I felt a great sense of relief."
>
> Maria J.

Societal expectations weigh heavily on most of us; the traditional family structure is deeply embedded in all aspects of our culture. Unmarried people, especially women, once reaching a certain age, have throughout history been viewed with pity, judgment, or even mockery. Women would be called spinsters, and while unattached men might be viewed as irresponsible or selfish, they were more easily accepted than unmarried women. Authors like Jane Austen or the Brontë sisters captured these societal attitudes during their time quite vividly. Financial independence was rare for women up until fairly recently (and even now, there is disparity between the sexes), so marriage was often a matter of survival.

Although the economic circumstances and legislative landscape have changed, the general expectations and societal norms remain centred around conventional family values. This can be a tricky environment to navigate for a person who has no interest in a romantic or sexual relationship. It's even harder when you don't understand why you are wired that way, and when you feel like something is lacking, or something is wrong with you; the stories we've received can attest to that. Hopefully, some of these heartfelt, moving narratives will help readers on the aro/ace spectrum feel seen and heard. Many of the stories shared commonalities, demonstrating, yet again, the critical importance of representation. To know someone, anyone, whose experience is similar to one's own, is a powerful aid in feeling less peculiar and isolated.

> "I realised I'm asexual. At the age of 47! I always thought that it's something wrong with me. Now, all this has become clear."
>
> Anna

It doesn't help when those around you invalidate your feelings constantly by saying things like, "How do you know you don't like it if you haven't even tried?" or, "You just haven't found the right person yet." We often bend and twist ourselves into something we're not in order to avoid prejudice or alienation, as evidenced by some of the stories we received where people felt they had to force themselves into physically intimate relationships even though it went against their nature. The pressure to conform in order to fit in affects us all.

> "The way the media and society modeled relationships and interactions just didn't seem right; I never had the urge to be particularly touchy-feely, nor did I have a strong desire to kiss someone, or to go further than that. I met the man who is now my husband when we were in high school, but I never told him about these feelings, which I have just recently come to understand mean that I am on the aromantic and asexual (aro/ace) spectrums. He knew I was bisexual; I told him, since he was my best friend all through high school, but he never knew about my lack of interest

in a sexual relationship. I've always put others above myself, and this was one of those things where I repressed my feelings to be what he needed."

Alexis

One thing is crucial to understand: people on the aro/ace spectrum have the same core human need for connection that everyone else does. I really liked the wording on the website: "Asexuality does not limit a person's emotional needs. As is the case for sexual people, we vary widely in how we fulfil those needs. Some asexual people may still desire romantic relationships. Other asexual people may be most satisfied with close friendships, or happier on their own."

When I looked up asexual representation in the media, just to see what Google would offer, I was thrilled, but not surprised, to see *Heartstopper* as the top result for positive ace representation. This show is groundbreakingly inclusive, and having a central character like Isaac go through a journey of discovering their asexuality is truly a gift. Not only did this portrayal raise awareness and motivate people to research and better understand this identity, but it also liberated people from their self-imposed mental and emotional confines.

> "I'd already questioned and sorta-considered myself asexual before watching it, but *Heartstopper* helped me feel more normal in my own body."

Benwvatt

Isaac's overall journey in *Heartstopper* throughout the three seasons is a poignant and beautifully told story. We hear him say early on that he wants to believe in romance (S1 E2), and we follow his gradual questioning and self-discovery throughout the episodes, with several painful moments along the way. We often see him look around the room, taking in the various couples he's surrounded by, and his facial expression is a bit forlorn. He tentatively asks Charlie what it feels like to *like* a person romantically while they are on the bus to Paris, which doesn't seem to help much, and when James plucks up the courage to confess his crush, and they exchange a brief kiss, confusion and emotional turmoil are writ across Isaac's features. I just wanted to hug him when he returned to the hotel room with tears on his cheeks. Over time, he gets increasingly frustrated with the friend group's badgering about the state of his relationship with James, and he finally snaps at them when he's had enough of their playful, teasing banter.

In true bookworm fashion, Isaac peruses some books along the way to help him understand asexuality, and the first person he opens up to about it is Charlie in Episode 1 of Season 3. His journey culminates in a heated argument with Tao, which finally leads to his coming out to the friend group as aromantic and asexual in Episode 3 of Season 3. Of course, as to be expected in this show, his friends are kind and accepting.

One scene in particular struck a chord with people, where an art student explains his exhibit to Isaac in Episode 7 of Season 2. He tells him that his piece is about his experience being aromantic and asexual, living in a world where romance and sex are of the highest value, while not feeling those forms of attraction himself. He explains that he grew up feeling that something was different about him, but was unable to describe it, and then found freedom in the euphoria of liberating himself from those expectations and pressures.

This moment is pivotal in Isaac's self-exploration, and in the next episode, he is seen picking up a book about asexuality and hugging it to his chest. Tobie Donovan, who plays Isaac, handled this subject matter with delicate care, pulling the viewer into his emotional journey. Many fans in all age groups have shared the relief they felt when realising that the absence of sexual or romantic attraction in their lives wasn't because they were lacking in something, but that there was an entire spectrum of asexuality where they could see themselves reflected.

> "This show changed the way I perceived myself. As a much younger person, I had relayed to my mother that I had no interest in being with someone or having children, and I remember she scoffed at me. [To her,] this was such a ridiculous way to think. So, I tamped it down and went on to marry, have children and now I'm a grandmother who, through this show, was able to rediscover and accept the truth of myself that I'm on the ace spectrum and have always been. There has been no coming out, as I told one person and was once again told, you can't be, you have children, so I tamped it back down again, but to myself I've been able to acknowledge my truth."
>
> Jenn

What is very important to note is that asexuality and aromanticism encompass a spectrum of various ways in which people experience different forms of attraction. Not everyone on the asexual spectrum feels romantic and sexual attraction in the same way. When I researched the aro/ace spectrum, I was amazed to find a label that seemed to describe my very own feelings and experience: demisexuality. I have never enjoyed casual sex, but once again had been led to believe that my past trauma had something to do with that. I've always needed a strong emotional connection to find true enjoyment in physical intimacy. When I was at university, many of my fellow students were having casual relations like that, and I tried it out to see what the fuss was all about, but left those encounters feeling gross and somewhat repulsed, even though my partners had been nice enough.

There are many identities on the asexual spectrum; in very general terms, some people do not feel sexual attraction at all (asexual), others feel it only rarely or under specific circumstances (greysexual), or only once they get to know a person better and form an emotional connection, like me (demisexual). And even within one "label", such as demisexual, not everyone finds the transition from becoming friends to feeling sexual attraction in the same manner. I've heard some people describe it as a switch being flicked, whereas others felt a gradual change over time. Researching this was a revelation – and I feel like I have barely scratched the surface.

I've always thought that almost everything about the human experience is so nuanced and varied that even two people truly feeling identical about themselves and the world around them is hard to imagine. We have no way of knowing what is happening inside someone else's mind, but even though so much literature exists that tries to describe and explain everything about our thoughts, feelings, instincts, needs, and desires, there just isn't a manual, a one-size-fits-all approach to going through life.

Fortunately, lots of resources are available to learn more about asexuality and aromanticism. One of the oldest websites I am aware of is the aforementioned asexuality.org, and for younger audiences, the Trevor Project has helpful and easy-to-read information on its website. There are many websites and books to learn more (some of which are included in the reference section at the end of this book), but more positive media representation is definitely needed.

"At the age of 36, the character of Issac is the only openly asexual person I have EVER seen on television!!! That's crazy to me!!"

Danielle J.

Alice's stories have validated, liberated, and empowered us all, but especially those on the asexual spectrum, who have never seen themselves reflected in mainstream media.

Jackie Ross-Lavender's Story
"Thank You, Alice Oseman!"

This is a transcript of Jackie's video[1] on YouTube, included in this book with his permission.

Jackie Ross-Lavender is a queer filmmaker and content creator hoping to inspire thought and change one video at a time.

"I love Charlie Spring in a romantic way, not just a friend way."

In 2022, *Heartstopper* was adapted to screen by Netflix, and the world exploded.

So, where do I enter this story? *Heartstopper* came into my life at the perfect time. At the point of watching *Heartstopper* for the first time, I was three years deep into a YouTube and creative hiatus. I lost my career due to COVID. I had no direction, no forward trajectory. I was just existing. And I was sinking further and further into, well, alcohol addiction.

I was at one of the lowest points of my life and struggling in silence. I felt like I was disappearing. Now here's where my life and *Heartstopper* cross paths. As I made my way through the eight episodes, I was filled with so many emotions. Happiness, anger, grieving. Just about every emotion you could think of. And when I reached the end of this series, which I adored for so many reasons, I was left with an overwhelming feeling of sadness.

---

1. http://bit.ly/47oQdg7

And at first, I couldn't figure out why. Why had I found this series both equally gratifying and traumatic? Well, I quickly realised that as the show went on, I was being forced to revisit my own experiences, and it made me realise that I've got a lot of healing to do. I'd spent so many years repressing so many emotions from the traumas of my childhood, and they were all now starting to surface. I knew I couldn't continue to repress these emotions if I was ever going to truly heal.

So I began to share in the only way that I knew how: By watching the show again and writing down all of my feelings in note form. And by the time I was done, I knew exactly what I had to do next.

I had to make a YouTube video.

For the first time in three years, I was inspired to pick up a camera and film a video. In that video, I talked about why *Heartstopper* is so special to me. How it helped me to grieve and finally let go of being estranged from my homophobic family. How it helped me to heal from my own very damaging coming-out experience.

Heartstopper has since changed my life in so many ways. I restarted my YouTube career, and I have once again begun chasing my dreams of being a voice for the LGBT community on the internet. I have a thriving Patreon community who are the most wonderful and supportive human beings I could ask to surround myself with. I've even recently moved to pursuing content creation full-time, which has been a dream five years in the making.

But every few weeks or so, I find myself back to where this chapter started. Watching that first *Heartstopper* video again, and every single time I'm filled with so much gratitude. Gratitude for how this incredible story and all the surrounding stories from the Osemanverse have helped me heal.

But there's something more, something I couldn't say. That changes today.

I wasn't ready to talk about it then, but I am now. And this is the first time that I'm saying this out loud, but Alice's work has helped me gain the confidence and the courage to revisit the trauma of being sexually abused at age 9. An experience that has affected me every single day for 22 years. An experience which led me to believe for so long that I was damaged, that I was abnormal. But through Alice and her work, I've learned at age 31 that I'm not damaged. I'm actually asexual.

I didn't really understand that that was even a thing. I didn't know that there was a word for it. But through the incredible representation in the Osemanverse, I have come to learn that I'm one of many and I'm whole. And I'm not to be defined by the loss of my innocence as a child. So not only has Alice's work allowed me to do an intense amount of healing around the issues so many of us in the LGBT community face when it comes to acceptance from our own family and our upbringing, but it has also allowed me to truly find myself. To find myself in ways I never thought possible.

To quote Mr. Ajayi: "Don't let anyone make you disappear, Charlie."[2]

I'm really understanding that now. So, thank you, Alice. Thank you for creating such a beautifully inclusive and diverse universe of stories and characters that are helping us all feel seen; that are helping us all to not disappear and are helping us all to heal the wounds from our childhoods. I wish so, so much that I had your work when I was a teenager or a child because I would have avoided so many years of hurting, but I'm grateful. I am so, so

---

2. Quotation of dialogue from the Netflix series *Heartstopper,* based on the original book by Alice Oseman.

grateful that the LGBT youth of today have your work to help support them through what can often be a very cruel world.

I want you to know that your work is, without a doubt, going to save so many lives in the LGBT community. I want you to know that you've saved mine.

Now, I'm sure many of you at the beginning of this video thought it was a misquote.

But it wasn't.

I don't like Charlie Spring.

I love him.

And Nick Nelson and Elle Argent and Aled Last and Tori Spring and all of these wonderful LGBT+ characters in the Osemanverse that are helping us all feel seen.

MP's Story

I have no specific history with the LGBTQA+ world. I've always thought of myself as straight. I have always supported my rainbow friends and taken part in Pride, for example, but I saw myself as an ally ("I'm not, like, homophobic,"[1] to quote Imogen from Season 1). Then I watched *Heartstopper* in May 2022. And I rewatched *Heartstopper*. And I kept watching *Heartstopper*. And when Nick and Charlie had their first kiss, I cried uncontrollably, time and time again. And I had no idea why that was.

I devoured everything *Heartstopper*-related. I dove headfirst into all things Alice Oseman. I read the graphic novels, and then I read all of Oseman's other works. I became obsessed with the cast and their careers. I listened to the music from the soundtrack. I took deep dives on Twitter. And then, when there were absolutely no more reaction videos or anything else to consume, I discovered fanfiction (this was in the summer of 2022). I've been a fan of things or people before (especially when I was younger), but I had never been in a fandom before. This has all been new to me.

I've been on a journey of self-discovery: turns out I'm not straight. I'm ace (asexual). I do have an allosexual[2] past, and that was true at the time, but I've since come to understand that sexuality is a

---

1. Quotation of dialogue from the Netflix series *Heartstopper*, based on the original book by Alice Oseman.

2. Allosexual means experiencing sexual attraction the way most people do.

thing that evolves and changes. I haven't found a microlabel that fits my current state; there are traces of many: gray, fray, aceflux, aego[3]. And that's okay. I know many people like labels and see them as things that help them, whereas I kind of feel the opposite.

I think that part of what triggered the exploration of my identity was seeing their friend group and how strong a bond they had, and feeling a longing to be a part of something so special. My reading and studying everything *Heartstopper* related was somewhat fueled by a small wish to find something that would feel **like me**. Of course, I understand that just because I have this new understanding of myself, I don't automatically get my own Isaac or Tara or Elle (or even Tao), especially since I'm only out to a couple of people in real life and can't really see that changing anytime soon. But in my online community, I've found something that resembles that bond remarkably well.

I've also learned a lot about my relationship with my body through the deep dives I've done to better understand my sexuality. I've realized that I have severe body dysmorphia, and that's why I'm averse to straight and lesbian love stories: I don't want to see anybody who I can personally relate to, as a cis woman, have any kind of physical relations.

I wholeheartedly support trans people and sapphic people (and even straight people!), but if someone's AFAB (assigned female at birth) and there are vaginas involved, I'm personally out; it is extremely triggering to me. I don't know if that is necessarily a

---

3. In very general terms: graysexuality means experiencing sexual attraction to a limited extent; fraysexuality means that attraction to someone is strongest initially, fading as an emotional bond develops; aceflux describes individuals whose degree of asexuality fluctuates over time; aegosexuality means someone may experience sexual attraction without the desire to act on it.

"positive" impact, but at least it's something I'm aware of now that I wasn't before.

Being part of a fan community has been life-altering. Being in a fandom with people of all ages, all backgrounds, and all over the world has been the most rewarding thing in my life. I'm actually in contact with several people all around the world on a daily basis. I've found a friend with whom I am close enough to tell them everything about myself. I've never been this honest with any of my real-life friends or my husband.

I've actually taken time for myself. After becoming a parent, I was lost for a long time. For years, I didn't have anything I felt so passionate about that I would prioritize it, or prioritize myself. But now I've travelled to different countries alone just to meet my online friends. I went to Poland to see three friends (Polish, Swiss, German), and this summer I'm travelling to Denmark to see the German friend again, as well as one from Australia. How incredibly cool is that?!

These friends are people I feel seen with, I feel safe with. It's **everything** to me. I never ever would have thought I would find new friends, let alone new friends who would become this important, at this age, and through the internet. If you'd told me three years ago that this would be my life, I'd have thought you were insane. It's unbelievable, really; I went to visit Auschwitz with someone I had just met in person for the first time the previous day! And all just because we both fell in love with two incredibly brave fictional teenage boys. I'm so grateful for that.

Heartstopper has also inspired me to write. I've always enjoyed writing. I write a lot in my job, but that's work-related and in my native language. Creative writing in English is not something I thought I'd ever do. But I found my voice and have even written something other than fanfiction. My self-esteem as a writer is not the best, and I haven't written anything new in months, but before *Heartstopper*, I had never done it, and now there are silly little stories in the world that I have made from scratch.

Heartstopper has changed my life in **all** the ways. And absolutely for the better.

A. Murray's Story

I watched *Heartstopper* for the first time in October of 2024, without knowing anything about it. I had been in search of queer TV shows and movies that had good representation. I live in a small conservative town, and I don't get to interact with many queer people. As I was looking for something to watch that I could feel part of, I turned on Season 1 of *Heartstopper*.

I had no clue what to expect, but I immediately knew I had found something very important. I remember thinking to myself that I wish I had found it so much sooner. I couldn't stop watching and ended up finishing the whole first season in one night. The show made me feel seen and understood in a way that I had never felt before, almost like it was a missing piece of my life that was finally put in place, and I knew instantly that *Heartstopper* would be so much more to me than just a show or a comic.

It helped me in so many ways. It helped me better understand myself and accept myself for who I am. It also gave me hope for a future with a community of friends that can be my own found family, and where I can experience joy no matter how hard life gets. *Heartstopper* changed my life from the moment that I pressed play.

This show helped me discover so many things about myself, and the biggest one was understanding my sexuality. I remember watching *Heartstopper* and feeling like I related to so many characters, but when Isaac came out as aromatic and asexual, something in my brain clicked. It started with the scene in Paris, where he shares his first kiss with James. His reaction on the screen was like the way I felt inside when I experienced my first kiss. It was very confusing, and afterwards I had an uncomfortable feeling about all of it. You would expect some sort of reaction, like the foot kick in *The Princess Diaries*, some kind of fireworks, but Isaac's face was expressing none of that, and my own experience mirrored that. I honestly had never heard of AroAce, and I wanted to know more. I had heard about asexuality before, but the aromantic aspect of it was new to me.

After researching and learning more about it, reflecting back on my own life, I finally realized that I am AroAce. I grew up around a hypersexual friend group, and it made me feel like I had to try very hard to feel similar emotions to them, and like I had to work extra hard to put myself out there in order to find "the one". After the show, I started talking to a group of AroAce people on Tumblr, and it made me feel like a weight was lifted off me in realizing that other people shared my experience. Instead of feeling stressed or scared about this realization, I felt comfort in knowing more about myself and in the fact that such a powerful show had representation that I finally felt like I could identify with. *Heartstopper* also made it easier for me to come out to my friends as AroAce and gave me the courage to seek out others.

Given the political events of the recent year, I had been feeling so scared of being myself and fearing that I would not be accepted, but *Heartstopper* helped me truly understand what "Queer joy is resistance" means. I attended World Pride in DC, my first time going to a Pride parade, and there was a tent dedicated to the Aro/Ace community, which made me feel so very happy. I spent a lot of my life worrying about other people and how the government might impact my rights, so going to Pride and sharing in the joy of being authentically who we are felt powerful.

This show made me become more open with my friends and family, and more comfortable with myself. It is a daily reminder not to let anyone make me disappear. Although there may be hard times and struggles in life, I will always have *Heartstopper* to turn to as my happy place, and a community of fans where I know I will be accepted for who I am.

Caecilia's Story

[Caecilia is Rowan's daughter.]

I've always felt different. I was never interested in sex or other intimate acts. When my peers would discuss things like that, I never saw the appeal, and when I would see things that involved sex in shows or movies, I would either feel nothing, think of it in a logical sense, or sometimes feel uncomfortable. I would get physically uncomfortable and literally cringe. I also never thought of people in a sexual way before, or in a way of wanting to do intimate acts with them.

I did date for a short period of time, but the thought of becoming intimate with them never crossed my mind. Whenever I would share these thoughts, people would tell me things like "well, you've never actually had sex, so you won't know if you like it or not," or "you just have to wait for the right person," or they would call me "naive".

It wasn't until a later point that I learned of the term asexual while researching LGBTQ+ information on the internet. What I read about it made it seem like it wasn't a good thing to identify as, or that people who identified with it were deemed "weird" in a bad connotation. I was actually in denial for a long time about being asexual and believed what people were telling me about my own feelings.

I've never seen asexual representation in any sort of media, so when I watched *Heartstopper* and read the graphic novel series, I was pleasantly surprised. It made me feel seen, and I absolutely related to Isaac's character. It was like I found someone just like me (especially since I had never actually met another asexual person before). When watching Isaac's story, I actually felt like a normal person. It also made me feel extremely emotional. Feeling seen like that is something I can't even describe. I had so many emotions going on at one time. It was very lovely seeing Isaac's friends accept him as being asexual, and I hope that I can find people like them, too, who will accept me like they did Isaac.

Heartstopper led me to reading another book by Alice Oseman, called *Loveless*. I was in an inpatient mental health treatment at the time that I read it. It was like I was reading my own thoughts and feelings written out on the pages. It felt like Alice had picked through my brain. Georgia's struggle of telling other people how she felt and seeing her go through the different emotions was extremely relatable to me. I was Georgia, and she was me. My reaction to this book was very, very emotional, but also liberating. Up to this point, I had wondered if other asexual people even existed.

Despite the relief of understanding myself and finally having an explanation, I was also sad, and a little jealous of the fact that Georgia had people to talk to about it who accepted her. There is still a little sadness about my future, because I envision a relationship that I don't think is achievable: Having a platonic relationship with someone who won't expect intimacy. I worry that I will just end up alone.

After watching *Heartstopper* and seeing Isaac's story arc, I ended up accepting that I am asexual. And of course, when I came out to one of my parents, who is one of the authors of this book, he wasn't surprised. Thankfully, he was very aware of the LGBTQIA+

community and is part of the community too. I still haven't come out to my other parent, as I don't think he would understand. Plus, we don't talk about that kind of stuff anyway.

I also haven't really told other people in my life after accepting myself. Not because I feel ashamed of being asexual, but sometimes, I do feel like I might be judged or just be told those same things that I've been told before, and I know that's not the case. I also don't want to have to argue with others about what my feelings actually are. I'm happy with being asexual myself, so I don't care what others think, but I don't want people I care about to judge me for something I can't control or change.

I'm so thankful to Alice Oseman for creating *Heartstopper* and showing such amazing representation not just for the LGBTQIA+ community but for asexuals in particular. It's thanks to her and her work that I was able to understand and accept myself.

Iris' Story

When I first saw *Heartstopper*, I thought it was just an awkward show for preteens, but the more episodes I watched (while reading the comic on the side), the more it both warmed my heart and made it ache, knowing these are real experiences many have gone through.

Heartstopper is a story for everyone, and I hope it has had a positive impact on both queer and cishet, young and old people alike. It shows such a heartwarming and important spectrum of queer identities and themes, but also deals with many other issues that youth have to face in today's world. It touches on mental health problems, both with oneself and especially in those around you, and on the pressure to drink or have sex. Bringing up these themes and taboos and discussing them in such a sensitive way, like *Heartstopper* does, is something incredibly important for our society.

I've become so much more comfortable in my own skin. It can be difficult being asexual when everyone around you is talking about dating and sex-related topics. Seeing asexuality represented like it is in *Heartstopper*, and showing that having people around you is just as important as having a partner, was a huge thing for me to see. The topic of eating disorders was treated so sensitively, and especially when Charlie read the letter to his parents, which was really touching and powerful.

I started to advocate for people around me who might not have the voice or the courage to speak, because there are still so many things wrong and unjust, even inside the queer community. One of my younger siblings is trans, and I have some other asexual people in my circle, so I've kind of taken them under my wing. For example, I have encountered misinformation in a post on Instagram and commented on it, and it resulted in someone actually reaching out to me to ask for advice on dealing with being asexual. A simple comment on a post, or pointing out when someone is undermining an identity, can be really impactful.

Heartstopper has had an immense effect on my journey dealing with mental health and with accepting my identity, and I will be eternally thankful for it, because being asexual can feel so alienating and lonely sometimes. When you feel really, really anxious, insecure in your body and uncomfortable in your own skin, stories like *Heartstopper* are a reminder that there are other people who deal with the same issues and give you a sense of hope. Tori's character has especially made me cry on multiple occasions because there are so many aspects to her that I can relate to, and seeing her be there and provide support for Charlie in her own way, and the impact it had on him, has been a huge comfort and inspiration for me.

Seeing these characters, who are younger than I am, struggle with the same things I've had to go through and seeing them overcome those struggles has had a big impact on me. Charlie's journey from the ages of 14 to 16 was so similar to my own, and I was 15 at the time I first watched it, so I was experiencing the same struggles at the same age. Watching it now at 20, in my flat, at uni, is such a powerful thing, seeing it from the other side. For people in that age group who are getting ready to finish school and start their path to uni, this story is a really good representation of how much of a struggle growing up can be, but also shows that they can do it, and it will be okay. When I got to the last season, I felt so overwhelmingly proud and happy just realising how far I've come myself from when I watched the first season to when the last season came out.

I don't think I would be here doing what I truly want to do in life, not caring too much about what others think, if it weren't for *Heartstopper*. I feel like I've grown up to be a quite brave person who is truly, unapologetically themself. I'm studying art education, and am currently working at a kids' summer camp, working with something that actually matters both on a personal level for the kids and on a societal level as preventive social work. Being brave enough to take your own path, no matter what others think, is something I want to model for future generations, and it is something I learned from Nick and *Heartstopper*.

Sophie Grudin's Story

It felt like a whole new world had opened up for me when I found *Heartstopper*. I had spent the last few years beforehand just existing but not really living. But the joy that *Heartstopper* brought, particularly Nick and Charlie's relationship, opened my mind to emotions I had not let myself feel in a very long time. The most notable among them was clearly love. I have never felt love more viscerally from an artistic medium than I did when watching this show.

I have never been in love, but the feelings this show evoked – I think I could now easily identify romantic love if I ever found it for another person. As I watched Season 1, I fell in love with the show in tandem with Nick and Charlie falling in love with each other. It created such a bond between me and the show – there is a reason why fans watch it over and over again.

I watched the entirety of the first Season six times in three days. It was filling a hole in myself that I had not even realized was there. I was finally experiencing my first teenage love story at the age of 37. It was cathartic and healing and also a little heart-breaking, knowing these emotions exist, and I was only now getting a hint of them for the first time. I was sucked into the world of *Heartstopper* with its beautiful romances, supportive friend groups and diverse sexualities (and lack thereof) and felt comforted and at home. I don't ever want to leave.

Heartstopper has impacted my life in several ways. The most noticeable initial change for me was actually physiological. I experience disordered eating – I binge eat, mostly for comfort/serotonin. I began watching Heartstopper on repeat in the spring of 2023 – Season 1 was the only season out at the time – and I found that I was not only less hungry, but some of my favorite binge foods no longer appealed. All the sweets I kept in the house remained untouched for months.

I lost 30 lbs. in six months. I also needed much less sleep – I would sleep for four hours at a time and not be tired when I woke. I had so much more energy. This didn't last, of course – I'm sure it was a sudden change in my chemical makeup, and it eventually evened out again, but the initial change to my mood and physiology was remarkable. I can't remember when I felt so alive.

The other impact *Heartstopper* made on my life was a desperate urge to create something beautiful. Alice created a world both with her comic and the show that has brought a community together with such joy and acceptance and representation that it inspired me to create something that does even just a fraction of that. It has made me want to write again after a decade of listlessness, in the hope that I can touch the mind of just one person in the way that Alice's work has touched me. To leave the world a little more beautiful than it was before.

Most recently, I have discovered that I am somewhere on the asexual spectrum because of this show. It took a solid year after finding *Heartstopper* to even realize it. But being confronted with a myriad of sexualities, including asexuality, sparked my curiosity to research what they all entailed. The idea of there being a wide spectrum hadn't really occurred to me before watching the show. There are different kinds of asexuals – it doesn't just mean that you are never interested in sex? Demisexuals, aegosexuals? Being asexual doesn't mean you can't experience romantic attraction? I never realized how caught in the binary I have been.

I know not everyone believes in labels, but realizing there are other people who feel like I do in the world, that I am not just an anomaly that is written off as a mistake among the heteronormative population, is deeply comforting. I have found an online community through the podcast *Why Are We Like This: A Heartstopper Podcast*, where I could interact with others also deeply affected by this show, many of whom identify as being on the ace spectrum as well.

I spent so many years thinking there was something wrong with me, not seeing any representation that I related to, assuming that I was alone in my perception of the world, and therefore not really able to integrate into it. But I found a niche where I can feel less alone now and the world of *Heartstopper* is the most comforting and accepting place, where I feel settled and whole.

Jae's Story

Upon watching *Heartstopper* for the first time, I immediately thought it was cute. And as the show went on, I felt a deeper connection forming, realising how this story paralleled my school experience in many ways.

Heartstopper literally saved my life, and it has led me to a fandom that I've fallen in love with. This show came to me in a very dark period of my life, and it shook me out of that state of mind. I've never been connected so deeply to a series in my 41 years of life. I've made lifelong friends through it. It also helped me realise that I'm ace/demi.

Watching Isaac's story arc is how the realisation came to me. Although I'm very much a romantic in the most tragically painful way possible, sex has just never been appealing to me. I have an idealistic view of romance, but in my experience, guys don't want to wait around for someone to be ready to have intimate relations. I had a bit of it in my late teens and early twenties, but because I was forcing my body to do something it didn't want to, I think I zoned out during those experiences. But because of it, I hit a real low and it sent me into a depression. I've only had two relationships in the last two decades and both guys left me for someone else because I wasn't sexually attracted to them. They couldn't understand it and back then, neither did I. So, once it clicked, I had a full-on sob for three days solid.

This series also helped me realise my love of writing. I'm currently writing a fiction book based on my life as a transgender Apache girl who was raised outside of her culture as she navigates life and love whilst reconnecting with her culture. Writing was never on my radar until I discovered *Heartstopper*, and the process is cathartic in the best way possible.

Discovering the show led to buying the books. Then I found the Facebook group many of us now belong to, which then led to reading someone's post about the fanfic they were reading. So, curious, I clicked the link and began to read it. I laughed and cried. That fic led to many, many more. I devoured so many of them that an idea sparked in my brain: I wanted to see the boys in my hometown of Phoenix. Soon after, I had an outline written. And then I wrote the story. Before I knew it, I had a full 28-chapter fiction posted for all to read. Then a couple of one-shots[1] and another multi-chapter story later, the idea of writing a fictional book based on my life as a transgender Apache girl came to mind.

If I hadn't discovered this universe, I can confidently say I don't think I would have discovered my love of writing. I'd never written before finding *Heartstopper*. It's both saved and changed my life for the better.

---

1. In fanfiction, a one-shot is a story told and published in a single instalment, as opposed to multi-chapter fanfiction stories that can be published over a period of weeks or even months.

Gender Journeys
By Rowan Murphy

This chapter is special to me, as *Heartstopper* was the catalyst behind my gender identity discovery and subsequent transition. And while we didn't receive as many stories related to gender identity as, say, bisexual or asexual orientation, I was not the only person who experienced a gender-related revelation.

Growing up in rural Germany in the 70s and 80s, I was surrounded by traditional family values and clearly defined gender roles. In my own home, this was slightly more relaxed; I was the youngest, and grew up with two older brothers in the house (there were older siblings, but they had already moved out), so I often wore hand-me-down clothes that were boy clothes, and I played with their toys as much as I did with my own. The games we played were definitely not girly tea parties with dolls and stuffed animals. When the neighbourhood found out that my mum was working an office job, there was gossip and plenty of commentary, because "a woman's place is at home, raising the children".

In my youth, the only time I remember coming across people who pushed the gender boundaries was when I saw men dressed as women, what people called "crossdressers" or "transvestites" back then, but what was essentially drag. As far as screen media, I don't recall seeing any main characters or key plotlines relating to the bending of gender norms in mainstream movies until *Tootsie* in 1982 (although *The Rocky Horror Picture Show* was released in 1975, I personally didn't see it until 1987).

The following year (1983), the movie *Yentl* came out. I had a powerful reaction to it. In retrospect, this makes a lot more sense now (by the time I saw it, I was twelve years old and deeply intrigued by Barbara Streisand's character, who impersonated a man in order to study the Talmud, as women weren't allowed).

About a decade later, there was *Mrs. Doubtfire*, and then *The Birdcage*. While these movies still maintain a heteronormative tone and sensibility, it was a start to seeing featured characters pushing the gender norms.

None of the mainstream media representation I remember seeing throughout my younger years ever painted a particularly positive picture of gender nonconforming people (that's not to say none existed; it was just extremely rare). I felt like the characters who dared to impersonate another gender (like in the above-referenced movies) always had to pay a price; it seemed like the moral of the story was that you shouldn't "deceive" others in such a way. And in the rare instances that an actual transgender character was portrayed (usually trans women played by cisgender male actors), they were either villain or victim, the punchline of a joke, or sensationalist shock value.

Without the internet and without a frame of reference or awareness of a term for what I felt, I simply forced myself to play a role and try to fit in – at a huge cost to my mental health. When I finally addressed my gender identity issues, I indulged my inner nerd: I researched, I read, I asked questions, and I discussed with other people. Nothing could have prepared me for the sheer size and volatility of this particular minefield. I think it is the most divisive topic of debate I have ever encountered.

The gender binary is deeply ingrained in modern civilisation, and I wanted to learn and understand its history. Using Google, like any self-respecting Nick Nelson fan, I found information on Muxe in Mexico, Māhū in Hawaii, and two-spirit Native Americans, to name just a few. I also found out that there seem to be records from 2000-1700 BCE in Mesopotamia that mention society and people's roles within it. These records are said to describe a variety of gender roles and sexual orientations. My mind was blown. I had known for some time that from a scientific perspective, dividing humans strictly into two sexes, male and female, was inherently wrong – the existence of intersex individuals proves that we are more diverse than that. But the roots of the gender binary are deep and permeate all aspects of life in Western societies.

German was my native language growing up, with nouns that are gendered (male, female, and neuter). When I learned French and English at a relatively young age, I made two amazing discoveries. The first was that the French used different genders for things than Germans did – who decides that the moon is male in German but female in French (and the reverse for the sun)? And secondly, the English language did not sort nouns into genders at all!

There are so many factors that contribute to the gender binary and restrictive views about gender roles. Unsurprisingly, religion played a significant part throughout history, especially the Catholic Church during medieval times. The belief that women, as descendants of Eve, were responsible for "the Fall" and were weak and prone to sin led to demands that they remain chaste and subservient. From there, it's a short leap to the idea that there is a "right" way to be a woman or a man.

All this is to say that gender is a social construct, and that gender is not the same as sex, which is "assigned" at birth solely based on the appearance of your genitals. Gender is a complex and innate sense of self, comprised of many factors that make up a person's identity. No two human beings are identical. We know this is true for our physical form; not even identical twins have the exact same fingerprint. Why, then, are we trying to force uniformity on our identities?

Sadly, the trans and non-binary community faces divisiveness not only externally, but within the LGBTQIA+ community as well. As with bisexuality and asexuality, there is resistance to including gender nonconforming individuals. This marginalisation is particularly frustrating when one considers the role the trans community, especially trans women of colour (Martha P. Johnson and Sylvia Rivera,[1] for example), have played in fighting for LGBTQ+ rights.

While there has been more trans representation in recent screen media, the majority of it is still portrayed by cisgender actors (whose gender identity corresponds with their birth sex), and most of it still carries stigma and prejudice. There are exceptions, of course (*Orange Is The New Black* is a good example), but *Heartstopper* was the first show where I felt like I saw an authentic, positive, and normalised portrayal of a transgender person.

Elle was one of the core friends, a central character, and her gender identity was simply part of who she was; it didn't dominate her storyline or become the vehicle for unnecessary drama or trauma. There was no big introduction, no major spotlight. We found out she was trans in passing [S1 E1], when her friends were talking about her changing schools (Tao mentioned it was better that she was at an all-girls school, especially since one of the teachers was refusing to call her Elle, to which Charlie responded that the teacher was a massive transphobe). If you didn't pay attention, you could easily miss it and only realise it later.

---

1. Marsha P. Johnson and Sylvia Rivera were pioneering transgender activists, drag queens, and close friends who were crucial to the early LGBTQ+ rights movement, particularly the Stonewall Uprising.

We saw Elle befriending Tara and Darcy at her new school, and they didn't bat an eye upon hearing she transferred from an all-boys school. Her gender identity wasn't a focal point of her character. On top of that, we got to witness a blossoming relationship between her and Tao, the self-proclaimed token straight friend, and her journey to self-actualisation by joining an art school for sixth form, where she made new friends who were also gender nonconforming. It was just beautiful.

> *Heartstopper* helped me put the pieces of the puzzle together. I always knew deep down that I was transgender, but with all of the stigma around it, I kept telling myself, 'No, I'm just not like other girls.' This show taught me to ignore the stigma and negativity around who I am, and that has allowed me to live my life as my most authentic self."
>
> Sammy

Heartstopper also set a wonderful example of how to interact with trans and non-binary people. A great example is in Episode 5 of Season 3, when Tao inadvertently triggered Elle's gender dysphoria. He immediately apologised, and when they talked about it, he emphasised how important it was for him to have her affirmative consent and for her to be comfortable. He wanted to reassure her and be sensitive to her needs. When I saw their interaction for the first time, I was on the edge of my seat. Tao said he didn't really think about her being trans, and this opened a crucial conversation between them, allowing Elle to express her feelings and concerns in a safe space. I felt so grateful to see communication like this on screen.

Yet, the show did not shy away from addressing the glaring issues the trans community is facing nowadays. The very next episode saw Elle being interviewed by a local radio station, ostensibly inviting her to speak about her art, which had gained a considerable following on social media. It became clear right away that the talk show host had ulterior motives; after a couple of perfunctory questions related to her art, Elle was blindsided with questions about trans identities and how they were the "hot topic" of the moment. This scene provided a small glimpse into the experience gender nonconforming people find themselves in nowadays. It was uncomfortable to watch, yet it only scratched the surface of what it's really like for us in the current political and social climate. I literally cheered when Elle said that trans people aren't a debate, they are human beings.

What *Heartstopper* does brilliantly is celebrate uniqueness and diversity. Not only does the breadth of representation expand in Seasons 2 and 3 to include several trans and non-binary characters, but we also get to observe Darcy's journey of discovering their non-binary identity first-hand, and witness the support of their girlfriend Tara, as well as the friend group. This plot development may have in part been related to Kizzy Edgell's real-life transition, or it may have been planned all along, but seeing these parallels playing out was truly inspiring to many fans.

> "In the third season, whilst watching Darcy discover their gender, it stirred some feelings I'd never realised I felt. Although I'm still unsure of my gender, I know I'm not cis, and that is thanks to them."
>
> River

> "After I realized I'm a demiboy, I watched in awe as Kizzy Edgell came out as within the nonbinary spectrum and changed their pronouns. And then season three was released, and I watched as Darcy changed their appearance and came out as nonbinary, and I felt so seen."
>
> Jordyn Lenz

Gender identities, just like sexual orientations, exist on a spectrum. There are many labels and descriptions, but what is hard for many people to understand is that one's identity isn't a fixed point on a chart – and that applies to sexual orientation as well. People grow and evolve over time, and once we let go of the binary view, there is a whole world of possibilities out there. *Heartstopper* sends a strong message that we don't owe anyone these core pieces of ourselves, and that we are allowed to take our time to figure things out.

> "*Heartstopper* helped me realize it's okay to be different, and it gave me the confidence to come out as pansexual and transgender."
>
> Ocean

Rose's Story

The first time I watched *Heartstopper*, I was instantly pulled in by the opening music, the colour palette, the pacing, and the story. I felt an immediate connection with the characters, and a sense of deep comfort and safety, which only grew as the show went on. I kept expecting the stereotypical angst seen in other queer stories, and time and again was delightedly surprised when it failed to appear, the characters for once allowed to experience joy and happiness with one another and in themselves.

I remember saying out loud so many times, "Oh my god, this is SO good!" and "Oh my god, I love this show SO much!" while I was watching it for the first time, and those feelings haven't lessened at all. I'd say I actually love it even more now than I did then, and becoming intimately familiar with the story has only deepened my abiding sense of comfort and queer joy.

Heartstopper has completely changed my life, and I do not say that lightly. When I first watched it, I was still married to and living with my abusive ex-husband, whom I had been married to for four years at that point, having lost all my self-confidence and feeling very isolated and scared, whilst trying to keep myself and my young baby safe.

Watching *Heartstopper* that first time was like a window opening out onto the light, and being shown a reminder of what healthy and loving relationships look like, and I suddenly just knew that

I could not continue to accept less for myself and my child any longer.

Nick and Charlie are my comfort couple, and feeling armed with them, within just one month of first watching the show, I found the strength to tell my ex to leave the house, and a couple of days later, he was gone. I felt truly free again for the first time in years, and my only tears at the ending of that relationship have been ones of joy.

Repeated viewing of the show on a loop, buying and reading all of the books, and joining online communities of fans have all helped me to regain my confidence, both as an individual and in my queer identity as an agender pansexual person.

Heartstopper opened my eyes to life beyond the gender binary, it pushed me to explore my own identity and examine why I had always felt that I was somehow failing at being a woman, despite always trying so hard to get it 'right'. In reading more about the gender spectrum, I was so relieved to discover the agender identity, for the first time feeling that there was a word that fit me, rather than me constantly trying (and failing) to fit myself into the wrong mould. Gender isn't something that I have any sense of for myself; I can't really relate to it as a concept, and it just doesn't factor into anything, not in terms of my own identity or the people whom I am attracted to.

I feel such an enormous debt of gratitude to Alice Oseman for creating these characters (friends!) whom I love so dearly, and to the cast and crew, for all making this truly life-changing show that brings me such ongoing comfort and happiness every single day.

Life as a queer, autistic, ADHD single parent is not at all easy, but having Heartstopper in my life makes even the hard times so much easier to bear, and I will be forever grateful for it.

Sammy's Story

I first started watching *Heartstopper* after the first season was released on Netflix, but I wasn't ready to fully absorb what this show really was, so I stopped after the first episode. I began actually watching it after season three was released, and it became my comfort show. I binge-watched from beginning to end within a two-day period, and the show felt like home to me then. It continues to be my number one comfort show, because it's beautiful.

My immediate reaction was a full range of emotions from start to finish. In the first season, I was rooting for Nick and Charlie to get together. When Nick walked off the field in the last episode, abandoning the rugby game to take Charlie to a private spot to talk and to convince him not to break up, and they finally kissed in the hallway, I was cheering.

Season two was fun, and I was laughing with them on their Paris adventure, while also becoming concerned about the bigger topics about to be uncovered. There were a lot of emotions, so many tense moments, a lot of "what ifs", but overall, it was heartfelt, and the ending left you on edge.

Luckily, I had season three available, so I didn't have to wait for the outcome. This season tugged at my heartstrings, but they really dealt with the topics being addressed in a beautiful way, and after watching all three seasons, I felt they did an outstanding job with this show.

Heartstopper has had a huge impact on my life. I met my best friend through the fandom on TikTok, and the show was the final key for me to accept that I am transgender. *Heartstopper* helped me put the pieces of the puzzle together. I always knew deep down that I was transgender, but with all the stigma around it, I kept telling myself, "No, I'm just not like other girls." *Heartstopper* taught me to ignore the stigma and negativity around who I am, and that has allowed me to live my life as my most authentic self.

Seeing all the trans and non-binary characters on the show, without shame or negativity, no overt bullying or transphobia, and then witnessing Darcy's journey in season three as they discover their true gender identity, was very freeing and relatable to me. If they could do it, why can't I?

I have actually moved to a more accepting state. Nobody was accepting of the trans community where I lived before; people were very negative and openly spoke out against transgender people. Where I live now, I feel safer, and I can be who I am without being criticized for simply existing. I have started working towards receiving the medical care that I need to continue to thrive.

Heartstopper influenced this decision. Before watching the show, I was unhappy with every aspect of my life back in my home state; I didn't have friends who understood me, I strongly disliked my job, and my home state is not accepting of trans rights. After watching *Heartstopper*, I realized that my life didn't have to be that way. I realized that I can be my authentic self and be happy while doing so.

Sunny's Story

My first reaction to *Heartstopper* was to feel a level of love, acceptance, and community I hadn't experienced before. I felt seen. I could relate to these characters and their struggles.

The way they supported each other through all of their challenges, rather than facing those struggles alone as so many of us queer kids had to do, was revolutionary to see. It healed a piece of my inner child that had been hurting for so long.

Growing up, we never saw positive queer representation for younger audiences. We only saw the struggles and hardships we were expected to face, and we were misrepresented and often portrayed as deviants in mainstream media. We were taught early on to feel ashamed of ourselves and to hide our true selves away from the world or risk being hurt or ostracized.

Heartstopper showed us that we are loved and that we aren't asking for too much when we say that we want to live happy, loving lives, just as anyone else does. It normalized being queer in a way that felt right, and it made me long for that normalcy in my life.

The show reminds me that I am deserving of that love, and that we need to be there for each other, to uplift each other and support each other, that we are all beautiful and strong. I believe that the message *Heartstopper* sends to our younger generation will save lives.

It also showed me that being queer is beautiful, and it gave me hope again. I was in a bad place for so long, I spent many years trying to be the perfect spouse to my ex-husband, and I finally reached the point where I couldn't lie to him, or to myself, anymore. It wasn't fair to either of us. I realized that I couldn't live this way anymore. I had these feelings buried deep down and keeping them to myself was killing me.

Heartstopper was one of the first positive representations of living as a trans person that I'd ever seen. Witnessing how Elle was treated normally by her friends and family, seeing a trans existence normalized, and a trans character having a friend group rather than being isolated, was giving me hope that I wouldn't have to be the outsider all the time. It also gave me hope that maybe I could survive transitioning, that I would still be worthy of love if I transitioned.

It wasn't long after watching the series that I started to research transitioning without having that gut reaction of dread and fear settle in the pit of my stomach like it used to. Over time, I didn't feel like I had to keep it to myself anymore like some dirty secret.

Eventually, I started transitioning and coming out to friends and family a little bit at a time. It was so scary at first. I lost relationships along the way, and there are family members who may never understand me, but I also found new relationships that I felt more connected to than I ever have. Presenting as my true self in public has helped me find my tribe and it is easier to connect with people on a deeper level when you both know where you're starting from. I feel more connected to myself and my own life than I ever have. I'm no longer living on autopilot; I'm in the driver seat.

It's been a really difficult transition; not everyone responded in a positive manner, but there was more support out there than I expected, and I wouldn't take it back for anything. I am the happiest I've ever been, and when times feel tough, *Heartstopper* reminds me that I'll be okay, and that there are good people in this world who love me and want to see me thrive.

Zack's Story

What resonated with me the most about *Heartstopper* is Charlie's story. When I first watched it and read the webcomic, I was just starting to figure out my identity, and I learned a lot from watching the show. I began to question my gender identity because I never really felt at home in my body before. Throughout that journey, I felt like an outcast from my family and that they would hate me if I ever told them. I hated myself then. But my friends were there to help, and they supported me the entire time. Most of my friends are also queer, so that also helped, knowing that I wasn't alone. When I first came out to my family, my parents weren't that supportive, and my brother was mean. When I tried to tell my mom I was bisexual and nonbinary, she wouldn't listen to me, and she only heard the bisexual part. She ended up outing me to a family friend I will call E for this story, whom I saw as an aunt. E took me out to get dinner one night, and she started talking about how I shouldn't like girls, and she made me cry. I started to distance myself from them all.

I got my hair cut short; it looked super masculine, and I loved it. I went to a summer church camp with my best friend, which was hosted by E's church. E was a youth pastor, and she was there at the camp. One night after service, we were sitting in a group talking, and E had us write down something that God told us that night. At that time, I didn't believe in God and was distancing myself from Christianity. So, I made stuff up and wrote down something to the effect of, 'God loves everyone, no matter their sexuality or identity. She pulled me aside after reading mine to say that I had to stop this 'lesbian and transgender thing', and she told me that I was 'made to be a mom'. All of that hurt me so much that I started to cry. After that camp, I never let myself call her my aunt anymore, and I made sure not to be alone with her. I was hurt, so I started isolating myself and falling into a deep depression. I just hid myself from my parents, but at school, I came out to my teachers and friends. It was so nice to be called my name and not my deadname.

I related to Charlie's experience of being bullied; that aspect of things is familiar to me because my brother would hit me and call me slurs, and yell at me all the time. This had been happening long before I came out, since I was little; there were times when he would randomly hit me. He would say things like nobody would ever love me, that one day a car was going to hit me, and no one would care. It got worse for a while after I came out. I understood what Charlie felt like, and I started to draw into myself more. I started self-harming because my emotional pain was too much. By the time Season 2 came out, I was having a very hard time staying clean of self-harm and had seriously considered killing myself twice. I never went through with it either time, but I had the intention to do it, and that scared me.

When I watched Season 2, I realized that it's okay to not be okay, and it's okay to ask for help. I started opening up more and telling my friends. They were the first people I came out to, and they were very accepting, so when I told them about my self-harm, they were very supportive and helped me a lot. I am so lucky to have them, and they are always there when I need help. The Halloween after Season 2 came out, we had suicide prevention at my school during our social studies class. They talked about depression and different disorders like OCD or eating disorders. At the end, they answered questions and had us anonymously take a test for depression and gave us the option to fill out a Google form to talk to the guidance counselor. I talked to her, and she then spoke to my mom, and that day, I went to the emergency room to see if I could get some help. I eventually went to a part-time hospitalization program, and that helped so much. I got my current therapist, and she is amazing.

I honestly don't know where I would be if I hadn't watched *Heartstopper* and started to ask for help. What gave me the push was Episode 8 of Season 2, when Charlie told Nick about his self-harm. It made me realize that I can ask for help or just talk to someone about things. Charlie talking about how he was bullied made me see that I shouldn't have to deal with the awful stuff my brother did to me by myself. I kept thinking about how Charlie shouldn't go through that, and neither should I. Then Charlie told Nick about his self-harm, and that was what pushed me. I remember reading that part in the webcomic, but that was before my depression got really bad. Seeing it portrayed like that, with actors who brought it to life, made me see that I could ask for help. If Charlie could ask for help, then so could I. It still took a couple of months for me to talk to an adult about it, but I eventually got there.

Another thing that resonated with me a lot was Nick's story. Watching him figure out his sexuality over time has helped me realize that I don't have to have everything figured out right away. I just have to be me. I am currently describing myself as trans and bisexual and use he/they pronouns. But I went through a long journey to fully figure that out, and that's okay. I tried different things, tried out different pronouns, and I used the name Everest for a bit. I tried various pronouns, but most of them didn't fully fit me, so I landed on he/they. I chose the name Zack, and I have stuck with it ever since. As for my sexuality, I first thought I was bisexual, and I questioned this over time, but I also thought I might be on the asexual spectrum. I still don't know if I am asexual or demisexual, but I know that I can figure that out later on. Another thing I learned from Nick is to support friends and people close to me who are struggling. When I was going through my depression, my best friend was also struggling, and I helped her in ways that I know helped me.

Heartstopper was the catalyst for me to start to heal from my self-harm and find ways to manage when my brain was always making me feel like shit. This show encouraged me to ask for help when everything got too hard and I was scared. It helped me get the therapist that I have right now, who has been an amazing helper in my journey with my identity and my depression, and even getting meds for my ADHD. It has also helped me to recognize signs of depression and self-harm in my friends and people around me. To help them and get them the help they need.

My life has changed a lot since I first watched *Heartstopper* because I figured out things about myself, and it has helped me stay alive, knowing that I can ask for help when I need it. I have changed and grown so much, and I am so grateful for *Heartstopper* and that I could find my true self.

Jordyn Lenz's Story

My initial thoughts after watching *Heartstopper* were that this is going to be an incredible source of queer joy and representation.

I was already out as queer when season one was released, but I was out as a cisgender queer woman. I'm AFAB (assigned female at birth), but after watching *Heartstopper* incessantly after season one was released, I realized maybe I'm not a woman. Since then, I have come out as a transmasculine nonbinary person (or demi-boy), and I'm comfortable identifying that way.

Honestly, I had never experienced gender envy before watching *Heartstopper*, but Kit Connor as Nick Nelson made me want to explore my gender identity. It wasn't just his physical appearance, but also his character traits. I'm not too worried about muscles, but seeing his flat chest made me feel strongly about wanting to have mine look like that. I wanted to look like him, to be seen like that, not to be seen as a woman (and also to have the beautiful queer romance that Nick and Charlie have, but that's beside the point).

So, I cut off all my waist-length hair, changed my name to Jordyn, and started presenting more masculine. I really like the way I feel when I indulge my more masculine side. I feel euphoric; using the new name and dressing more masculine makes me feel more in tune with myself. Using they/he pronouns and changing my technically unisex birth-name to something I feel more comfortable with and attached to has been so euphoric. My mom used to tell me she always wanted a daughter with my birth name, so the association of that name with the female gender is what made me want to change it. I wouldn't be here the way that I am, more authentically myself, if it weren't for *Heartstopper* and Kit Connor. I would still be wondering if something was missing. Looking back, there had always been something that I couldn't quite reach, and *Heartstopper* allowed me to identify what that was. So, I want to take a moment to thank Alice Oseman for creating *Heartstopper* and allowing it to be made into a Netflix series.

After I realized I'm a demiboy, I watched in awe as Kizzy Edgell came out as being on the nonbinary spectrum and changed their pronouns. When season three was released, I watched as Darcy changed their appearance and came out as nonbinary, and I felt so seen. Especially that part where the lady at the zoo says, "Excuse me, ladies," and Darcy says, "Don't you hate when people call you ladies?"[1] [S3 E3]. For me, it was the word "ma'am," but I always assumed it was because it made me feel older than I am, so I never thought much of it until *Heartstopper*. And then Darcy said they hated being called a lady and I was in awe. So, I also want to thank Kizzy Edgell, as well as Alice Oseman, for opening the door for Darcy to be nonbinary in the show and in the comics thus far. I don't think I've ever seen anything representing a nonbinary transition, and it made me feel like I wasn't alone in how I was feeling.

This show means the world to me and I'm so sad it's ending but I understand why. I'm going to miss the entire cast as their respective characters but because it's on Netflix, I know I'll be able to rewatch it for ages to come, and I'm so grateful for that.

---

1. Quotation of dialogue from the Netflix series *Heartstopper*, based on the original book by Alice Oseman.

Marieke's Story

When I first watched *Heartstopper*, I was deep in the throes of parenting young kids and barely out of restrictive pandemic life. I remember thinking that it was a really sweet show with an innocent coming-of-age storyline. At the time, I simply went on with my life, not giving it another thought. In the fall of 2023, I noticed that a second season had come out, so I decided to watch it. Within the space of a couple of days, I watched all of season two, but this time I couldn't get it out of my mind.

I rewatched seasons one and two, then listened to the soundtrack on repeat, went on to find a couple of *Heartstopper* podcasts, and bought and read all of the comics. I couldn't wrap my head around why I was being so obsessive. And then one day it dawned on me: I wasn't straight. I felt relieved to have figured out the root of the intense preoccupation, but also scared and sad to have potentially missed out on a part of myself until my forties. I also felt desperate to try to piece together which feelings I'd repressed over the years.

The next few weeks were a whirlwind, as I came to terms with comphet and what being in a long-term heterosexual relationship since I was twenty meant in regard to knowing myself. Over the course of the next two months, I came out as bisexual to my husband and a couple of close friends. My husband was very supportive, but I felt like I had more to discuss and figure out, and it felt difficult to discuss with him. I spent the next six months in a depressive state, overwhelmed with the grief of only having figured out that I am queer in my early forties.

When season three came out, I binged the whole season within 12 hours of its release, sobbing all the way through. Once again, I couldn't stop thinking about it; this time, I resonated immensely with Darcy's storyline. All of the feelings I'd had with never really identifying with womanhood surfaced, and I realized that in addition to being bi, I'm also probably somewhere on the nonbinary spectrum.

Heartstopper was what I needed to realize that I'm queer. I'm still in the process of figuring out what being queer means to me, especially since on the surface, my life looks so straight. I've gotten closer to a couple of bi friends, and we've formed a little support group. The three of us have started going to a monthly "Bisexual Brunch", hosted by a local bisexual Facebook group.

Through this group, I've also gotten to chat with a few nonbinary people for the first time in real life. I've also been experimenting with more androgynous styles and undoing so much of the societally imposed femininity that I always felt pressured to adopt. In the last few months, I've cut my hair short, revamped my wardrobe with several thrifted outfits that I feel good in, and I even got a half sleeve tattoo. A few close friends are also trying out she/they pronouns for me, but unfortunately, I am not around to hear them using those at the moment.

I'm currently on a life break, biking through Europe with my family. It's been a relief to step away from my usual life and its expectations and to have some more time to think. My hope is to come back with a clearer idea of how I want to move through the world as a queer person, freeing myself of expectations, of self-imposed restrictions, allowing myself to live unencumbered and to feel comfortable in myself, unapologetically.

Heartstopper awakened something in me. I've had other obsessions in the past that now make a lot of sense (Eddie Izzard, for instance), but not to the same level. This show is unique in that it allows the characters' journeys, including their struggles, to happen without the overly sexualised or traumatic plot lines we have gotten used to for queer characters in the media. The journeys of self-discovery are allowed to evolve naturally and without being rushed, so they feel like they could actually occur in real life.

There is a sense of sadness in having missed out on a time in my youth when something like *Heartstopper* would have been possible. Even still, it helped me understand that I don't have to be stuck; it's never too late to be who you are and live authentically. Funnily enough, I had said to a friend of mine, "Who knows what I would identify as if I were twenty years younger," a few months before I saw *Heartstopper*. Of course, she reminded me of this after I came out to her...

A Message of Hope for Viewers with Mental Health Conditions

By Rowan Murphy

In addition to its unparalleled representation and innovative LGBTQIA+ storytelling, *Heartstopper* also stood out because it managed to handle serious mental health topics without detracting from its hopeful tone or optimistic outlook. It was a fresh take on mental health representation, which screen media usually tends to skew toward either stigmatisation or trivialisation, often perpetuating specific stereotypes[1] by casting people with mental health disorders as villains. I don't recall ever seeing an entirely unbiased and optimistic portrayal of a person with mental health challenges on screen.

Not only is mental health generally misrepresented, but it is also underrepresented: Although mental health conditions impact a significant portion of the population, their depiction in movies and television is disproportionately low. In 2023, the University of Southern California Annenberg School for Communication and Journalism studied the "prevalence and portrayals of mental health conditions across the 100 top-grossing films from 2022."[2] Of the 3,815 characters they examined, only roughly 2% reportedly had a mental health condition. This is in stark contrast to

---

1. Naveed Saleh, "How Mass Media Contributes to Mental Health Stigma", http://verywellmind.com, 5 March 2025

2. Communication and Marketing Staff at Annenberg USC, "Distorted depictions: Popular movies misrepresent the reality of mental health conditions", 17 November 2023

the estimated 1 in 8 people worldwide who are affected by a mental disorder, as published by the World Health Organization,[3] or the approximation that 20-25% of the US population experiences mental health issues, according to the National Institute of Mental Health.[4] Numbers in the UK are about the same, with most sources estimating between 20 and 25%.

Similar to LGBTQIA+ identities, mental health conditions are typically used on screen to establish sensationalist or violent plot lines, or as an element of ridicule. Villains and criminals are often called "crazy" or "psycho"; this occurs not only in movies or TV shows, but in casual everyday conversations where these terms are downplayed and bandied about without second thought (somehow the first thing that came to mind as I wrote this was Katy Perry's lyrics "Someone call the doctor/Got a case of a love bipolar" in her song *Hot N Cold*. Bipolar disorder is a complex condition that can vastly impact a person's life). Serious conditions are often trivialised in everyday life – for example, OCD isn't just about being a neat-freak or germophobe, and depression isn't just being sad; it can be absolutely debilitating.

Media portrayals are not helping public perception; they feed into stereotypes and reinforce the belief that individuals with mental health conditions are unstable at best, and dangerous at worst, and that they pose a risk to society. The perpetuation of this stigma can contribute to the avoidance of open conversations and prevent people from seeking help. Admitting the problem is the first and scariest step in the healing process, but the fear of being viewed as inadequate or unstable is a valid concern for many.

---

3. Fact sheet on mental disorders, http://who.int, 8 June 2022

4. https://www.nimh.nih.gov/health/statistics/mental-illness

Men, in particular, are reluctant to ask for help, as this could be perceived as a sign of weakness. Physical strength, emotional fortitude, dominance, and control are considered cornerstones of "masculinity" as defined by modern societal norms. Vulnerability is seen as weakness; after all, *boys don't cry*. Meanwhile, headlines are citing depression and suicide as a leading cause of death for men – and there have certainly been enough prominent cases in recent history. For example, Alexander McQueen, Robin Williams, Chester Bennington, and Anthony Bourdain each reportedly struggled with mental health before they died by suicide.

In beautiful contrast to the predictable patterns of mental health storylines in film and TV, *Heartstopper's* sensitive and optimistic treatment of this topic was a source of inspiration and hope to many. Viewers were slowly and gently introduced to Charlie's underlying mental health problems – Season 1 touched on some of the fallout from the bullying and the way Ben (the boy he was secretly seeing) had treated him, which set the stage for events in the subsequent seasons.

Toward the end of Season 1, Nick got into an altercation with one of his rugby teammates, Harry, who had been needling Charlie and his friend Tao relentlessly throughout the preceding episodes. The ongoing tension between Harry and Charlie had been a source of conflict for Nick, and this scene was the culmination: Harry called Charlie a horrible slur, and Nick lost control and punched him.

When Charlie found out and saw Nick's bruised eye, he began to spiral, and viewers were drawn into his struggle as we watched him withdraw. At the beginning of the last episode, he confided in Tori, his sister. He told her about his secret relationship with Ben before he met Nick and shared that Ben had made him feel like he was ruining his life, and how he had started to believe him, thinking that the world might be better off without him.

As heartbreaking as this scene was, it was giving us only a glimpse into the negative thought patterns that plagued Charlie. Viewers might have noticed several instances throughout Season 1 where he didn't eat or finish his food, giving hints at what would be revealed as an eating disorder in Season 2. During a school trip to Paris [S2 E4&5], Nick noticed with growing concern how Charlie skipped meals or ate very little. This culminated in a scene where Charlie lost consciousness after going too long with too little sustenance, and after he recovered, Nick asked him about it directly. He approached this entirely without judgment, showing only care and compassion.

Throughout the show, Nick and Charlie had mature and emotionally intelligent conversations, modelling open and honest communication between young people. This is so important nowadays, when many teen TV shows are centred around sex, drugs, and unnecessary drama. The ending scenes of Season 2 were especially heartbreaking and tender: Nick finally got Charlie to open up about how the bullying had affected him, and Charlie shared his feelings of self-hatred and episodes of self-harm, telling Nick that he used to sometimes cut himself. We witnessed raw vulnerability and honest emotional connection, a true and equal partnership. Nick's pain at hearing how much Charlie had endured was as palpable as Charlie's fear of being viewed as broken or as a burden.

These emotional confessions at the end of Season 2 prepared viewers for what was to come, as Charlie's mental health became a central plot line in Season 3. Despite kicking off with adorable, reciprocated confessions of love, Charlie's problems escalated by the end of the second episode, when Nick was on vacation with his family. During a tear-filled phone call, Charlie finally admitted to having an eating disorder after months of being in denial.

Nick's careful handling of the situation helped Charlie to acknowledge how serious his problems were, and Nick supported him in finding a way to tell his parents. In one poignant scene, they sat on the sofa together, and Nick held Charlie's hand as he read aloud to his parents what he had written down to say to them [S3 E3]. It was one of the most emotionally impactful scenes of the entire show, demonstrating stellar acting skills and produced with obvious care and attention to detail. The significance of this moment was only heightened by the fact that it was a male character asking for help with his mental health in a depiction of courage and strength.

> "When it touches on mental health, it makes me realise it is okay not to be okay."
>
> Ocean

> "Charlie's story in particular also helped me admit that I wasn't doing as okay as I pretended to be, and I got help."
>
> Michelle W.

> "It also helped me through serious dark times, and I honestly don't know if I'd be alive right now if I didn't find *Heartstopper* when I did. It helped me realise that it's okay to ask for help when you're struggling."
>
> Kylee

What followed was a journey of healing and recovery in a brilliant portrayal that not only showed Charlie's side but also gave some insight into how deeply a loved one can be impacted. Nick struggled with feelings of helplessness and inadequacy, at times neglecting his own emotional needs. As wonderful as it was to see unconditional love and support, there is an important message here: Self-care is crucial while supporting a loved one; you cannot pour from an empty cup. Luckily, some of the friends in their little group were observant and made an effort to support Nick as well. Joe and Kit delivered authentic, convincing performances with real emotional depth.

> "It pushed me to go back to therapy, as in recent years I have relapsed and not taken accountability for my mental health. If Charlie could do it, then so could I!"
>
> Laura

I experienced some level of catharsis, especially during episodes three and four. I remember feeling a powerful mix of emotions; some were rooted in the utter lack of support I had in my teenage years, when I was hanging by a thread. While watching these episodes, I felt torn between strong sympathy for Charlie and envy of seeing him go through these battles with the support of friends and family. My tears were partly due to remembered pain and partly out of compassion for my younger self; I wished I could go back in time to give comfort and instil hope for the future. *Heartstopper* showed the possibility of a very different journey and outcome, and it was like a healing balm on the wounds of my past (a sentiment shared by many people who wrote to us).

Nick's conversation with his aunt Diane at the beach in Menorca was an absolutely brilliant element. She provided support and gave advice on how to be there for Charlie, helping Nick understand that his boyfriend needed more support than he would be able to provide. Caring for a person with a mental health condition can be very difficult if you haven't studied psychology or psychiatry. Google searches can only get you so far, and Nick needed support from a capable and informed adult, which he found in her – it certainly helped that she was a qualified psychiatrist!

Of all the programmes I've seen that touched on mental health, I don't recall ever watching one that handled the subject so sensitively, and through both the lens of the affected person as well as the main caregiver. *Heartstopper* took a very thoughtful, sensitive approach to both Charlie's and Nick's journeys, including the issues with codependency they both had to work through.

Throughout the fandom, I have seen open and honest discourse about mental health issues, with fans confiding in each other about their own struggles. The level of candour and mutual support in some of the chats and message threads was truly astonishing. Furthermore, *Heartstopper* gave people the courage to seek help.

> "I have, after 20 years, decided to seek therapy for my self-harm."
>
> Geolover

> "I started therapy to fully process all of these traumas. It's difficult but necessary to finally live, after 50 years of suffering."
>
> Hughe

> "*Heartstopper* saved my life. I've had an eating disorder since I was 10 years old, and I never knew how to put it into words. It was with season 3 of *Heartstopper* that

I was able to put it into words. It was a very difficult time for me, but *Heartstopper* was there, like a person telling me that I wasn't alone."

Kit

As I was working through the stories submitted for this book, I found something that is much more common than I expected: The conflation of mental health and LGBTQIA+ identities, which came up in my own story. What I didn't expect was to see how many others had similar thoughts and experiences.

One of the first stories I reviewed was Harry's, which is included in this chapter. As she described the process of discovering that she was on the asexual spectrum, she brought up past trauma as something she considered to be the cause. I've heard others express similar thoughts, somehow correlating their queerness to trauma or mental health issues.

LGBTQIA+ individuals often feel forced to conform to societal expectations and norms, and this leads to inner conflict, which can cause serious mental health issues. The National Alliance on Mental Health Issues (NAMI) estimates that "LGBTQ+ adults are more than twice as likely as heterosexual adults to experience a mental health condition. Transgender individuals are nearly four times as likely as cisgender individuals to experience a mental health condition."[5] If we were simply allowed to exist as our authentic selves, if society could stop obsessing about private matters, such as who we love or what we do with our own bodies, and not be dehumanised and vilified, one can't help but wonder if the risk of mental health impacts associated with LGBTQIA+ identities would be drastically reduced.

---

5. https://www.nami.org/your-journey > identity and cultural dimensions > lgbtq

Political narrative in recent months might lead one to believe that not being straight, or identifying with a gender other than one that aligns with their sex assigned at birth, is indeed related to, or even in itself a form of, mental illness. Some politicians are certainly weaponising these ideas, painting the LGBTQIA+ community as mentally unstable to fuel the fire and use its members as the perfect scapegoats. This vicious cycle leads to even more marginalisation and various forms of phobia, which in turn increases the targeting of LGBTQIA+ people. Hate crime is on the rise in the U.S., and according to GLAAD,[6] LGBTQ individuals "were the third-most targeted group in 2024". The statistics are bleak and will continue to worsen in the current environment, which in turn impacts our mental health through added stress, anxiety, and fear.

Unfortunately, many mental healthcare providers are not educated and/or trained to work effectively with members of the community. My own experience with therapists is a prime example: I was told on numerous occasions that hating my female form and feeling this huge disconnect between who I was in my head and my physical appearance was due to the sexual abuse I experienced in my childhood; it didn't feel accurate, but I assumed they knew what they were talking about.

Thankfully, I've since learnt that one's sexual orientation or gender identity is not a trauma response. It's just who we are, how we were born. There's a reason conversion therapy doesn't work: you can't change a person's intrinsic nature. The best we can do in the face of a society that still won't simply let us live our lives is to find a way to embrace ourselves fully, and to find a supportive, accepting community where we can get a sense of belonging.

---

6. Press office at GLAAD, "GLAAD responds to 2024 FBI hate crime statistics documenting over 2,400 anti-LGBTQ hate crime incidents", 13 August 2025

Heartstopper allowed viewers to examine their trauma and issues without stigma, without judgment. It freed us of the expectations to "carry on", to grin and bear it, and it obliterated the idea of mental health issues being a weakness. While Charlie might have viewed himself as weak sometimes, we all witnessed his undeniable inner strength and courage. *Heartstopper* empowered us to acknowledge our wounds and scars, to embrace broken pieces of ourselves so we could reintegrate them, and to emerge stronger than ever.

Ruth K's Story

When I first watched Heartstopper, I was in a very bad place both mentally and physically. I was 17, and I had just recently been diagnosed with two chronic disabilities. I was bedridden due to my health issues and was really struggling with my mental health. Just when I thought it was never going to get better, and I was feeling hopeless, I found *Heartstopper*.

It had just come out on Netflix, and I had read the first volume of the graphic novel a little while before. I remembered how much I had enjoyed the book and decided to try out the show in hopes of a little joy. Little did I know how much the world Alice Oseman had created would change my whole life for years to come. There are differences to the graphic novel, but I wasn't very focused on that, because the way it was filmed, and the little elements of the comic that were incorporated, made it feel very comforting.

I binge-watched the whole series in a day and bought the rest of the books immediately. By the time I finished the show for the first time, I was completely hooked. It brought me so much joy during such a dark time in my life. Nick and Charlie and the rest of the gang's story filled me with so much hope for the first time in longer than I could remember. I knew from the very beginning that I related to Charlie a lot, specifically when it came to the bullying and the situation with Ben.

After reading the rest of the books that were published at the time, I realized just how much I related to him. I had struggled with self-harm, depression, OCD, eating disorders, and other mental health disorders from a young age. Finding this representation now, which was something I never had before, gave me hope that I could find friends and be loved despite the cards I had been dealt.

From the very first time I experienced *Heartstopper* on Netflix, it impacted me deeply. I think I knew immediately that it was going to be a light in my life, which, at the time, I truly believed I would never find. I was still very ill, and I was almost completely immobile for many months after.

There were still many times in the following months when I started to feel hopeless again, but now I had *Heartstopper* right by my side. I didn't have many friends at that time, and my family life wasn't always the best. For about six months, my whole life revolved around watching and rewatching the show or reading and rereading the books.

When I was feeling up to it, I would draw the characters or make a new *Heartstopper*-themed decoration for my room. I created a *Heartstopper* fan account on social media, where I ended up meeting my first really good friend in a long time, thanks to the show. Eventually, I started gradually feeling a little better; it was a slow process, and it was still a very stressful time in my life.

Alice Oseman and the beautiful world of characters that she created were what gave me the strength to keep going and try to get better. When I was 18, I was able to work again for the first time. This was also when I found my first girlfriend. Funnily enough, her mom was obsessed with *Heartstopper* as well! We've had a few battles over the years about who is a bigger fan, and I proudly win every time.

While my life overall was starting to improve, I still struggled a lot with my health, experienced periods of unemployment and went through emotional ups and downs. I also broke up with my girlfriend after about six months, but we remained the very best of friends. She's the Tao to my Charlie, or the Tara to my Nick. She even has a new girlfriend now, who turned into my other very best friend, and I love them both very dearly. Although I suppose I shouldn't call her a "new" girlfriend anymore, as they've been dating for well over a year now.

Both of them put up with my crazy *Heartstopper* obsession because they know how much it means to me. They've gone with me several times when I had the chance to see Joe Locke and Kit Connor performing on Broadway. *Heartstopper* has become an essential part of my life. It gave me the opportunity to experience the intense joy and suspense of anticipating a new season or a new book release, the excitement of seeing the actors perform my favorite scenes from the books, and maybe a little bit of dread sometimes as I mentally prepared for some scenes that I knew would break my heart.

I've watched my collection of *Heartstopper* merchandise grow to what some may consider a bit of an insane amount, buying every new item that came out. I've also forced everyone I love to watch *Heartstopper*, because I want them to experience the joy I feel when I watch it. Even now, after what must be my 200th watch, I still feel the same emotions I had the very first time I watched it. It still feels like I can feel what the characters are feeling, which I believe is in large part due to the amazing performances by the actors, and also because of Alice Oseman's superb writing skills.

Although I still have most of the same struggles today as I did when I was that ill, depressed, seventeen-year-old, I now have all of the things *Heartstopper* has taught me about life and also about myself. When I first came out to my family, they weren't very supportive. I thought something was wrong with me, but *Heartstopper* demonstrated to me that the very opposite of that is true. I thought that I was unlovable, but *Heartstopper* helped me see that I can be loved for who I am. I didn't think that I would make it to the age of 20, but here I am, and that is because of the huge impact this story has had on my life.

I have a lot of life left to live. *Heartstopper* has inspired me to use my life to stick up for other people like me. I'm a political science major, and I have become an activist for the rights of all of the people who find themselves relating to *Heartstopper* as well, which goes beyond the LGBTQ+ community (human rights). I know that no matter what, this story and the community attached to it will have a lasting impact on my life forever.

Harry's Story

When I first watched *Heartstopper*, I thought it was cute. My friend had recommended it, and I found the main character, Charlie Spring, very endearing and sweet as soon as I turned it on. I thought, *okay, I'll like this. It's obvious what is going to happen, and I'm all for cutesy happy endings.*

But then I saw the end scene of episode one, where Ben restrains Charlie and forces a kiss upon him. It made me feel a bit, for lack of a better word, angry, but I pushed it aside. I figured I was probably just empathising in places I'm expected to, based on the dramatic storyline.

I finished the first four episodes in one sitting, thoroughly invested in Nick and Charlie's love story. But I couldn't get an image out of my mind. It was Charlie's face, just his face, as he was being pinned against the wall by Ben. He was looking up, and the look in his eyes triggered a feeling, something I had buried: Desperation, fear, but also a macabre sort of acceptance that this was happening, and I just wanted it to be over quickly.

When I was 14, someone pushed me into a concrete wall and forced me to kiss them. I told everyone afterwards, but nobody cared. My best friends would use phrases like "it was just a kiss" and "don't be so dramatic". By the time a year had passed, my virginity was taken from me, and the forced kiss was long forgotten. Until I watched *Heartstopper*. And maybe it was because of where I was in my life at the time – early 30s with a newborn baby and a recent relapse into my own depression – or maybe *Heartstopper* would always have opened up that part of my psychological make-up I hadn't faced. Either way, I went on for months not getting that boy's face out of my mind.

When I'd worked up the courage to watch the final four episodes (life with a newborn is hectic, okay?), the opening scene of episode eight with Charlie and Tori at the drum set broke me. It was like the writers had torn pages out of my diary from when I was a suicidal teen. And I realised that I still felt like that, like I was better off if I didn't exist. I often thought I was put on this earth to be someone's punching bag. That I've spent my whole entire life never being wanted.

Heartstopper has made me reevaluate my whole life. I had difficult conversations with people from my teen years and stood up for myself. Some friendships are now stronger than ever, some have ended, and it's for the best. Mostly, I fight the good fight wherever I can because I want my children to grow up knowing they have a voice and they matter. I want to be a role model for them.

I'm still in therapy. It's still a very long road, and I have more historical trauma than I realised. I feel like I'm discovering who I actually am for the first time, and not just who I think I need to be for others. I'm no longer just existing, I'm living.

Until I met my husband, I didn't know what it felt like to have another person genuinely want me there. I think I buried all of this to live in the false security of finding my own soulmate. But just because I am happily married, it doesn't mean the trauma isn't there.

I experienced something terrible like Charlie, and it affected me. It affected how I saw myself, and it set up how I processed and understood my own sexual relationships, desires and expectations.

I also grew up believing that I was disgusting and that people didn't care about or want me. I self-harmed from the age of twelve, because that was the way I was brought up to react by my own abusive father, who abandoned me when I was five; hello Nick Nelson, I see you too.

Through therapy and a lot of tearful conversations with my husband, I realised that I'm on the ace (asexual) spectrum. I thought that perhaps I always had been, or perhaps my early-in-life intimate experiences had played a part in it – who knows. But I have spent my life doing what I thought was expected of me, finding it easier to go along with it instead of saying no. The only person I have ever been truly attracted to and desired is my husband. He's been so patient with me. He even watched all of *Heartstopper* to try and understand me better, which is a lot for him (unless it's a war film or travel documentary, it's a no from him).

I could wax on lyrically about all the parallels I draw with *Heartstopper* and the different characters and storylines. But this is the most significant for me. This was the most impactful on my life.

I know people got a lot from *Heartstopper* because of its queer joy – but even if you take away the queerness of it all, it still meant so much to me. It still does. It made me feel seen and heard, and that what happened **did** matter. I matter.

Author's Note

As referenced in the introduction to this chapter, this story illustrates how we often blend LGBTQIA+ identities with trauma. When Harry mentions her thought process as she realised that she is on the ace spectrum, she references the consideration of past trauma as a potential determining factor of being ace. Since telling her story, Harry has come to terms with the fact that her asexuality has always been a part of her, and shared the following update:

"I think my trauma made it more difficult for me to see that it's okay to not want the same things as everyone else. I think 'asexuality' ten to fifteen years ago wasn't heard of, and that probably didn't help either. Most of all, I think the intrusive thoughts of 'no one else will want me, so I may as well take it' overshadowed me realising what I actually wanted in terms of relationships and sexual experiences. This is why the Ben/Charlie storyline hit home so deeply with me.

I also want to add that through *Heartstopper*, I found community. I found friends and people who make me feel less alone. I found hope and a drive to live my most authentic self."

Luke Adams' Story
The Gift of Heartstopper

I just don't have enough thanks and praise for Alice Oseman. I have frequently referred to them as a lovely, subversive genius. In 2022, *Heartstopper* was recommended to me by a fellow psychotherapist. I am 62 years old at this writing, and a bisexual, cisgender man — not exactly the original target demographic.

I am a trauma survivor — of child abuse, sexual assault, the ravages of the AIDS pandemic, bi-phobia, and a heterosexist environment in general. I've done a lot of therapeutic work for many years to overcome it. That's why, at age 45, after a career in progressive political organizing, campaigning, fundraising, and other activism, I began a new career path in mental health and in social and sexual health. Now I'm consulted internationally by fellow mental health colleagues. But I never imagined how a written and screen series, billed as a sweet coming-of-age love story, would rock my world.

I watched the first episode, and I had a bit of an out-of-body experience at the scene in which Ben assaults Charlie. Immediately, I purchased and voraciously read every book Alice Oseman had written. I wasn't a person who cried at books or shows. As I continued to watch the first season and to read Alice's writing, the floodgates opened. I asked myself why I was responding so emotionally to a British show about teenagers, and why I was identifying with both Nick and Charlie.

Then, patients in the age range of 35-70 began to tell me that the show was deeply moving to them and was transforming their lives. Colleagues began to contact me to report the same phenomenon with their clients. Friends began to talk about it as if it were life-changing. Today, I literally know of lives saved, relationships salvaged and grown, disorders treated, healthier love and expression undertaken, boundaries and healthy communication improved, loving partnerships that had endured since high school represented, and queer joy that had been out of reach finally experienced, because of *Heartstopper* and the public lives of the cast.

And one need only look at the thousands of thank-you messages that Alice and the cast receive on social media to see people declaring all of that again and again.

I find the people who work on *Heartstopper* to be profoundly inspiring as well as entertaining. They are accomplishing on a massive scale some of the same objectives I had many years ago with my pet project, New Pacific Academy. We made history at our Academy, and the model now pervades the LGBTIA2Q+ movement, but we had nowhere near the immediacy, reach, and leverage that *Heartstopper* has at this writing.

Supposedly, it was just a little love story. But in the UK, Members of Parliament have spoken about *Heartstopper* on the floor of the House of Commons. Dictators around the world have banned it. Book-burners in various parts of the US have prioritized removing it from schools and libraries (where they can get away with that). Laws were changed at Tynwald on the Isle of Man because of a direct hit speech by Joe Locke. Meanwhile, the awards and kudos for the stories and the ensemble just kept rolling in.

In 2023, the second season of the show premiered. The story began to shed light on Charlie's need to do certain things precisely, and on his eating disorder and associated self-harm. At one point, I spent a sleepless night having an internal argument about whether I was having a trauma reaction to it.

I'd spent much of my life telling myself my experience had so many big, awful parts to it that my teenage issues with OCD about food, and the cutting and food restriction just weren't important enough to worry about in the scheme of things. I'd buried it and had rarely realized that I was having reactions because of it. Suddenly, it had become front and center, and I was rattled. I had to go back to it with my own therapist to work through what happened and how it had affected my actions in life. I am deeply grateful that I could do so, finally.

In the fall of 2023, Chetna Pandya (who portrays the rugby coach on the show) posted an Instagram reel discussing the difficulty she'd had being a single parent, especially with the intense schedule of working on *Heartstopper*. She praised the mental health and production teams of the show for helping in any way they could to make things easier for her and her daughter, and to help her cope. I wrote to her and told her that it was one of the bravest things I'd ever seen on the internet. That started a periodic exchange that has occasionally been hilarious, but always inspiring.

This was also the tipping point for me to write my own queer fiction novel, *Chance Harvest*, which was a story I'd had in my mind since 1984. I had seen watershed books and shows come forth over 2022-2023, but the *Heartstopper* phenomenon sealed this thought: "If Alice could write Solitaire when she was only 17, then I can get this damn book done now." So, I did.

In the midst of all this, I began to become friendly with members of the online *Heartstopper* fan community. At the time, I didn't realize that some of us would have amazing experiences together and become important parts of each other's lives. I now have

Heartstopper friends in several countries — a number of whom are amazing artists, photographers, educators, and actors.

Beyond "chats with Chetna," I've had opportunities to meet and talk with several other members of the cast. Then came season three, and because of it, many fans bonded more closely than ever, while new people were just discovering the show.

When Joe received his Human Rights Campaign Impact Award in the spring of 2025, he noted, "What makes me the most emotional is the reaction from the older generation of queer people." All along, it has struck me that although Alice wrote *Heartstopper* for a Young Adult audience, the story has strongly resonated with people of all ages. Regardless of age, the scenes at the end of season two shattered most of us. I watched it in a room full of fans, all of whom wept at those last scenes. Showing, as they really see each other fully, the intensity of Nick and Charlie's story of enduring love, Joe and Kit turned in performances that pushed the bounds of the craft.

Because of the show, I went to New York to see Joe's Broadway debut in *Sweeney Todd* — and his closing — with US *Heartstopper* friends. We also saw Will Gao and his sister, Olivia Hardy, at the New York and Chicago debuts of their band, Wasia Project. I went to London to see Rhea Norwood's West End debut in *Cabaret*, and Fisayo Akinade's turn in *Slave Play*, with UK *Heartstopper* friends. I was back in New York with these friends to see Kit Connor's Broadway debut in *Romeo + Juliet*. My horizons and my network have broadened; my life is changed. Right now, we are all eagerly anticipating the forthcoming *Heartstopper* movie, which will wrap up that part of the Osemanverse in which the story of Nick and Charlie is the center of the orbit.

The show couldn't have happened without its stunningly talented writers, producers, crew, and ensemble cast. They have created a truly moving, life-changing, global force for good. And many of us in the fandom have picked up that baton and run with it. Individually, jointly, and collectively, their efforts and ours continue the impact of the show (and books) through our lives. Perhaps most importantly, *Heartstopper* makes it possible for queerlings of all flavors, in many little pockets of the world, to hear a very crucial message: You are not alone.

Heather's Story

When I first started watching *Heartstopper* in February 2024, I was in the darkest period of my life. I was ready to end it all. I had seen it on my "suggested for you" list on Netflix for a while. I started watching, and over the course of each episode, it brought me so much joy. My first watch through of the show, which had released seasons 1 and 2 at that time, was very enlightening, but at the same time, it was hard for me to watch.

What Charlie faces throughout the series feels like glimpses into my own past. I relate to Charlie a lot, having struggled with anxiety, depression, and an eating disorder most of my life. In addition, my husband has very similar energy to Nick, which felt like another connection - I have literally said to him, "My life is way better because I met you."[1]

Heartstopper quickly became my comfort to turn to when I was feeling down. For the longest time, it was the only thing that brought me joy.

My first marriage was toxic, my ex-husband was in the military, and I was young when we got together. Our marriage lasted about three years. He was verbally and mentally abusive, which was a traumatic experience for me. I never really confronted that trauma, and as a result, I had anxiety, depression, and control issues.

---

1. Quotation of dialogue from the Netflix series *Heartstopper*, based on the original book by Alice Oseman.

I grew up in church as a preacher's daughter. I knew early on in my life that something was different about me, but at about eleven years of age, you can't really figure yourself out. I knew I liked boys, but also found girls attractive, but due to my religious environment, I suppressed this for a very long time. I was probably about 18 when I realized I was bisexual, but I couldn't tell anyone. I never came out to my dad, who passed away in 2019, and I don't regret it. He probably wouldn't have shunned me, but I never wanted to risk it. I had to hide that part of myself for a very long time, which contributed to my mental health problems. Watching Nick's journey and the arc from discovery to coming out was like standing in the sunshine.

In late 2023, I had a confrontation with a friend of mine on the praise team at church. The way he talked to me was so much like my ex-husband, and it triggered my trauma, causing me to descend into the worst depressive state I've ever had. It affected every aspect of my life. At work, I have to interact with customers a lot, and I struggled because I felt like I was moving through fog. My brain couldn't handle talking to people, and I didn't have the energy that's required to do my job. My husband wanted to help me, but I withdrew, feeling like there was nothing he could do.

I tried several times afterwards to go back to that church but ended up having a panic attack every time. I'd had some difficult experiences with church before, and this additional trigger fractured my relationship with church and God even further. Time will tell to what extent this will heal.

I have come out of that dark place; it took a while, but *Heartstopper* is a big part of that; it was the catalyst to understanding how bad my mental health actually was, and that I needed to get help. I started therapy, as well as a regimen of medications, and I firmly believe it saved my life. Without *Heartstopper*, I don't think I would have sought help, and I would not be here.

I see myself in Charlie so much. There were so many times that he would say or do something, and I would just crumble because I knew what he was going through. For instance, the last episode of Season 2, where Charlie tells Nick, "I just don't want you to think that I'm this fragile, broken mess, that you have to fix me. I would hate that."[2] I have literally said the same thing to my husband in the past. Watching Charlie say this made me break down crying; it was like reliving that conversation. Another example is in Season 1, when Charlie tells Tori, "Maybe I do just ruin people's lives, and it would be better if I didn't exist."[3] I know I have felt that exact way in the past. I may not have said it out loud, but I could completely relate to him in that moment. *Heartstopper* helped me process my trauma. To me, it's more than this little Netflix show.

Heartstopper brought me out of my darkest days. It allowed me to see that I do have trauma, but it doesn't define me. It helped me see that, even though it is a long road, there is light at the end of the tunnel. It also helped me recognize that I am enough just being me.

---

2. Quotation of dialogue from the Netflix series *Heartstopper*, based on the original book by Alice Oseman.

3. Quotation of dialogue from the Netflix series *Heartstopper*, based on the original book by Alice Oseman.

Izzy's Story

When I first watched *Heartstopper*, I thought it was so beautifully done. The colours were so pretty, the storylines were so well executed. Everything about it was just really comforting.

Season 1 came out when I was in year eight and getting terribly bullied. I remember watching it in year nine after we had to analyse the promo picture, the one of Nick and Charlie sitting at the school desk, for my media class. That day I went home and watched all of Season 1 and I remember thinking it was lovely, and then I moved on, like you would with any TV show.

It wasn't until around the time Season 2 came out that I really got into *Heartstopper*. I remember it came out during the summer holidays the year I had dropped out of school. Midway through year ten, school became unbearable for me; I would confide in teachers and instead of offering me support, they advised I take a three-month break and return the next year. To no surprise, the bullying continued, to a worse degree. I once again tried to talk to staff about the way I was being treated but was told by the principal that it was my fault for returning, and that I knew what I was getting myself into, almost as if I was asking to face this every day. Their lack of support and understanding further eroded my self-esteem and made me begin to blame myself for the things I was enduring. I was beginning to resent myself but that's when I watched Season 2, and I just remember feeling seen for the first time.

I fell in love with these complex characters. I saw myself in Charlie, but also Nick in some ways too. I loved watching Tao and Elle's relationship blossoming and witnessing Tara and Darcy's struggles with family and coming to terms with the fact they're in love, and the beginning of Isaac's journey of discovering he was aro/ace. It was all just so beautifully done, and the show was something that brought me joy for the first time in a long time.

The night I finished Season 2, I went out and bought Volume 1 of the graphic novel. That weekend, I bought the rest of them, and I read them all in a day. To be honest, it became a regular routine for 15-year-old me to reread them all about once a month.

That Christmas, I was given the novellas *This Winter* and *Nick and Charlie*, as well as the novel *Solitaire*. Let's just say Tori quickly became my favourite character. I adore her storyline, which is one of my favourites in the whole Osemanverse. I waited in anticipation the whole next year for Season 3, as I knew it was going to be the most complex season so far, and volumes 4 and 5, which Season 3 is primarily based on, were so amazingly written.

As I expected, Season 3 turned out to be my favourite season. I loved the way Alice depicted Episode 4, taken from the journal scenes in the comics; the way we can see not only Charlie's journey as he worked through his mental health issues and his inpatient treatment, but we can also see it through Nick's eyes. We can observe what a toll caring for Charlie takes on him, which we don't often see in the media to this degree. His level of support was unusual to see on screen, and the way he actually took the time to understand or try and understand Charlie's struggles was inspiring and moving.

Another character I began to see myself in was Tao and his struggles with abandonment, worrying that he'd be left behind. At the time, I felt like that too. I felt lonely; I had friends, but I felt like they didn't see me, and they didn't understand how badly my years at school affected me. It felt like I was going through something no one ever had before.

I didn't realise bullying could affect someone long-term until I saw Charlie's story and the way he was still suffering from the consequences of other people's actions years after they occurred. I also suffered, pretending everything was ok, and struggled with self-harm. I felt crazy, as blunt as that sounds, until *Heartstopper*, where I finally began to see that everything could and would be okay.

We only have Alice's writing to thank for this. Though it's romanticised, the way the teenage experience is depicted in *Heartstopper* is so real. All these characters have a story. I never got to experience a healthy friend group, and it's so lovely to watch in *Heartstopper*, how everyone's there for one another and how they care for each other.

Without *Heartstopper's* help, I wouldn't have been able to reintegrate into sixth form, for which I transferred to a different school. I'm about to start my second year. I'm almost at peace with myself, but as Geoff says, "recovery isn't a straight line"[1] . I now have some close, supportive friends now who understand and are there for me.

I don't know where I'd be without *Heartstopper*. It truly has changed my life for the better, so thank you, Alice, for this beautiful world you have created. I am also very excited for the movie and for volume 6, to be able to see this magical story come to an end on and off screen.

---

1. Quotation of dialogue from the Netflix series *Heartstopper*, based on the original book by Alice Oseman.

Though I'm slightly dreading letting it go, I can rewatch and reread the completed story as many times as I want now, which is nice. *Heartstopper* will always be there for people, and for future kids like me who are going through tough times. It's nice to know they'll have something to see themselves represented in, and hopefully it can help get them through things they're going through, whatever that may be.

C's Story

I had been a casual reader of the comics for a little bit before the show came out. I honestly didn't even know it was being made into a show until it popped up on my Netflix. I remember pressing play on the first episode, and then minutes later, I was cancelling my plans to watch the entire thing in one sitting. At the time, I was 22 years old and really struggling to accept my own sexuality. I was overwhelmed after I finished watching it for the first time.

Although I was a few years older than these characters, it was the first time I felt truly represented in the media. Watching Nick go through things that I'd been going through at that age, and dealing with it so bravely, made me emotional. I didn't really have any characters like this when I was growing up, and I think it made me feel sentimental to know that teenagers now have someone like this to look up to.

Heartstopper has changed me completely. After watching Season 1, I did a lot of work to become my true self and come out to my friends and family as bisexual. I also loved the subtlety of Charlie's mental health in S1 and related hugely to his struggles with depression and an eating disorder. I, too, had a pretty severe eating disorder from ages 14-16 and have been in recovery for ten years. I think it was beautifully captured, and the series has done such an important job of showing that people are not their mental illnesses, that people suffering are also capable and deserving of love.

It has changed the way I see myself. I remember feeling exactly like Charlie does, that everybody around me would see me as a burden for the things I was struggling with, and while people did their best to assure me that wasn't true, I had a very hard time believing that. I think watching the series and watching how Charlie's loved ones handled it, especially seeing it from Nick's perspective, helped me to understand that my family and friends were doing their best to navigate something they might not have completely understood, but they loved me regardless. I definitely give myself a lot more grace than I used to when I'm struggling. While I know that I'll never be fully recovered from my eating disorder and other mental health issues, I can understand that blips in my recovery are completely normal, and I shouldn't feel any shame around that.

It's encouraged me to go back into therapy and really address underlying issues so I can be who I want to be and not who my mental illnesses have made me. Although I went through treatment as a teenager, I stopped going once I felt 'recovered'. Going back has completely changed my life. It's been an incredibly difficult journey accepting that my mental illnesses are something that will always be with me, but I have the tools to not let it control my life the way it used to. The main difference is that I'm now an out and proud bisexual woman. It's something I struggled with a lot, and I always had the mindset that it was something I could just hide away and never acknowledge. I recognise this as somewhat of a privilege, to have the 'option' as a queer person to hide it, but at the same time, it was this huge part of myself that I was hiding away. I never felt like I was being completely myself around my friends or family. I've been out for a couple of years now, and it's been life-changing for me. I finally feel like myself, and I have found a community of people that I love and cherish with my whole heart because of it.

I'm 26 years old now, and I have not been able to find another piece of media that has had even half the impact that *Heartstopper* has had on me. I think it's one of the most influential, important, beautiful stories that has ever been created. It will be a show that I will encourage my children to watch, to teach them that this is how love and friendships can be with the right people.

Kayla P's Story

I kept seeing the prompt for *Heartstopper* Season 2 on Netflix and finally decided to watch it, knowing nothing about the show. At the time, I was 27 and had just realized the year prior that I was in fact NOT a straight woman. I am from a conservative town in Upstate NY and had no concept of... well, anything queer, until I lived in Massachusetts as an adult, made important queer friends, fell head-over-heels with one of my female friends (while in a long-term relationship with a good man), and learned about compulsory heterosexuality.

My immediate reaction to watching *Heartstopper* (other than Ben Hope needing therapy) was along the lines of "Wow, I love this story, and I wish I had this when I was younger, because maybe I would have known myself sooner". Watching Nick's confusion over his feelings for Charlie and what that meant for him, but ultimately not running away from those feelings in order to discover his true self, made me feel so seen. I remember watching the episode "Kiss" (S1 E3) for the first time and being struck by how impactful their conversation right before their first kiss was: Nick was not sure if he would date a boy or kiss a boy, he could only say "maybe", but when Charlie asked if he would kiss him, that was the one thing Nick knew he wanted – Charlie. Despite our age difference, Nick's journey made me feel validated in my own identity and that it was okay that I was not like Charlie, or other people I know who have just "always known" they were LGBTQ+.

Nick, at one point, says that when he realized he had feelings for Charlie and figured out that he was bisexual, he felt like he woke up. I have felt the same way over the past 3 years: I am finally awake and happier and more in love with life and myself than before. This show sparked a chain of events where I was drawn to learning more about the queer community and how I felt within it, enough to come out as lesbian and end a 6-year relationship with a good man who deserves love just as much as I do. Showing myself that much care is new. We parted amicably, and we are still part of each other's lives.

Charlie's entire journey has impacted me in more ways than one, but the most important is his battle with mental illness. My own battle with an eating disorder monopolized my late teens and the bulk of my 20s. Watching Nick and Charlie in Seasons 2 and 3 was so difficult and in many ways triggering, but it was also so important to my own healing. I wish *Heartstopper* had been around when I was growing up, for a plethora of reasons, but especially to witness not only Charlie's strength and resilience, but also Nick's love, support, and care for Charlie through it all.

I needed a person like Nick during my own dark times, and I did not have that then, but something still broken in me was healed seeing *Heartstopper* when I did. Their relationship, as well as the love they share with their friends and supportive family members, is most important because the world needs to see our stories now more than ever. People in the LGBTQ+ community are here, they have always been here, and the true gay agenda is to be loved, lift each other up, give love to whomever you feel compelled to, and live happily. *Heartstopper* is an incredible beacon for that message.

I feel like I cannot accurately describe what this show means to me. *Heartstopper* helped me wake up and see my true self and is a guiding light for what a life celebrating and embracing that could look like. This story is so important and needed right now and always. Thank you, Alice, and everyone who is a part of creating this masterpiece.

Michaell K Herrera's Story

When I first watched *Heartstopper*, I thought I was going to see something like Skins 2025, with stories about teens involving drugs, alcohol, and sex – but I was completely wrong. I finished all three seasons in just three days despite my limited free time because I work in a drive-through that belongs to my family, and my mum is blind, and there's always something to do here in Grandma's house. It felt like a bucket of cold water had been poured over me. I woke up from an eternal sleep. It was as if a swimming pool had broken inside me. I cried so much, but I understood why. Watching *Heartstopper* made me realize that innocent, tender, "white" love really does exist (what we call blanco in Mexico, meaning pure and without malice). But for many reasons – my own naivety, the older men who gaslighted me (and no, I don't see myself as a victim, but they told me it was normal, so I believed them), or maybe just the desperate need to be loved – I fell into a trap.

I wish *Heartstopper* had been published when I was 14. Maybe I would've thought twice about some things. But it's okay. Today, my eyes are open. And if I'm given the chance, I want to tell the story of a different 14-year-old: Michael – the one who did have a boyfriend, who was happy, who was cared for and truly loved, not treated like just an object.

I don't have scars on my body, but my heart has so many thorns. And every time I pull one out, it helps me breathe and keep going.

I don't want anyone to think I'm looking for attention. Watching *Heartstopper* was the best therapy – it made me realize it was never about my age.

I'll be honest, I never had a teenage romance. When I was 12, I lost my virginity to a 34-year-old man, and deep down, I thought that was love. I was always surrounded by older men (over 30) and classmates who harassed me, touched me and bullied me, and made me believe that was affection. But it wasn't.

When I watched *Heartstopper*, I cried because I regretted everything I had lived through. I looked back at so many things, some of which I had blocked out. I finally understood why. That kind of gentle, innocent love was something I never had. I got lost among older men, and today, June 25, 2025, I forgive myself. I embrace my 14-year-old self and tell him, "You survived. Now heal, and move forward."

Just yesterday, I cried with my best friend. We talked about how intense and powerful the show was, and how it opened something inside me. She sat next to me in class for years and only found out a month ago that three boys used to harass me, and I never realized it was harassment. Of course, if the same thing had happened to a girl, I would've defended her. But when it happened to me, I stayed silent. Partly because I was "the weird one" at school, and partly because... who would've believed me?

I have to admit that I used to be very hypersexual. But when I watched *Heartstopper* and began this journey of healing, my libido disappeared. I didn't become asexual – I just realized that the version of me who acted like a Samantha Jones type, always into sex, wasn't really me. That was just a character, a defense mechanism I used so people wouldn't see how fragile and vulnerable I truly was. I haven't stopped crying – but not because I want pity. It's because today, I finally embrace that 14-year-old boy and tell him: "You're going to be okay. Your mom is proud of you. You have friends around you, people who love you. You won't be alone. Just wait, and be still. Love comes when we're ready."

I love all the *Heartstopper* characters – not in a sexual or crush kind of way, but in a deep, emotional one. Charlie feels like me. He can't express himself or ask for help. And that... hit me hard. Charlie's sister, who steals the scene every time she shows up, reminds me of my friend Fernanda – always protecting me.

I see myself in so many *Heartstopper* characters. Tao, with his hipster taste in films – I was like that as a teenager (if "hipster" is still a word that's used). Nick is bisexual, and so am I. I used to think I was just gay, but I've had girlfriends... though they weren't good to me. Darcy is my wacky, extroverted side. James, working at a young age – I've been working since I was 12. And Ben... well, Ben. I relate to him, too. He was lost, just like I was, getting involved with older men. He confused Charlie, and I was confused too. Maybe that's why I don't hate him or judge him. I was him, too.

I decided to tell my story the way I wished it had been – like a farewell letter, giving advice to that 14-year-old Michael and telling him: you are not alone. So, I've been secretly writing an illustrated book – not a comic, because I don't know how to draw. It's about a teenager like me, who never had any of that innocent love. But now, as a closeted writer, I get to give him the dreams I never lived. I know it might sound silly, but I'm working on it quietly.

I just want to say... *Heartstopper* is the best thing Netflix has ever made. And if I ever get the chance to meet Alice, the first thing I'd do is thank her – over and over – for creating something so healing. Because I healed. And it's thanks to her that today, I feel more alive, with my eyes wide open.

Bellerine's Story

When I first watched *Heartstopper*, I was not familiar with the comics, so I did not really know what to expect.

At first glance, I thought I might be too old for a series that is about teenagers (I was 27 when I first saw it), but I quickly realized that it was very much for any age group because of how many important messages it contains. To me, this wasn't just another teen show, and I have never felt such an intense connection and so much care and love for fictional characters before. *Heartstopper* feels like the biggest hug that you never got when you were young and going through stuff. It feels like the most wholesome, empathetic, but also very powerful and kind story that I think everyone needs to see, whether you are young and queer, or older, or straight. Its message is really important in so many ways, and I believe that everyone can take something away from it.

My whole life, I felt like an outcast, and I was bullied as a kid, so Charlie's storyline very much resonated with me. *Heartstopper* helped me find some actual self-compassion and self-acceptance, which is something I truly never had before.

I have been struggling with mental health issues since I was 15 (OCD & anorexia), and seeing that so authentically and sensitively portrayed was honestly life-changing to me. It was a part of my life that I thought I would want to erase from my memory, until I saw it reflected through Charlie's lens. I never wanted real recovery as much as I did after season 3, and the impact it had on me to see these struggles AND recovery shown in such a beautiful way was honestly life-saving. Seeing how incredible recovery can be made me want to experience it for myself. Before, I had gone through the process because I felt like it was something I had to do, but after watching Charlie's journey, I began to believe that I deserved it.

The way Charlie's eating disorder was portrayed was different from what I had seen in other media. It's not always purely about body image; sometimes it stems from other trauma someone has experienced. It captured how much deeper the causes of it can go.

I had also never seen asexuality represented either, which is also a very personal one to me. I really think *Heartstopper* is incredibly unique in that it celebrates queerness in such a beautiful and loving way, showing how important it is to have a support system and that you can be queer and HAPPY. Even if it's hard to exist as a queer person, there is so much joy in friendships and communities that have your back, and you can find your people, who will love you for who you are. It also doesn't shy away from very serious topics, either, which is a difficult balance to find.

I love these characters with all my heart, and I care about them so, so deeply. I can't go without mentioning how unbelievably talented the whole cast is. It is a big deal to portray such beloved characters so perfectly, and they couldn't have done a better job.

I am eternally grateful to *Heartstopper* for all the warmth and hope it brought me, and to countless other people, too, for demonstrating how much of a gift it is to show people love, to be kind, and to **care**. For making so many people feel **seen** and understood, for showing them they matter, and they are **loved**, no matter what they are going through, what their identities are and all the complexities that come with those. For giving people hope and letting them see what they could become if they had someone around them who let them be themselves and explicitly showed them love and true **acceptance**. For letting people see pride in their identities and allowing them to imagine a future for themselves that they might never have thought they could have. For sending the message that people with mental illness are worthy of love, even when we least feel like we deserve it.

Just thinking of how many people have found community and understanding, and representation through this beautiful story makes me feel very emotional. It changed my life, and I am sure it saved many.

From Surviving to Thriving
By Rowan Murphy

"I'm no longer just existing, I'm living."

Harry

Heartstopper inspired many people to challenge the status quo in a world where we often find it easiest to acquiesce and try to make the best out of less-than-ideal circumstances. Our hopes and dreams are constantly diminished and trivialised; if we cling to them, we are told that we're ungrateful or unrealistic. "You have a spouse and children, you own a home, you're successful in your career (soul-crushing as it might be). You should appreciate the things you have!" Yearning for a sense of purpose, of fulfilment, makes you a dreamer, an idealist, or someone who expects too much from life.

It feels safer to accept things as they are than to rock the boat, lest we fall overboard and risk drowning. Many of us grew up being told how much worse things could be ("Just look at the starving children in third-world countries!"), and that we should be grateful for what we have. This is especially true for members of the LGBTQIA+ community, as we constantly receive the message through various channels and media that we are abnormal, that our identity is an affliction, and we can't expect to live happy, fulfilling lives.

As a society, we have learned to accept inequity. We might watch reality TV featuring people who have more money than sense, thinking how easy they have it, or how unfair it is that wealth is distributed so unevenly, while at the same time accepting this as a fact of life. We watch fairy tale romances, dreaming of loving, mutually supportive relationships with an equal partner, but walk away thinking that those dreams are unrealistic. We use stories as a distraction because they often make us feel better in the moment. Sometimes they show how much worse life could be; other times they allow us to escape into beautiful fantasy worlds where anything seems possible, although we don't permit ourselves to believe it. But rarely do we see something that makes us think, "Why not? Why shouldn't I get to be happy/fulfilled/loved like that?"

Media and society are shaping our perception of what is normal, practical, and realistic, and as a result, we lower our expectations. Priorities are starting a family, buying a house, and saving for retirement; if your identity as an LGBTQIA+ person presents a hurdle to achieving these goals, you are further marginalised. The fight for equal rights includes things others take for granted, like same-sex marriage, adoption or surrogacy, and equal opportunity in the job market; just when we think we might have reached some level of equality, things start to backslide again.

Heartstopper is not a fairy tale; it illustrates many shared, common human experiences. We observe the hierarchical structure of teenage students, the cliques and groups that form, sometimes out of necessity. We witness the impacts of bullying without seeing much of the actual bullying happening on screen, which is just as effective in conveying the story. But when Charlie tells Nick that he's become used to it, Nick responds, quite emphatically, that he should not have to put up with it. It was such a simple statement, yet so powerful, so necessary for us to hear.

Throughout the series, we can witness Nick's gradual realisation that he had been burying his true personality to please others and fit in – something many of us can relate to – and his bravery in the process of breaking free from this cycle. It starts after he spends time outside of school with Charlie for the first time, when Nick's mum tells him in S1 E2 that Charlie is quite different from his other friends, and that Nick seems much more himself around him. We can see that this gives him pause, and he becomes quite thoughtful, even when he's around his friends in front of the school building.

Fear of change is one of the most common human experiences, and as frustrating as it can be to watch Tao grapple with the need to maintain the friend group's dynamic and his anger when he realises that change is inevitable, we can all relate on some level. At our core, humans are afraid of the unknown and prefer to stick with what is familiar. The familiar feels safe; we have survived it so far, so even if it's uncomfortable or painful, we know what we're dealing with, and we know how to survive it. Tao experienced a profound loss at a young age, and the fallout manifests in a deep fear of losing his friends. At first, his behaviour might be somewhat bewildering, but once we learn about his father's death, we understand him a bit better.

Darcy's struggle with parental acceptance is yet another example of a challenge many of us have faced, especially in the LGBTQIA+ community. While the confrontation between Darcy and their mother is painful to witness, their journey of breaking free and choosing to be around people who accept and love them illustrates the importance of found family, reassuring us that we can all find acceptance if we surround ourselves with the right people.

Most of the main characters in *Heartstopper* go through a significant journey of self-discovery, healing, and/or self-actualisation. Nick, Isaac, and Darcy discover key parts of their identities and overcome challenges as they embrace who they truly are. Despite painful moments along the way, they all end up more emotionally stable and find joy in being true to themselves by the end of the series. Charlie and Tao achieve personal growth as they work on confronting their pain and fear and begin the healing process. And Elle not only pursues her passion and talent by attending an art school, but she also finds kindred spirits in her new environment, with other trans and non-binary students. Each of these characters is on a trajectory to reach their full potential and live authentic, fulfilling lives by the end of Season 3.

> "*Heartstopper* is what helped clear the path for me to live my life freely."
>
> Spencer Milcheson

> "I truly believe if it wasn't for *Heartstopper*, I would still be closeted. Just seeing all the joy I had missed in my life gave me the push to live my best life."
>
> William Paul Miller

Witnessing these journeys and observing the rewarding outcomes prompted many fans to examine their lives through a critical lens. We got to see marginalised characters receiving support and learning that they have the right to be happy. Charlie, at his lowest moments, believed he deserved the way Ben treated him, and carried immense feelings of guilt, worried that he was a burden or ruined other people's lives. He even expressed at one point that he thought it would be better if he didn't exist. Many of us recognised parts of ourselves in Charlie and could relate to some of his experiences, yet his courage and strength were truly inspiring. None of us felt like he didn't deserve the support he received, yet we often believe the worst of ourselves.

Many fans who submitted their stories said things like, "If Charlie could do it, so could I," or referenced a specific action or decision one of the characters made, stating that these scenes inspired them to be brave, to no longer accept a life where they felt constrained, unhappy, or burdened. They felt empowered to make changes, to pursue happiness and fulfilment.

> "I got a *Heartstopper* tattoo to help me remember my strength, confidence and bravery that I got from the show, and I live my life openly and honestly."
>
> Sarah

> "Heartstopper has given me the confidence to truly be myself and love with my entire heart, not just that tiny scrap of it."
>
> Anonymous Anne

Heartstopper held up a mirror to people, and it said: These characters are much like you, and just like them, you **deserve** to be happy. You **are** worth it. It is **not** too much to ask. You **shouldn't** have to put up with anything like that. You're **allowed** to demand more from life. Believe in yourself. Stop being passive, allowing life to happen to you, and take action, own your happiness.

> "Before watching *Heartstopper*, I had been in a relationship with a toxic person and hadn't realized how

much they hurt me. She was always mean, and I went with it because I thought it was what I deserved."

Lilly

"*Heartstopper* made me realize I was in a toxic relationship and needed to get out of it. Seeing that there are people out there who don't use your sexuality against you helped me realize my ex shouldn't be doing it to me."

Karra

"I decided at age 60 to 'get back out there.' I went on PrEP for the first time and have allowed myself the possibility of dating and finding my own loving and mutually respectful partner."

Anthony C

This hopeful, unassuming TV show has given us permission to break free from the shackles of societal expectations and seek fulfilment in all areas of life. Leaving toxic or abusive relationships, changing careers, living authentically, restoring worthwhile relationships, developing talents, pursuing passions, finding purpose, living true to our values and beliefs – the list of ways in which *Heartstopper* has improved lives is endless.

"I have stopped doing things blindly just to do them. *Heartstopper* has taught me to at least try to live rather than just exist."

Gloria C. L.

"I'm no longer living on autopilot; I'm in the driver's seat."

Sunny

Ann-Marie's Story
Heartstopper and Me

I'm a sucker for a love story, so *Heartstopper* naturally appeared on my "recommended for you" page. I watched the first two episodes with my husband, who spent the whole time huffing and puffing and muttering under his breath, "Not another fucking teenage angsty love story."

I managed to watch the rest of the show after he went to bed, sneaking an episode or two each evening. I was hooked. I watched it constantly. The credits went up on episode 8, and I'd go straight back into episode 1. There wasn't a day that went by during which I didn't watch at least one episode. Three complete season rewatches on Saturdays while my husband was at work. Then came Tobie Donavan's Vlogs, the cast interviews, and promotional work, then TikToks, YouTube reaction videos, magazines, and any content I could get my hands on.

I've always tended to become fixated on things, but this was on a whole different level. I bought all of Alice's books and created a Pride display outside my classroom devoted to the show. I bought cut-outs of Kit Connor and Joe Locke, the actors playing the main couple, Nick and Charlie, and placed them on both sides of the display board. My friend crocheted me leaves, which are a staple of the show, and I wrote a piece about *Heartstopper* for the college blog Pride month page.

I joined a *Heartstopper* Facebook page in June 2022, and it was amazing. Finally, I had a tribe with whom I could talk *Heartstopper*, and they didn't think I was mad. The group grew quickly, and it became very apparent that some people on there needed protecting. It had a worldwide reach, and a lot of members were from countries where they were not safe being a part of the LGBTQIA+ community. Admins made it a private group and set strict ground rules. No sexualisation of cast members, be kind, homophobic comments would result in removal and blockage from the page, to name but a few. Members range from teenagers to those in their eighties. Younger members and those in homophobic countries are supported if/when they reach out. It *really* is a safe space.

Fast forward to the summer holidays, and I'm still obsessed. We go on a family holiday to Spain – me and my husband, four children and two partners, and a gorgeous villa in the mountains. Halfway through the second week, my stepdaughter joined me by the pool and said, "Ann, do you think you're so obsessed with the show because you're part of the community?"

"No, don't be silly!"

"Okay," she replied, and off she went.

I sat there, feeling puzzled and started reflecting. I was 52 years old. I was married to my second husband. I'd always liked boys/men.

That evening, we walked down to the local bar (me channelling my inner Nick Nelson with a yellow Adidas t-shirt and denim shorts). The Golden Retriever element not kicking in because, on the way to the bar, I was bitten by a dog (this is relevant to the story). Patched up, tetanus and antibiotics. All good.

The next evening, everyone headed to the nearest beach (about an hour away). I stayed back at the villa under the premise that I didn't want to get sand in the wound. That bought me at least four hours on my own.

I started to think about when I was younger again. *Come on, Annie, open your mind up.* Ok, there was a girl a year above you at school. She was brilliant at hockey, and although you never spoke to her, you really liked her and wanted her to like you. The thing is, she was a lesbian, and I couldn't be a lesbian because I fancied the boy next door. I grew up under Maggie's [Margaret Thatcher's] reign. No LGBTQIA+ education at all.

Then there was the woman at the pub I worked in when my first son was a baby. Again, I really liked her but just pushed it to the back of my mind. I was married after all. Two more babies, and then the marriage ended. I met my second husband quite soon after. He had been my first boyfriend. We spent the summer of '79 climbing trees, eating ice cream and playing with our friends. I think I got caught up in the romance of this, and he moved in with me and the boys.

A couple of years later, we went to a party at a friend's house. I spent hours talking to this woman, and I would have done anything to make her like me. I'd never felt like this before. She was there with her girlfriend. I had had a couple of drinks, and apparently, I told another friend that "she (the woman) could turn me."

So, there I am, sat by a pool, the sun's starting to set, and I was like 'FUCK'. I was Nick Nelson in the form of a 52-year-old woman.

I started spiralling. I didn't know what to do. Who could I speak to? How could I process this?

I immediately drafted an anonymous, slightly hysterical post to the *Heartstopper* FB group. Someone had posted a link to an article about realising you're bisexual later in life, and I couldn't find it. The response was so supportive. Total strangers reaching out from all over the world. They embraced me and made me feel valid despite my protestations that I had never kissed a girl before.

We returned home a couple of days later. Me in a bi-panic daze, my husband as angry as ever, and the kids all sun-kissed and ready to see their other parent.

Soon, I was back at work and able to catch up with my best friend. For about two weeks, I walked into her office, talked a load of shit, burst into tears and walked out again. She eventually said that she thought I wanted to tell her something, but I was scared of her response. She told me that she loved me and that that wouldn't change, whatever I told her. She knew.

I came out to my husband a couple of weeks later, and again, he told me he already knew! WTAF – how come everyone knew but me! Our marriage hadn't been happy for years. I had been sleeping on the sofa for at least a year and had been hurting myself pretty much since we first got married. Mainly head-butting walls, sometimes picking things up and smashing them against my head. Anything to stop the noise. I was subjected to verbal abuse on an almost daily basis. Having all my shortcomings shouted at me, spitting in my face because he was so angry. Accusing me of loving my students more than him. He had a point there. I taught 16- to 25-year-olds with special needs.

It got to the point that I was going into work, crying all the way, going over the events of the night before. On a couple of occasions, I got it into my head that I'd go up to the top floor and... well. I never did. I'd walk in and see my students in the atrium, singing and dancing, and I knew I couldn't do that.

At the end of October, I went to stay at a friend's B&B. My husband and I were supposed to go together, but he didn't want to go because everyone would be drinking. I drove off, and he decided to go to my parents to speak to them about me. This resulted in him screaming and shouting at them, and in the process, telling them I was gay. My mum called me, and all I could hear in the background was my dad shouting, "He said you're gay, Annie. I know my daughter. You're not gay!"

This was two days before Kit posted his final tweet [the one where he felt forced to publicly come out as bisexual after months of online bullying], after which he closed his Twitter account. I was devastated. I cried for days. I cried for me, I cried for Kit, and I cried for every other person who has ever been outed or forced out.

By this point, my marriage was well and truly over. My support network was my family, friends and the people on the *Heartstopper* Facebook page, although I hadn't confirmed my sexuality to my parents. I came out to my middle son, who was absolutely amazing. At the age of 18, he simply said, "You have nothing to be sorry about. You owe no apologies. I love you."

I spent the weekends over the next couple of months staying at friends' houses before I could find myself a place of my own. My grown-up sons moved in with their dad. I moved into my sanctuary, my safe space, at the end of May 2023, and attended my first London Pride that summer with friends I had made from the Facebook page. The week before Pride, my parents came to visit, and my dad asked me about the abundance of rainbows in my house, and whether I'd "gone over to the other side?". I told him that I thought I'd always been there, just didn't realise. We hugged, I cried, and after an open and honest chat, they left, only to come back the following day with a rainbow doormat and gnome. Instant acceptance. I had been so scared to tell them because of my dad's initial reaction when my ex outed me, when all I had to do was speak to them.

If I hadn't found *Heartstopper*, I honestly believe I wouldn't have had the strength to leave my marriage and would have continued to spiral until it was too late to save myself. *Heartstopper* didn't just awaken my sexuality; it showed me just how toxic my marriage was. Seeing the behaviours I had been experiencing for years, being portrayed on the screen as part of Charlie's story, literally saved my life.

I will be forever thankful to Alice Oseman for creating such a beautiful world, and the cast and crew for bringing it to life. I have made some amazing friends and shared some incredible experiences with them because of *Heartstopper*. And even now, at almost 55, I absolutely adore everything to do with *Heartstopper* and the Osemanverse. I've found my tribe.

Narnia's Story

I started watching *Heartstopper* about a week after Season 2 aired; I saw it featured on Gogglebox, and then it popped up on my Netflix suggestions. I watched the very first episode and recognised immediately that it was something very special and different to a lot of the queer shows I'd seen previously. I vowed to savour it and not binge both series; I wanted to drag it out, but I watched all 16 episodes within 5 days.

The scene where Nick types "Am I Gay?" into the search engine hit me like a thunderbolt and will still reduce me to tears even after watching it hundreds of times. Seeing these characters (albeit much younger than me) pondering the same questions I had been asking myself was amazing. I remember getting to the end of both series for the first time and thinking that it was a lovely show, and that I couldn't wait to see the third series. I thought that would be it, but it had gotten under my skin, and I watched them all again twice over the next week. It wouldn't leave me alone; I identified with so many aspects of the different characters, and over the following weeks, I downloaded the soundtrack, devoured all the books, and found the Facebook community. I had no idea then just how big a part of my life it would become and how much it would help me.

I kept a journal on and off for a couple of years before I found *Heartstopper*. It had been a tricky few years for my mental health, and I was really struggling at times. On the very last page of that journal, I wrote, "I feel like I'm waiting for something to happen, almost like I'm on the brink of something that's going to reveal itself, it's within touching distance..."

A few weeks after I wrote that, I found *Heartstopper*, and it has changed my life. I feel like my life is split into 2 parts: the life before *Heartstopper* and the life after; and the life after is so much fuller. After watching the show, reading the books, and finding the Facebook group, I discovered fanfiction, and that was a revelation. I have always wanted to write fiction; it has been my biggest ambition, but I never believed that I could, never had the courage to do it.

As a direct result of grieving the younger, closeted me, I went back to therapy and through that, I started to write again. For the first time ever, I showed my writing to someone else, and that was a massive step for me. The confidence that gave me was immense, and I realised that through fanfiction I had a purpose, a reason to write, and an audience. I have made so many friends from all over the world from the Facebook group and, more recently, the Discord group. These are people who feel like my people, my tribe, people who understand me in a way that nobody else does, because we share something very special: our queerness, and *Heartstopper*.

The feedback I have received for my writing has boosted my confidence better than years of therapy ever did. I feel like I have my purpose now, and I know I will go on to write more and be published one day. *Heartstopper* has influenced me to learn more about all aspects of the LGBT community and has changed the way I work, so I now help other people through their own journeys of self-discovery. I've been a therapist for 15 years, focussed on anxiety and trauma, and have been wanting to change directions. I've toyed with different ideas, but now I know I want to focus on working with the queer community.

Reading fan fiction has also taught me so much. I thought I'd known I was bisexual for a number of years, but by reading up about different queer identities and examining different experiences in my past, I discovered that I'm actually gender fluid. So many puzzle pieces slipped into place when I discovered gender euphoria!

Through discovering *Heartstopper* and Kit Connor, I visited New York, travelling across the Atlantic, which was an adventure I wouldn't have had the confidence to do in the past. That week in New York was one of the best weeks of my life.

So the writing, finding friends, changing my business to help other queer people, solo travel, finding my true self...all of these things changed me beyond recognition. I am a very different person today because of *Heartstopper*, but it doesn't end there, because the confidence I feel in myself now has helped me through a massive challenge.

In January, I was diagnosed with Breast Cancer. The day after my diagnosis, I fell apart. I thought that all of this good stuff, all the confidence, the new me, and my new identity was over; I'd only just found it, and it was being taken away. But that evening, something changed. I decided that I wasn't willing to let the new me go, that cancer was just one part of my life, not my whole life.

I put on the *Heartstopper* soundtrack, pulled up my favourite fanfic, surrounded myself with the support of my Discord group friends, and fought back. Through each surgery and each round of treatment, my focus has been on *Heartstopper* (there's nothing like an imaginary Nick Nelson hug to get you through yet another injection or anaesthetic), and I'm officially in remission.

Heartstopper and its wider influence gave me the strength to fight for my life and win.

Joanne's story
How Heartstopper Changed My Life

I am a 52-year-old cis white middle-class woman. My life changed utterly and completely beyond all reason within a year of first seeing this little show called *Heartstopper*, a teen show about romance and friendship. How was it possible for this enchanting, sweet love story to change everything?

My friend told me her son was playing an extra in a teen live-action show, so I tuned in to spot him. I had no way of knowing this sheer coincidence would be such a major turning point in my humdrum life. My first impression was that it was this very watchable rom-com, which drew me in, and then watchable turned into awe and wonder, and then into obsession.

I've never been obsessed with anything, and this really intrigued me; I wanted to understand the reasons for my obsession. I was rewatching it every other night, hooked beyond measure with no reasonable explanation, like a love-struck youth. I had fallen hook, line and sinker in a way I couldn't fathom. I've always considered myself a cynical independent – what on earth was happening?!

Well, first of all, it is the sweetest, most enchanting love story you'll ever see, with joy at its heart and a feel-good sensation that's hard to beat. Love is love. More than that, it is incredibly well told in every way. From the script to the acting, to the lighting, to the music, to the props...every single department got the memo and further enhanced the storytelling, creating something that was better than it needed to be. For the first time ever, I found myself dissecting all aspects of storytelling in a television show and how all members of the production crew contributed to portraying the essence of the story.

On top of that, each character was portrayed as someone valuable and worth knowing. When I was bullied at school, I remember feeling worthless; this series was shining a light on the opposite being true. I wish that I had been able to see myself through the same lens as the production team viewed these characters. Of course, there are hardships and challenges, but every character at some point in time feels seen and heard in a way many of us never were. But still, this didn't fully explain the extent of my fascination.

It made me ponder the purpose of obsession. Why do people become obsessed? What does our subconscious crave? Like dreams, it's our brain telling us something we have yet to fully understand.

Having embarked on this journey, I craved to connect with others who felt like I did, not even knowing if there were others. I joined a *Heartstopper* fan group on Facebook, all the while not being sure I could possibly belong. I just wanted to unravel the mystery of my obsession and talk to others who loved the same thing I did. What I absolutely didn't expect was to be wrapped in acceptance by a community which my own cis white community has historically rejected, abused, and derided. I mean, what right did I have to infiltrate the safe space of the queer community? And yet I was met with nothing but love, empathy, and care. We discussed, analysed, and validated each other in a way I had never imagined possible.

So, what is the point of obsession? Why do humans return to the same thing again and again? Safety? Definitely. Feel good sensations? Of course. But there's more; so much more. I didn't know it at the time, but it helped me come to terms with my own challenges and provided answers I didn't know I was brave enough to face. More than anything, it said to me, "Want more!", "Don't settle!", and "You are valid!".

Nick Nelson, played by Kit Connor, comes out to his mum with such bravery and heart in the show. It's unbelievably heartbreaking and lovely at the same time. Kit talks about a profound moment when a teen fan found their strength to come out of the closet to their own family all because of our lovely, beautiful show and God damn it, if he has the courage to do it, then I surely had to find the strength to leave a crumbling, soul destroying marriage of 23 years to find the person I deserve to be. And that, I realised, was the reason for my obsession.

Within a year of first watching *Heartstopper*, I travelled from the mundane to the extraordinary. Instead of settling for less than I deserved and living a life my teenage self would have been appalled by, I reclaimed my right to happiness, left my loveless marriage, bought my own house, went back to work full-time and am now able to live independently. Not only that, but I also found a partner who makes me feel special, who finds me interesting, and who wants to see me happy.

Although this show was intended for LGBT+ teenagers, it transcends all boundaries. If this show could change my life, being so far outside of the target audience, we as humans clearly have much more in common than it would first appear.

Rebecca P's Story

I first watched *Heartstopper* on the eve of my 20th wedding anniversary. My husband was ill, and I was sleeping downstairs so as not to disturb him. I'd heard people speaking about it as a good adaptation of a graphic novel, but I didn't know much else. This was in August 2023, shortly after Season 2 had been released.

I watched the first season pretty much straight through. I then turned off the light, tried to fall asleep, gave up, and watched the second season. By the time I was done, it was 3 in the morning.

I didn't really understand why the story gripped me so hard. But it was all I could think about. I went online looking at stuff about the cast. I read the webcomics through. I looked up the music and started listening to it. About the same time, I lost my appetite and began having trouble sleeping.

I'm bi. I had suspected that since high school, when I had crushes on girls and boys, but I didn't really know the language to put to it. The summer after my first year in college, I went to Lilith Fair with a friend. I remember standing in front of one of the tables, looking at a display of buttons. One of them was clearly a Pride button. Another one said Ally. I didn't know which one to choose. I knew the Pride button was mine. But I chose to buy the Ally button. I was scared to claim who I was.

I think that's why Nick's journey in *Heartstopper* resonated so much with me. Kit Connor does such a fabulous job of portraying that mix of yearning and fear as Nick grapples with his identity. I felt it in my gut – I remembered that feeling of yearning for something but being afraid to claim it. I was shoved back to high school and rooming with a close friend, whom I also had a crush on. I was shoved back to college and that button table at Lilith Fair. I felt it viscerally.

Suddenly, my bi-ness became something precious that had been buried for years but was suddenly unearthed. It was beautiful and tender in a way I felt I needed to protect and cherish. At that moment, it didn't really have to do with who I wanted to be in a romantic relationship with. It had to do with me and my uniqueness as a child of God.

About ten days after I first watched *Heartstopper*, I was trying to explain to a fellow queer friend why this show was so important to me. How this story has shown me parts of myself I hadn't looked at in decades. I expressed my desire to watch *Heartstopper* with my children to show them the hope and joy that can come with being queer. There's so much pain and fear – not from being queer but from the world we live in. We need to hold onto that joy and beauty with both hands.

And *Heartstopper* is so full of that joy. A joy I didn't even realize I was starving for. Not just teenage Rebecca, so full of uncertainty about who she was and what it means to be bi in a heteronormative world. But Rebecca of today, who, unbeknownst to me, had carried that hunger hidden inside her for decades. A hunger to be herself – to fully claim all of her.

I didn't realize how much I needed to see Tara and Darcy kiss on that dance floor. To see their joy in being together, in showing affection for each other, in just being them. Something hetero couples take for granted. To see the pure joy reflected in Nick's eyes as the knowledge hits him – *this*, this can be joyful too. To be reminded that there is so much joy in being you – in letting down that mask and showing your full self. Of letting go of that fear.

I shared with my friend that I don't know where my girls are going to end up in terms of their sexuality, but that I was concerned about their father's reaction if they turned out to be queer in any way. I worried that he might not be able to accept them as their full selves. He is generally a kind, welcoming man, and would love our kids no matter what, but he would likely question whether we did something wrong if they turned out to be queer. I'd talked to him about *Heartstopper*, but he wasn't keen on watching it. He's kind to queer people we know, but not necessarily fully accepting.

A few days later, I was alone for the first time in several weeks. In that space, as I sat in an empty, still house, listening to songs from the soundtrack, I was hit with a wave of clarity that left me reeling. If I worried that my husband would not accept my girls if they were queer, what did that mean for me? He wouldn't possibly accept this part of me – my bi-ness, this precious, tender piece of what made me, me. And the waves of grief came as I mourned what my marriage was not – a place where I was seen, known fully, and loved for it. I did not have a husband who saw me, in all of my individual, specific awesomeness and thought, "Wow! I get to be married to HER?"

I'd been skirting around that knowledge for years. As I entered my forties and came across more people who saw me and truly perceived and valued me for who I am at my core, I became more and more aware that I did not have that in my marriage. In so many spaces, I saw people who knew me deeply and loved me for it. My marriage was not one of them.

The grief was the tearing off of a scab over an infected wound. It was sharp and overwhelming. I lived in that place of grief for about two weeks, after which I was hit with a second wave of clarity. Standing here waiting for my husband to fully see me and know me was weighing me down with pain. At the same time, I did not believe that he desired a marriage with any of the connection and vulnerability I craved. I needed to let go of any expectation of receiving that type of love from my husband, so as not to have my hopes dashed again and again. And so, I did. I let go. And I felt lighter. And the lightness hurt . . . but it wasn't that infected ache. It was a sharp, clear pain marking the beginning of healing.

Two years on, that healing continues. My husband and I are now divorced and co-parenting our kids. I've continued to lean into my queerness, attending Pride for the first time in more than 20 years. I'm surrounded by people who know me and love me: at work, at church, in my family, with my friends. My life is rich and full. I'm grateful to all who brought *Heartstopper* to my laptop screen two years ago and created a story that pushed me towards joy.

Rhyn's Story

Initially, I just thought *Heartstopper* was an adorably sweet and lovely story. When I finally heeded my friend's recommendation to watch it, I got hooked and devoured it like any good binge-worthy Netflix show. But I didn't think about the deep meaning of it at first, until I noticed I was downloading the entire season to watch on a plane trip again just a few days later. I then spent that entire trip (what was supposed to be a family vacation) crying every night in the hotel after everyone had gone to sleep. After several rewatches, I started checking out some related fanfiction on the advice of that same friend and ended up spending my days consuming more and more of it as another source of *Heartstopper*-related content (I had literally never read fanfiction before in my life!). Before we even came home from the trip, I had reported back to the friend that something was definitely happening inside me and that I needed therapy, stat!

This whole experience 100% ended up being a catalyst for life-shattering changes. For many years before that, I had been in a marriage where we weren't happy, and I just figured I'd never do anything about it, because I didn't want to rock the boat. But something about *Heartstopper* wouldn't let my emotions go and it drove me to therapy, to talking it out with friends, to making new friends in the fandom. I still can't put my finger on just exactly what about this show grabbed me, but it somehow convinced me that I shouldn't settle anymore.

The first time I saw the show was in July 2022. Now, almost exactly three years later, my ex and I have separated, and we are both much happier in our own lives while working together to be good co-parents. I have been with my new partner (whom I met through the *Heartstopper* fanfiction community!) for over a year and am incredibly happy. Both of us are learning more about ourselves and healing old, entrenched trauma as we deepen our relationship, surrounded by an incredible community in the fandom. I am slowly learning that it is important to recognize my own desires, and to ask for what I want, a lesson I ignored for most of my life.

Overall, I have seen and been a part of the *Heartstopper* community which is very supportive of one another, openly sharing their journeys and challenges, and serving each other as resources for many life questions and issues. The connections I have made in this fandom are very meaningful to me in so many new ways, as we learn about all the different kinds of connections that can help make us who we are, and help us love who we are.

I suspect even more growth and wonderful things lie ahead, but I am amazed that I've come this far, and that it all started when my friend Ryan texted "if you haven't seen *Heartstopper* on Netflix yet, you have to. It's the most joyful, beautiful queer series I have consumed, ever." And I have tons of friends within the fandom who have gone through similar total life upheaval for the same reason! We all saw something that was simple but powerful, a group of young people learning how to be true to themselves and challenging all us viewers to do the same.

Molly Robins' Story

Initially, I thought the first few episodes of *Heartstopper* were totally cringe - but once I (and my wife) reminded my Xennial brain that this was a show about teenage love (and subsequently learned it was based on a webcomic), I really started to enjoy it.

My life is so much better because of *Heartstopper*, and I only came into the community in early 2025, about 3 months ago, as I am writing this. Before my wife and I had even finished the first season, I'd caught up on the webcomic. I almost immediately joined Alice's Patreon at the highest membership level and started participating in the chats there and on the *Heartstopper* Discord.

Sweet love stories usually fall into two categories: fairy tale or Hallmark. Hallmark love stories tend to feel like any tension they try to build is so ridiculously contrived that it feels forced. Fairy tales are magical; there tends to be less tension and more of an elaborate meeting of destined lovers in over-the-top scenarios, like in Disney movies.

Heartstopper (both the show and the comic) saved my 12-year marriage/16-year relationship. "Lesbian bed-death" is a real thing, and combined with my own mental health, it started relatively early in my relationship. Much of this is due to societal expectations that have shaped our way of thinking and interacting; friendship takes a front seat and often overrides other aspects of the relationship, including physical intimacy. It was a point of stress, which tends to have a way of expanding itself.

The way that love and relationships with family, friends, and partners are addressed in *Heartstopper* (even with the rose-ish tinted glasses we watch/read through) dug into my brain. Looking at their friendships within the Paris Squad, there is a protectiveness, akin to siblinghood; no matter how bad things are, they are there for each other even when they don't agree. They embrace each other despite, or maybe even because of, their differences.

I have been living with and treating depression and anxiety for over 30 years. I can trace my anxieties back to when I was nine years old, and have been in and out of therapy since I was fourteen. It hasn't always been easy, but I've learned to adapt and function, and my anxieties about not being good enough or taking myself too seriously have started to weaken.

My wife and I have had more intimacy in 3 months than we've had in the last 10 years. I've started thinking about why I've been closed off and where it came from, and I'm TALKING to her about it. Low self-esteem can kill the desire to be intimate, and then the guilt kicks in, and it keeps eating into itself. Before I realized I was a lesbian, I sort of molded myself into someone who could be liked, could be attractive to men, but it was lacking depth. The lack of meaning in those relationships bled into other aspects of my life and was a hard pattern to break.

Heartstopper has also brought music into my life. I joke that if an artist wasn't making music before 2003, I have not heard it. But the soundtrack brings such visceral feelings that I found myself listening to some songs on repeat, foregoing my podcasts and audiobooks. I've even become an active participant in a Patreon playlist project.

If *Heartstopper* had only been a TV show or only a webcomic, I'm not sure I would have been so affected by it. I read/watch/listen to Alice's words and images, then discuss and analyze with other fans. Experiencing it in so many ways made this story bigger, deeper, becoming another branch on my "tree of stories" that have made me who I am.

Bob's Story

My first reactions to *Heartstopper* happened as the episodes progressed: I was aligning the story with the normal tropes of gay and young male films that I had seen. When Nick and Charlie kissed in the rain and Charlie walked back into school the next day, I expected Nick to be tragically gone (aka *Dead Poets Society*). I expected Charlie to be beaten up by Ben in a gay-panic "I'm not that way" kind of scene (aka *Beautiful Thing*). I was expecting Elle to be outed in some horrible way (aka *Boys Don't Cry*). I expected Imogen to out Charlie or sabotage their friendship when she had suspicions about Nick (*Brokeback Mountain*). I was expecting Isaac to attempt unaliving or to be the best friend secretly in love with Charlie. There were so many commonly portrayed things that could have happened.

I was expecting one of them to start doing drugs, turn to sex work, or be exposed to HIV. All the "normal" things that happen in gay stories. Those are the narratives we have been led to expect in our lives.

What *Heartstopper* did brilliantly was NOT turning to that weak, expected storyline, but instead giving us a positive narrative. I was crying at the end. I had to watch it again. And again. I had to find the *Heartstopper* community. I had to buy the clothes from the show. I considered, for the first time in my life, getting a tattoo of the leaves that feature heavily in the show and graphic novels. I told EVERYONE who would listen to go watch the show. I listened to the soundtrack. I told my therapist that I was not watching anything else for about 5 weeks, and he was fine with that.

Additionally, I was struck by the characters asking permission to kiss and permission to touch. They modeled permission and consent so that the young people watching would understand how adults should interact in romantic and sexual situations.

Heartstopper also affirmed my love for all things British. I already had plans to leave the US as soon as I was able, and I wanted to get to the UK. *Heartstopper* was just one more reason for me to make England my goal.

Heartstopper came into my life during my mother's last 18 months. It was a very difficult time, and the show was my respite and my safe space. Nick and Charlie were both teens and new to their emotions, and it was so relatable because even at my age, every time you go out with someone new, you feel those emotions. It was beautiful to watch them navigate their feelings and figure themselves out, even making mistakes, but without any of the unnecessary drama and trauma that pervades most LGBTQ+ shows and movies. It was wonderful to see Nick openly explore his identity and sexuality, without shutting it down. It was hopeful, joyous, and delightful to see these characters modeling something we all wish for.

In 2023, my mother passed away after 9 years of illness. I packed my things, moved out of Texas, which had turned very toxic for LGBTQ people. I moved to Virginia (where I grew up) and took several months to settle out estate issues, and then moved to the UK, and I now live in London. *Heartstopper* has helped give me a vision for being in a place where LGBTQ people are accepted and embraced.

While I was here visiting London, before the move, I was wearing a *Heartstopper* tee shirt with leaves and the words "Hi" / "Hi" and it was recognized by other fans in front of Buckingham Palace. We shared a bit of our favorite moments from the show. When I get time to explore, I'd love to go to the beach where the end of Season 1 takes place, the "we're boyfriends" scene, and see the water.

I also met up with a man from the *Heartstopper* Facebook page. We met for two dates. He's also from the US and is looking for a relationship like Nick and Charlie share. Right now, we're still just friends, but who knows? Having this show as a template gives us both a guide for what our future might hold.

I watch the show on a loop, especially when new seasons are released. I am very alone and would love having someone around to make me tea and for me to fuss over, someone who understands that "Hi" really means "I love you". There's no other show that delivers the feeling of companionship that *Heartstopper* brings. Currently, my Netflix is at Season 2 Episode 5 when Charlie faints; it makes me think about how I want someone who will catch me if I falter, someone I can defend against the rugby lads of our lives.

If there were a *Heartstopper* dating service, I would sign up right away. We all have our issues: For Charlie, it's an eating disorder, for Darcy, it's her mom and family issues. For me, it's feeling unworthy of sharing my world with someone. Part of that is in the evidence that there aren't a lot of people asking me out; the other is that I've been cheated on, so trusting a new relationship will be hard. But having someone who sits patiently by, smiling, like Nick....that would be lovely.

Claire's Story

When I first finished watching *Heartstopper*, my initial thought was, "Oh, hmm, ok, wow! I need to rewatch this immediately". I did not understand my visceral reaction, but the beauty of the story unfolding had grabbed my attention.

It was the perfect catalyst to wake me up from my life and save me from the burnout I was having at work. It gave me a way to shift my focus away from my job, which had been the centre of my life; it had become very small after making it through the pandemic. Within the first weekend, I had rewatched the show 5 times. Three weeks later, I realised why Nick googling "am I gay" and the soundtrack of the song *Why Am I Like This* kept driving me to tears, bringing that scene and the emotion I felt watching it back to the surface anytime I heard it. I had been ignoring that I am bi, and it went so far that I thought I was an ally. I think I wasn't ready to explore the niggling feeling, and there hadn't been a pressing reason for me to look into it.

I started talking to my friends about my obsession with *Heartstopper*, and after a little while, I mentioned that I also like women. Every time I talked about it, the responses were lovely, which helped alleviate some of my fears. I gradually came out to friends and family, and went to Pride, which was quite emotional to attend as an openly bi person for the first time. Strangely, I felt imposter syndrome this time, when previously attending as an ally didn't have the same effect.

In the meantime, I found out about fanfiction and delved right in. I saw mention of it on Reddit, and it sparked my interest immediately; the idea of having more of Nick and Charlie was enticing. I just needed more. I had never been part of a fandom before or interacted with other fans on such a large scale. Yet now I had found an online community I wanted to be part of. I joined groups on Reddit, Twitter, and later Discord, where I found a community of fanfiction readers and writers. I made friends, talked about sexuality and gender, and found myself questioning my gender identity, too. I began to realise that I am not strongly attached to my gender as something fixed, probably leaning more toward being nonbinary.

I met an online friend to go to a concert in London to see Baby Queen (who contributed many songs to the *Heartstopper* soundtrack), then to an event with Alice Oseman, the author of *Heartstopper*, in Manchester. The online fandom entered my real life; it became more real. I went to Pride in London with other fans; it stayed more real, and throughout this period, I began feeling more and more like myself.

I got my first tattoo, then a second one, both depicting iconic elements of *Heartstopper*. A year later, I was talking to a friend from the *Heartstopper* community, questioning whether I was on the neurodivergent spectrum, and was advised to look up Complex PTSD. Another bulb lit up... This was bigger than realising I was bi; it took me about nine months to decide to start therapy. I broke out of my shell, and it feels damn good.

In the past two and a half years, I have written, read, shared, and edited stories, and in the process, I got another chance at rewriting my own story, too. Being an active part of a creative community like that has brought me joy in a different way; interacting with other writers through editing and through discussions about the stories enhanced the experience beyond the mere reading of fiction.

I don't know what my life would be like if I had kept watching *Selling Sunset* that evening, instead of switching to *Heartstopper*. I hope something else would have knocked me out of the slumber I was stuck in. But I don't have to know, I can just be grateful for all the good things that have filled my life since. *Heartstopper* and the community gave me life, hope, strength and acceptance. I'm better because of it. And when I doubt it, I can just look up at the shelves, see the books, and pins and tokens of happiness. It's not magic, it's "just" good.

Brandon Ford's Story

Heartstopper had me hooked from the minute Nick and Charlie played in the snow in Episode 2. It was so pure and sweet and the opposite of every other teen show and piece of gay media. It was innocent and true. I found that line after line throughout the series was something I had uttered at least once in my life.

I binged all three seasons in one day. I was at a low moment in my life, having had a difficult year prior to this that affected pretty much all aspects of my life (work, relationships, etc.). When I finished the series the first time, there was a hole in my heart, an ache I couldn't soothe or make go away. The only thing I could do to stop the pain in my heart was to start the series over and watch it again. After seeing Charlie's journey (and the toll it was taking on Nick) in Season 3 Episode 4, I got a therapist and entered therapy for eight weeks. I started working again, got promoted, moved to a bigger place and started dating.

I live in North Hollywood. I'm 39 years old. I had heard of *Heartstopper* because the hallway scene from the season 1 finale kept coming up in my Facebook feed. I decided to watch it on January 7, 2025. When I got to the kiss in episode 3, my power went out. As I said, I live in North Hollywood, and January 7 was the day of the Palisades fire, which I lived 4 miles away from. I would be without power for three days.

But my phone still worked, and I have several battery phone chargers, so I picked *Heartstopper* up on my phone where I left off and watched the entire series all night. The only light I had for three days was my phone playing – and replaying – *Heartstopper*.

I fell in love with it instantly. The perfection of the casting. The innocence and purity. The fact that there's no salacious teen show storylines – no drug habits or orgies or affairs or students with teachers or fires or shootings – just kids getting to be kids and having the chance to figure things out.

As I turn 40 later this year, this whole year has been this introspection of my life and its direction (or lack thereof), and after 40 years, in this tiny British show, I saw 14-year-old me, terrified anyone would know my real feelings. The anxiety. The pain of first love. The terror of losing it.

More than anything, the show reignited a fire I thought had gone out. I'd resigned myself that true love wasn't for me. I gave up being the hopeless romantic and settled into the reality of being a single queer man in his late 30s... "dead". I stopped looking for that permanent relationship, finding that one person to spend the rest of my life with. I had simply given in to the belief that it wouldn't happen for me. Then I saw these two kids, and it reminded me that that's all I ever wanted and NEVER could have gotten when I was their age.

I'm glad kids today can be free. I'm glad this show can show them the way. I wish I could send this back to 14-year-old me... I could have saved myself a lot of time and pain. Seeing Charlie return home, still carrying the weight of his challenges on his shoulders, but determined to move forward with optimism, allowed me to reopen the door to permit myself to actively look for that connection again. If Charlie could do it, then so could I.

Community and Meaningful Human Connections

By Rowan Murphy

Heartstopper came into our lives at the tail end of lockdowns, quarantines, and travel bans due to a worldwide pandemic, which had catastrophic impacts on our social lives and relationships. On top of the ongoing terror of mounting death tolls and rapid spread of the virus, we lost key elements of our emotional support system. Social distancing, bans on gatherings (which are deeply ingrained in our culture), isolation due to remote work mandates, and periodic lockdowns or quarantines all created a very lonely and isolating environment. Everyone was affected, regardless of age or socio-economic background.

Many lost their sources of income, businesses went under, and mental health suffered. People felt trapped, caged in, and became angry or depressed; something as simple as a discussion about wearing masks could destroy friendships. A recent poll[1] showed that most Americans believe COVID-19 drove the U.S. apart, and the chasm has only grown in the past three years.

COVID-19 forced us to fundamentally change the way we seek and maintain social connections. As we found ourselves in isolation, unable to meet up with friends and family the way we had previously, we turned to the internet. Video calling and social media use increased and became a lifeline for many, and the way we

---

1. Alec Tyson, Michael Lipka, Claudia Deane, "5 Years Later: America Looks Back at the Impact of COVID-19, 12 February 2025

interacted with these tools evolved. While this could not replace in-person contact, the establishment and maintenance of social connections via online tools were gradually normalised.

The majority of stories we received made references to finding community and forging new friendships, even if their focus was on other topics. In fact, roughly 80% of narratives we received included mention of new friendships or online groups where fans were able to find connections that were sorely needed. Community is especially important for members of the LGBTQIA+ community as we seek and find acceptance, support, and affirmation to help balance out the stigmatisation and marginalisation we experience in our everyday lives.

Human connection is fundamental to our existence. This goes beyond the simple instinct to procreate and maintain a population; as I've mentioned before, it is recognised as a psychological need that ranks almost as high as our basic physiological needs for survival. Family is the nucleus in which we start to experience feelings of safety and security, and as we grow, we find many other ways of connecting with others, forging friendships and building our own networks. Humans are social creatures; isolation breeds anxiety and despair. Studies have found that during adolescence, isolation can lead to cognitive deficits, emotional pain, and even physical health problems; these impacts are no less severe in our adult lives.

Considering the criticality of community and social interaction, rejection by one's own family becomes an existential threat. The psychological impacts are vast and extremely harmful; this is the type of trauma that leads to negative self-perception and serious mental health issues. In a 2023 *Psychology Today* article, a study found that "nearly half of LGBTQ+ young adults are estranged from at least one family member, and one-third are 'not confident' that their parent/guardian would accept them if they came out."[2]

In this context, it becomes crucial to find connections outside of the immediate family circle. "Found family" is a term commonly used by members of the community who have experienced rejection within their biological family. It is deeply rooted within LGBTQIA+ history and necessary for our very survival. Found family can be many things, but at the heart of it is acceptance and validation, a common understanding of our shared experiences. Typically, found family emerges from friend groups, possibly from community organisations and shared safe spaces. I never expected to find it in a fandom.

> "I landed on Tumblr and found great like-minded people and got a newfound feeling of belonging. I especially found one very important friend (or did she find me?), who is still very important to me today."
>
> Bethaven

> "The growing love and appreciation for this programme led me to find the most meaningful relationships with people who understood me and with whom I felt connected."
>
> DD

---

2. Fern Schumer Chapman, "New Study Finds Half of LGBTQ+ Are Estranged From Family", blog on https://www.psychologytoday.com/us, 10 October 2023

> "I found a community of like-minded people who understand and share my obsession with *Heartstopper*. I have made friends literally around the world, and there is always someone awake to chat and flail with."
>
> Shannan

I have thought long and hard about what makes the *Heartstopper* connections so special and unique. I have never in my 53 years made such deeply meaningful friendships on the internet, and I have been trying to pinpoint the reasons. All fandom communities are built on the same foundation: A shared passion and appreciation for the film, show, book, characters, or celebrities we admire. So, what is it that sets this fandom apart?

Many fans I have spoken with agree that there is something special about the *Heartstopper* community. Yes, we all love the show and the graphic novels, and we greatly admire Alice, the production team, and the cast who brought it to life, but we are connected by more than that. Most of us are part of the LGBTQIA+ community, but the bond goes beyond this: Our lives have been irrevocably changed for the better. We freed ourselves from societal expectations and constraints, and we made deliberate choices to improve our quality of life.

> "*Heartstopper* has brought me a new community of people with whom I feel I can share my experience, and who support each other. It has helped my confidence level and encouraged me to put myself out there more, to move forward with life rather than dwell in the past and remain stagnant."
>
> Frank Drake Jr.

> "I have made so many amazing friends that I bonded with because of *Heartstopper*, but our friendships have now gone beyond that connection."
>
> Zee

Humans can form bonds through many deliberate actions, such as planned social activities or shared hobbies, travelling together, or even something as simple as having a meal together. Many of us stumbled into *Heartstopper* and its fandom by sheer coincidence, and yet we formed deep emotional connections that many described as being closer than those we had in our lives before. Somehow, we found the courage to be vulnerable and authentic with each other despite the relative anonymity of online environments, and as a result, we established a foundation of trust.

Many of the stories we received describe profoundly emotional responses to the show which seemed to have no logical explanation. I certainly experienced this, and it left me floundering for a while, unable to figure out what on earth was happening to me.

> "My first watch through broke me and healed me at the same time. I was sobbing through scenes and not understanding my intense reaction to this beautiful show."
>
> Sarah

> "I was very confused as to why this sweet little queer show completely rocked me to the core, but I was

about to have a (slightly early) midlife crisis because of it."

Skasi6

"I experienced a Tsunami of emotions, I cried, my heart sank, and dozens of doors in my brain opened."

Hughe

Not everyone experienced emotional upheaval quite like this. Many fans described their initial reaction as one of feeling safe, uplifted, or captivated by the beautiful story, but the universal response was one of intense fascination. The show touched something deep inside of us, and we all wondered: "Why are we like this?" We connected through discussions where we shared our innermost thoughts and feelings, trying to help each other understand the extraordinary response to this sweet, unpretentious show, which we all shared.

Some of the strongest connections are formed when people share authentic pieces of themselves, dropping the protective shields we often carry to keep ourselves safe from judgment or alienation. Within the fandom, groups have formed where people help each other in overcoming challenges, working through difficult realisations and acknowledging pieces of ourselves that we had never dared to even look at before. These types of interactions lead to deep, honest friendships based on mutual trust and acceptance.

Some groups created dedicated chats for "deep talk", where people could open up in a safe environment, and where group members actively listened, intending to truly understand and support each other. Fandom conversations span every topic imaginable, from the best recipe for apple sauce to personal experiences with mental health conditions and trauma. The honesty and vulnerability modelled in *Heartstopper* is being replicated within the fan community, and it has enabled us to form friendship groups that rival those in the show.

I remember when my own little friend group formed, just over three years ago now, in August of 2022. We started a group chat, initially intending to form a book club for LGBTQIA+ literature. There might have been the occasional discussion about books – we did read *The Song of Achilles*, which made most of us sob uncontrollably at the end, and we discussed Alice's novels – but for the most part, we chatted about our lives, our hopes and fears and challenges. Our group chat has turned into a little family and has been going strong ever since. And I know it isn't the only one, I have heard of quite a few friend groups like ours that have formed over the years. Of course, we still interact with the larger social media groups, which feel like a sort of extended family.

As with everything in life, there are exceptions, but generally, we share a fierce protectiveness of each other; there is zero tolerance for bullying or any kind of bigotry. Most of the time, disagreements are worked out amongst ourselves, and where needed, administrators will step in to mediate. It's almost like we cannot bear the loveliness and purity of the story to be tainted by anything mean or ugly, and when something causes discord, the impact is deeply emotional.

Of course, there are occasional differences in opinion or unpleasant encounters, but rarely have I seen groups of over 100,000 members that were mutually supportive and accepting to this degree. The positive environment is carefully guarded and monitored to ensure everyone's safety and emotional well-being. It's as if the spirit of *Heartstopper*, with its healthy communication models and general approach of celebrating uniqueness and authenticity, has carried over into the fandom.

The profound effect of this show not only changed our lives, it touched the lives of those around us as well; the ripple effect is spreading waves of love, acceptance and support to our families, friends, and acquaintances. Quite a few fans have made it their mission to support the LGBTQIA+ community through podcasts or YouTube videos, decided to volunteer for LGBTQIA+ organisations, or incorporated the credo of *Heartstopper* into parenting, teaching, and general allyship.

> "This show has shaped the way I would like to parent, so that my future children will feel accepted and loved, no matter who they are and who they love. Everyone around me assumed I was straight, so I did too. There will be no assuming with my future children, and there will be open discussions and representation of queer people and people who are different from them."
>
> Chantal

> "Another thing that came from *Heartstopper* is that I have been able to use this beautiful story to teach my 9-year-old about the LGBTQI+ community and normalise it all for her."
>
> Zoë R.

This book has brought me into contact with many new people, and I hope that it will continue to do so. The *Heartstopper* fan community is the safest, most open-minded and accepting environment I have ever experienced, and I hope the ripple effect Alice Oseman has created will carry on in perpetuity.

Ashley Hullett's Story

When I first watched season one of *Heartstopper*, I watched all of it in one sitting because I could not stop. I thought it was so wholesome and beautiful. As someone who watches a lot of TV shows, this was unlike anything I had seen before. It had a fresh and new feel to it, from the music to the cinematography. I was completely surprised when I realized the cast were mostly unknown, yet the acting blew me away. As a bisexual person, I was thrilled to see such beautiful bi representation in a character like Nick Nelson. Watching his journey throughout the series was so beautiful and lovely, and unlike most bisexual stories we see in the media. I knew right away that this series was gold and would become very meaningful for me.

It is hard to put into words the full impact that *Heartstopper* has had on me. The show came out at a time in my life when I was going through something completely distressing and difficult. My mom had just been diagnosed with stage 4 cancer. We were very close, despite some contentious years, and this diagnosis made me want to set aside any differences and be close to her again. She decided against treatment, and I spiraled into a deep depression. *Heartstopper* was this little ray of sunshine that I didn't know I needed until I had it, and it was so healing for me and my inner child, who did not have this queer experience. Seeing a show with such wholesome and vast representation was new for me, and I quickly became completely obsessed.

It didn't matter if I was celebrating a win or needing comfort after a tough day, *Heartstopper* always made me feel better. I could not stop watching season one and reading the comics on repeat. I decided that since I was constantly talking about it to anyone who would listen to me, I should start a podcast and just never stop talking about it. It began in the fall of 2022 and has followed the series in real time.

It was actually my therapist who encouraged me to do the podcast, to share the joy and comfort the show brought me. I have a background in producing and editing podcasts but had always been more comfortable remaining behind the scenes. She encouraged me to step outside my comfort zone, and I don't have a large queer community locally, so this was a way to connect with other LGBTQ+ individuals. I had some friends who watched *Heartstopper*, but they did not have such a strong reaction to it like I did.

I reached out to a couple of friends who I knew had podcast experience, and one of them agreed to start it with me. I never wanted it to be an empty rewatch podcast; I wanted to be vulnerable and honest, and really dig into it, and share how strong my connection to and feelings about the show and the characters were.

On top of that, *Heartstopper* is so rich with tiny little details, and there is so much to analyze in the show, so I decided to make it a deep-dive analysis type of podcast. The community that has developed from this has been astounding. People from all over the world have written to share how they felt seen for the first time in their lives, and it has been incredible to be a part of that shared experience.

Since then, I have laughed and cried with friends and strangers alike, and I have been lucky enough to watch a beautiful little community form. So many others reached out in one way or another to tell their story and their perspective on the show. It made me feel seen in such a unique way to hear from people of all ages, cultures, and backgrounds feeling just as intensely about these characters and this story.

Connecting with people around this series has been the greatest gift. I have met people from all over the world who have made such a lasting impact on my life that they have become friends with whom I speak every day. Through the most difficult years of my life, *Heartstopper* helped me find a community to support me and help me through the trenches. As my mom got worse, I moved back in with her part-time to take care of her throughout the week. Having the show and podcast to escape from the reality of it, along with the Discord community, where someone was always active to talk to me or support me, was really helpful.

Watching Charlie go through his mental health journey was revolutionary for me in that it helped me understand that it is okay to lean on your friends and to get support. This helped me to be more vulnerable and open with the people in my life about how I was actually doing. I will forever be grateful for what *Heartstopper* has given me, but also for what it has given everyone who has found or healed a part of themselves in it.

ZH's Story

This story *should* have started on 22 May 2022. But perhaps if it had, the story would not be the same.

See, 22 May 2022 was the first time I ever saw the word *Heartstopper*. At some point previously, I had seen a trailer and thought *"that's cute"*, though I had no idea there were any comics, and I'd never heard the name Alice Oseman. But on 22 May 2022, sometime after the kids were in bed, as I was looking for something to watch while winding down for the night, the title *Heartstopper* was under the heading of 'Just Released' and without thinking about it, I clicked play.

I made it as far as Mr Lange telling Charlie, "I'm sure you'll get along swimmingly" when mentioning he'd be seated next to rugby lad Nick Nelson, before it cut out and I couldn't watch anymore.

I shared my Netflix account with my parents and a friend, so on this same night, they were both watching something, meaning I was kicked out. I didn't think much of it. I was happy for them to be utilising my subscription, so I shifted over to another streaming platform and started a different series. I had no issue with it.

I was just shy of 12 months since leaving an 11-year abusive marriage. I was socialising again. I was finding new interests. I was parenting and working and keeping house just how I had always wanted. I was thriving!

So, getting booted out of a Netflix show at 10 pm on a random Sunday night wasn't upsetting or even anything worth thinking about.

My *Heartstopper* journey was over.

The series I began on the other streaming service was a full six seasons. I binged the crap out of it, and by the time I was done, I needed something new.

Cue Sunday, 19 June 2022.

By this stage, cracks had begun to form in my 'thriving self'. My ex had been mistreating my kids terribly, and I had finally been given some proof. I stopped them from seeing him, which caused stress for everyone involved. The busy season at work was ramping up. I just needed something feel-good with short episodes.

As I scrolled through Netflix, *Heartstopper* once again flashed at me. By this stage, I'd almost forgotten it existed. I played the trailer and remembered starting it and how much I'd wanted to watch it. And with 25-minute episodes, it was a no-brainer. One episode before bed was all I was going to need to wind me down so I could sleep. It was 11:30 pm on a work night after all.

I was not prepared.

Approximately 3 hours and 45 minutes later, I was a sobbing, bawling mess. I didn't understand. So, I hit play on episode 1 again. I think I only got an hour's sleep that night. If that.

While I was in the midst of my first rewatch at stupid o'clock in the morning, trying to figure out what the hell was going on, why this show was making me so uncontrollably upset and pained and intrigued and in love, I did what any good Nick Nelson would do. I turned to Google. (I hadn't yet worked out my Nick Nelson parallels).

I discovered a Facebook group with thousands of people. I discovered the series had been developed from an online webcomic. By the time I was at the end of episode 2, my heart was aching for Nick, I was shazaming the song *Why Am I Like This* (and then subsequently *My Own Person*) and trying desperately to hold shut the barrier I could see bursting with every repressed memory and feeling. The tears were back, and I don't know how long it took for them to stop. (To be honest, I'm not sure they actually stopped after the first watch.)

I silently joined the Facebook group and commenced reading the comics on Webtoon.

I spent the next day at work reading every single released comic panel, discovering the story wasn't done. I needed more. Nick and Charlie had a grip on me, and I still didn't understand why.

I scoured the Facebook group for answers, not finding many. I went online and, without thinking about my bank account, purchased on click and collect[1] Volumes 1-4 of the graphic novels, the Netflix edition of Volume 1, *Nick and Charlie* novella, *This Winter* novella, *Solitaire*, *Radio Silence*, and *Loveless*. I picked them up on the way home, not blinking twice at my out-of-character impulsivity.

Once home, I read through all the graphic novels again and returned to the Facebook group, just looking for *something*. Season 1 played again that night, and then at least once every night for the next 86 days.

---

1. Click and collect basically means you order online and then collect at a store, rather than having the item shipped.

It probably only took the first watch for me to link in with the term *bisexual*, but it took at least three more watches for me to acknowledge it. I didn't *want* to acknowledge it.

I was raised Christian. Christian household, Christian schooling, regular church attendance, and I was doing the same for my kids. And there was *nothing* that was going to take me away from that. And let me just mention right now that still hasn't changed. I am a Christian, and proud to be a Christian. But you can probably understand where my dilemma lay.

Being raised a Christian, I was taught homosexuality was wrong. Anything LGBTQIA+ was wrong. And whilst it was something that never fully sat right with me, I didn't question it.

Queer community and queer culture have always fascinated me. My favourite characters in books and TV shows were always the queer ones. Theirs were the stories I replayed. People watching is my favourite pastime. My gaze would always linger longer on those who were queer. I always befriended queer people in any social or work space. I never would have been able to tell you why.

I never hated the queer community, although I was raised to believe it wasn't right, and we *"love the sinner, but hate the sin"*. Even so, it was a community I couldn't seem to stay away from.

I reflect back now and recognise many things: There had been instances where I had behaved homophobically. I was plainly and obviously queer. I was seeking connection to my community. I repressed so many thoughts and emotions about who I really am.

So the crisis of culture and identity was a massive slap in the face I wasn't expecting when I switched on *Heartstopper*. But it was there. And it was unavoidable. I'd watched queer TV and movies before, so why was it *Heartstopper* that reached inside me and brought my queer AF self to the surface? (I'm still not sure I fully understand.)

When I joined the Facebook group, it was public, and there was no way I was going to make myself known when it had the potential to expose me to the rest of my Facebook friends. I still didn't totally know what was happening. I managed to submit an anonymous post asking if anyone else was having a Nick Nelson-themed *proper full-on gay crisis,* but quickly discovered anon posts weren't being approved. I was trapped in my own self-discovery with nowhere to find any support. So, I continued to cry in my spiral of repeatedly watching Season 1, reading the graphic novels, begging God for answers and searching Facebook for *anything* that could help.

Not long after, calls were made by active group members to make the group private, and the group owner did just that. As soon as the group went private, I started to engage. And oh boy, it was the best thing I could have done.

By this stage, I had watched the show multiple times, could quote each episode word for word, and was able to converse with other fans, discussing our love for our favourite characters, arguing over our favourite set pieces, deliberating the finer details, and competing in trivia games. Eventually, I even became a moderator for the group and finally an admin.

I discovered a group of people who very quickly became friends as we commented in the same posts over and over again. I reached out and became friends with another member, who very quickly became one of the most important people in my life. I still refer to him as my *Heartstopper* husband. It doesn't matter that he lives on the other side of the world; we FaceTimed almost daily, chatted daily, and eventually produced content for the group together, still keeping regular contact to this day.

I was asked to join a book club with several other group members with whom I'd been regularly interacting. These people lived all across the world, spanning seven countries across four continents, one of whom is an author of this book. A group chat was formed, and we talked all day, every day, for months and months. The group chat is still active, and those people are my family. (We may have only read one book together, but it was my introduction to queer literature – outside the Osemanverse – which has since continued to expand).

This family I found has been integral to me learning who I am. They have supported me through the absolute *worst* moments of my life. They know more about me than my "in real life" friends do. They have taken risks for me, metaphorically held me together when I thought I was falling apart, and celebrated big moments with me.

I've been fortunate to meet one of them face to face and have plans to eventually meet the rest. But they are so much my family that my kids have even met them on FaceTime chats.

There is much more in my life that has opened up and flourished since finding *Heartstopper*. Very quickly, I remembered my love for all things creative. My ex had removed my freedoms and independence on so many things over our 11 years; I hadn't realised how much I was no longer "allowed" to do.

But through *Heartstopper* and its community, I rediscovered my passion for writing. For drawing. For media manipulation. I rediscovered *me*. I began to write fanfic, something I'd never even heard of before, and that opened up new connections with new people on new platforms.

I joined a Discord server where I met many more wonderful people and was enthusiastically supported on my writing journey.

I learned so much about the queer community and even more about myself, finally naming and understanding my neurodivergences. I learnt so much about gender and sexuality. About asexuality, and how there is far more involved in gender than biology.

I learnt I wasn't weird, unusual, wrong, stupid or *alone*. I am me. And there is nothing wrong with who I am.

I'm still not out. It's not entirely safe for me to be out, even in a "white, first-world, western country". I don't fear for my life. But I am still Christian. And whilst there is a Christian community that is accepting and affirming, and I have finally made it to the same place as them, the community is small, and the wider Christian community are still not so accepting.

My faith cannot be swayed. I know who I am in Christ, but I also know who I am in myself. I am proudly Christian. I am proudly bisexual. I am proudly acespec [on the asexual spectrum]. I am proudly fluid. It still feels scary to acknowledge in writing sometimes, but if I can't be brave enough to put it to words, then the movement stops.

One day, I hope – I pray – that the Christian community will catch up. Queer is beautiful. Queer is natural. Queer is how God made me. And maybe there are Christians reading this who are angry now and are saddened to "see another Christian fall". To them I say, pray, research, discuss, investigate. Don't just shut it down. There is so much we have been mis-taught. Blind faith is not faith. Blind faith is not free thinking; it's rule following. Blind faith isn't conviction, it's religion.

Conversely, there may be Christians reading this who are scared and lonely, feeling very much the same way I did. To them I say, you're not alone. You are valid. God made you this way, and He loves you. Welcome to the family.

There is so much more I could say about my journey, and how *Heartstopper* was the catalyst for it all, how *Heartstopper* has given me the community I needed, and how even though the hyperfixation has dulled and my fandom involvement has slowed, *Heartstopper* will always be so important to me. While my journey started with Season 1, Seasons 2 and 3 have been equally impactful (especially Charlie's mental health journey), and I am eagerly anticipating the movie.

All in all, this is to say, I'm so thankful to Alice for creating Nick and Charlie. Those two boys stole my heart, and I don't ever want it back. Everything that has come with them has been far more than I ever thought I deserved, and I have so much confidence in myself now because of them.

Perhaps the most poignant quote from the entire series, when Nick is on his own journey of self-discovery, falling down the Google and YouTube rabbit holes, and is watching videos by a vlogger played by Courtney-Jai Niner, the words that hit me like a freight train and imprinted on me, words that are true both for Nick's/my bisexuality and also for my initial crisis of faith:

"You can have both and it be okay."

Harrison Taylor's Story

When my friend on Snapchat told me that *Heartstopper* was on her watch list, I didn't even know what it was. A Google search and a trip to my Netflix account quickly changed my life.

When I first watched it, I honestly didn't watch with a detailed or analytical eye, but was still captivated and ended up watching the whole season in one night. For me, this show was different from all the other LGBT+ shows I had watched before, simply because everything I wanted to happen, happened.

Seeing Charlie and Nick interacting and all the cute moments they had just melted my heart. I suddenly felt a mixture of emotions, so happy for Nick and Charlie that this romance could blossom for them at such a young age, but also angry that I wasn't able to have that when I was their age (I didn't come out until I was in my 20's, I felt like it would not have been safe to do so, even though it probably would have been here in Canada).

I decided to re-watch it again the next day. And then the next. And then I found myself watching it every day, sometimes multiple times a day. I was so drawn to the characters and their emotional intelligence, especially the way Nick gradually becomes just SO obsessed with Charlie, when at first you only notice Charlie's obsession. I started watching with more of an analytical eye, and I kept finding new things every episode.

I began to develop such an attachment to the characters that I began feeling their emotions with them. Tears started forming in my eyes when I watched the magical first kisses. The music definitely played a role, too; what an amazing score that show has. As soon as I hear that soft score in Season 1 Episode 3, I just fall apart. It is such an amazingly put-together show, and I am so glad I found it. I hope it continues to be a legend around the world and can keep spreading its legacy day after day. We all need this show and its books in our lives. Thank you, Alice, for making this masterpiece and for changing my life forever.

After a few watches of Season 1, I discovered a wonderful little Facebook group that I am still a part of to this day. I needed a place to gush about this show, since no one in my personal life seemed as interested in it. I quickly became a regular contributor in the group, even coming up with trivia questions and sparking conversations. It was awesome, I honestly enjoyed the mornings when I would open my Facebook and thumb through hundreds of notifications. I felt like I had found my new home. And it got better from there.

I met an amazing person with whom I connected and quickly became fast friends. Meeting this person led to me meeting even more incredible people from ALL around the world (one of whom is co-creating this book). The friendships I have with these people have been so helpful in my life; there have been moments where they have pulled me out of the darkness, and sometimes I did the same for them. I don't know what I would do without them, honestly. We have had video calls and endless Messenger conversations. So many moments of laughter, sadness, and anxiety, we all lifted each other up. And we still do.

I have learned so many things about the rest of the world, and I still want to manifest that my little *Heartstopper* family and I can meet somewhere in the world in person one day. I am so proud of my newfound family and the accomplishments they have made, the things they have endured; it is really incredible. Even as I type this now, I think about how everyone is doing, what they are up to. The friendships created by *Heartstopper* are lifelong ones, no matter what.

Another great impact *Heartstopper* had on my life is the newfound obsession with reading AND writing! I read all of Alice's novels and novellas, some of them more than once. I created my happy little gay bookshelf in my living room, where I have all the books displayed, and I love it so much. Now, I had heard of fanfiction before, but never really explored it. I figured that this could be my time to finally delve into it to see what all the fuss was about. I thought maybe I would find one or two really captivating fanfic stories. Was I ever wrong. I found SO many great masterpieces on the fanfic website; it's amazing to see how talented everyone is. Just like the show had me in tears sometimes, so did these fanfics. I even wrote a few of my own (and one of them is getting a sequel soon), and the response I received for my stories was so incredible. I never knew I had it in me. I wish my life weren't so busy and chaotic right now, or I would be writing a chapter every day!

Finally, this *Heartstopper* community has made me realize how to be a better fan (not an oscillating one that is keeping the heat down in my bedroom right now, mind you). I have learned not to trust everything on the internet and also how to separate actors from the characters they play and respect them more so. Alice's book *I Was Born For This* is a great example of how toxic fandoms can be. There are toxic people in this fandom; there's no denying that. I am so happy to have learned more emotional intelligence when it comes to this fandom and its actors and writers. The *Heartstopper* universe has truly made me an even better person, as I am sure it has done for so many.

AJ's Story

I watched *Heartstopper* for the first time on the recommendation of a dear friend who correctly assumed I would love it. I watched all eight episodes in one go about a month after Season 1 came out and immediately fell in love with all the characters, but particularly Nick and Charlie. Their journey from friends to boyfriends was incredibly heartwarming, and the back half of episode eight had me crying happy tears the whole way through.

I was in my late thirties when Season 1 came out, and had only recently begun to understand that I was somewhere under the queer umbrella. I assumed that the extreme warm-fuzzy feelings the show provoked were simply because I had a desire to consume more queer media as a late bloomer. I dove directly into other queer series, hoping for the same effect, but it didn't come. So, after a few weeks, I watched Season 1 again, and that's when I realized that *Heartstopper* itself was special to me.

After that second watch, I immediately went down the rabbit hole, following all the cast and crew on Instagram and watching any interviews I could find on YouTube. Once I discovered the show was based on a comic book series, I devoured all of those as well, reading and rereading them. When there was no more source material for me to consume, I started reading *Heartstopper* fanfiction. I'd never read a single word of fanfiction in my life before then, and I will admit I had held uncharitable beliefs about both the quality of writing and the people who write it. I couldn't have been more wrong, and I have made some very dear friends through that community.

I have never in my entire life been as obsessed with or affected by a piece of media as I am with *Heartstopper*. I have watched all three seasons countless times, subscribed to Alice's Patreon, and have traveled to New York to see Kit and Joe on Broadway. Though my hyperfixation has waned slightly since its apex, I'm still going strong in the fandom three years later.

Heartstopper has changed my life through two different mediums: the source material and the fandom.

The *Heartstopper* comic and TV series have allowed me to finally accept myself as I am, in no small part by providing representation not usually seen on TV. Using Google search abilities that would make Nick Nelson proud, the show helped me realize that I am a biromantic asexual, and also that I'm non-binary. These are aspects of myself that have always been inherently true, but that I'd previously lacked terminology to define. I may have never fully understood these truths without *Heartstopper*.

I've also experienced a bit of what some folks on Reddit refer to as "*Heartstopper* Syndrome," which is the profound sadness that comes shortly after consuming the source material for the first time. It seems to be quite common amongst older fans, which I believe is directly related to a longing for a childhood that could have been.

While no character's journey is completely smooth, the *Heartstopper* friends always have one another for support, and with the exception of Darcy (and Nick, to a certain extent), all of the parents are also supportive. This is very different from the childhoods many of us had, and it's hard not to feel a panging sense of loss for what never was. It's also impossible not to wonder what might have been different in our lives if we'd had a show like this growing up. But my prevailing feeling is that it's better late than never, and I'm so grateful to have *Heartstopper* in my life now!

My experience of *Heartstopper* Syndrome served as a catalyst for me to become a volunteer crisis counselor with The Trevor Project. I also work one-on-one with young people in my job in the education field, and use both what I've learned from *Heartstopper* and my Trevor Project training to try to be a positive influence and help create a *Heartstopper*-like world for my students.

The fandom has equally changed my life. I'd never been part of a fandom before *Heartstopper*, and now I've seen it all: the good, the bad, and the ugly. Thankfully, the good prevails, and I've enjoyed every major *Heartstopper* milestone since Season 1 with friends online. I work in an all-consuming and insular field, and becoming part of the *Heartstopper* fandom helped me make friends outside of my career for the first time in two decades. I've met several of my closest *Heartstopper* friends in person on multiple occasions.

Before I found the fandom, I treated my love of *Heartstopper* like a dirty little secret. Because of my age, I thought it was weird or shameful for me to be obsessed with a story about two teenage boys in love. I didn't tell anyone except my partner about my extreme love for the material. Once I found the fandom, I discovered there were plenty of invested fans my age and older. I learned there was nothing wrong with me, and that I'm allowed to be excited about things that bring me joy.

There is a large percentage of neurodivergent individuals in my fandom circles. Through those folks sharing their experiences, I have come to understand that I am also neurodivergent. My late-bloomer queer awakening and neurodivergent awakening have gone hand in hand. They have both caused a sometimes painful longing, knowing that my life would have made much more sense if I'd realized and accepted these aspects of myself when I was younger.

I always felt different growing up but didn't understand why. I thought there was something wrong with me. When I look back on the numerous awkward situations in which I ended up throughout my youth, most of them can be explained by the fact that I'm bi, autistic, or both! I likely would've been much kinder to myself at the time if I had a full comprehension of who I am as a person. But, as with my queer awakening, I'm happy to have learned about my neurodivergence late as opposed to never. It has opened a new window of understanding of myself for which I'll be forever grateful.

Michelle W's Story

I was first introduced to *Heartstopper* by my best friend Heather (Hi bestie!) and was instantly told I had Charlie energy. It was not long after the death of my partner of over ten years. I was at an all-time low – broken, isolated, and lost. I felt like I had lost one of the only people who truly understood me.

That all began to change when I found the *Heartstopper* community on Facebook, Patreon, and Instagram. They welcomed me with open arms and made me feel like I was home. This community truly is like one big family.

Nick Nelson's journey – discovering his bisexuality and coming out to his mum in that beautiful, emotional scene (which had me in tears) – made me take a long, hard look at what I had been suppressing for years. It gave me the courage to open up about who I really am, first to my best friend, and then to my parents and sister. Not everyone in my life knows – and that's okay, because as Coach Singh reminds us: I don't owe that information to anyone. For the first time, I've felt truly seen, loved, and accepted, all thanks to the amazing community that Alice Oseman has created.

With the support of that community, my confidence grew. I went to my local Pride, and even to London Pride! I've also found the strength to speak out against transphobia, homophobia, biphobia, and all forms of hate. *Heartstopper* gave me that voice and the confidence to stand up for others.

I also connected deeply with Charlie's character, especially his experiences with bullying, his complicated relationship with his mum, and his struggles with mental health. Though our diagnoses differ, I saw myself in him. He made me realise how damaging it can be to keep silent, and how important it is to ask for help. Charlie gave me the courage to do that, and I'm proud to say I've now been two months free from self-harm. I'm hopeful about staying on this path, and thanks to Geoff, I understand that healing isn't linear. There will be bumps in the road, and that's okay.

Finally, the supportive teachers – Mr. Ajayi, Mr. Farouk, and Coach Singh – each helped Nick and Charlie in their own unique ways. They inspired me so much that I decided to go back to college. I took an access course (which I passed with flying colours!), and in September, I'll be starting my journey to become a teacher myself. I want to be there for young people who need the kind of support and understanding these characters received.

To Alice and the entire cast and crew of *Heartstopper* – thank you. Watching your story come to life on screen led me to this amazing community, and through that, I've found strength, purpose, and connection. I honestly don't know where I would be today without it.

A. Fletcher's Story

Heartstopper opened up something new for me. Could I watch it in front of my parents? Nope. But did I watch it all on a sick day and realise that queer stories don't have to be the doom and gloom I'd come to associate them with? Yes. Yes, I did.

It was warm, and a level of comfort I hadn't found in any other story. For once, I had a story that I could relate to that wasn't spicy or tragic or hiding behind metaphors and ambiguity. It was open. Kind. Awkward. Soft. I hadn't seen that before.

Before *Heartstopper*, queerness in the media felt like something I had to squint to find, or something that was always followed by heartbreak, abandonment, shame, or worse. If it wasn't devastating, it was oversexualised. There was no space for the in-between — for the teenagers who didn't know how to say things aloud yet, for the ones who thought maybe, just maybe, this feeling means something but couldn't quite name it.

Watching Nick go through that process — of realising, questioning, sitting in the quiet discomfort of "what if?" — was like watching the inside of my own head played out on screen, only gentler. Safer. The show didn't rush him. It didn't need to label him right away. That mattered.

It made me feel like I could breathe, just a little. Like I didn't have to be all the way out, or all the way certain, to be real.

It also reminded me what it could feel like to be chosen. To be looked at with a kind of softness I hadn't known how to want before. Not dramatic or cinematic or perfect — just honest. And for a teenager who had learned to make herself small and careful, that meant more than I expected.

No, I couldn't share it with anyone at the time. I couldn't even talk about it. But I think *Heartstopper* still met me exactly where I was. And in doing so, it gave me hope that maybe — just maybe — stories like mine could be told too.

Not as a tragedy. Not as a metaphor. But as something living. As something good.

When I say *Heartstopper* changed my life, I really mean it in a way that goes far beyond just a TV show. I had just come out when the show premiered — and it didn't go well. It was awkward and painful, and I felt more alone than ever. The fear and confusion I carried felt heavy, and at times, I thought maybe this was just my story — a story full of struggle and heartbreak, the kind of queer narratives I'd come to expect. But then *Heartstopper* arrived, and everything shifted.

Heartstopper gave me something new: a queer story that was soft and safe and full of hope. It showed that queer love can be messy and uncertain but still warm and kind. It wasn't a story about tragedy or despair — it was about small moments of joy, awkwardness, and finding yourself through connection. This felt revolutionary to me. It gave me permission to believe that my story would be alright, that my identity didn't need to be a big thing.

Not long after watching it, I wrote an article for my school paper about the importance of queer narratives in the media, and I'll be frank, I was a little scared because it was one of, if not the first, openly queer article ever published in our paper. But the reaction surprised me, and something unexpected happened: through that article, I met my best friend. She was a year above me, and we connected because she asked me to help edit her article about the dangers of outing and queerbaiting. From there, we began writing together about queer history, aro/ace perspectives on Valentine's Day, and other stories that mattered to us.

Our friendship has lasted 3 years now. It's a deep, real connection, and I honestly don't think we would've found each other without *Heartstopper*. The show gave us shared language, shared experiences, and a safe space to explore complicated feelings. In many ways, it was the catalyst for one of the most important friendships of my life.

Heartstopper has also helped us navigate mental health struggles. When student life feels overwhelming — when anxiety or depression cloud everything — the show is a light in the darkness. It reminds us there's softness and kindness to be found, even in the hardest moments. That honesty, born from the gentle vulnerability the show models, has been freeing. It's okay to feel complicated things, to hold uncertainty and affection without rushing to define it.

Beyond friendships and feelings, *Heartstopper* influenced my creative voice. There's a sincerity and tenderness in the show's storytelling that shows me vulnerability is powerful, not a weakness. It encouraged me to write openly and honestly — to trust that being authentic matters more than being guarded or perfect. This has shaped my work in school and beyond, inspiring me to tell stories that honour nuance and emotional truth.

Most of all, *Heartstopper* became a safe place I return to — a steady anchor amid life's storms. When I rewatch it, I'm reminded of the gentle unfolding of identity and the importance of kindness, to yourself and others. It's a story that reminds me of how far I've come in both self-acceptance and connection. It's not just a show. For me, it's a turning point — a quiet revolution that made space for my story and gave me hope that I'm not alone.

If anyone is reading this and recognises the loneliness, I promise there is someone who will make space for you. Until then, remember that there are queer kids like you who can attest to this: you'll be found somewhere.

And should Alice Oseman ever read this, thank you. For inspiring as many queer kids as you have, for opening discussions, giving us a safe place to land, and more importantly, showing us that it's ok to ask "why am I like this" - and come up a little empty.

PF's Story

My 12-year-old came home with *Heartstopper* Volume One at the beginning of 2022 and read it cover to cover in a single sitting.

"You'd probably like this, mum," she said. If only she knew just how much she was shaping the next few years of my life with that statement.

It was a revelation. The first graphic novel I had ever read, the first comic I enjoyed, my first fangirl obsession that is now in its 3rd year of existence. I fell in love that day and have not fallen out of love yet. Too impatient to wait for my daughter to be able to borrow the next volume from her school library, I followed the links in the book to Webtoon and read every page available, reading each additional chapter and finding myself diving headfirst into Nick and Charlie's love story until I reached the final chapter available, only to find...it was not finished. It was not finished! Aarrrghhh!

I felt the despair hit me like a punch to the stomach when I clicked the 'next' arrow on the last published page, and nothing happened! That is how I joined the legions of other fans waiting for weekly updates and letting my imagination run wild about what future adventures awaited Nick and Charlie. Just writing 'legions of fans' makes me giggle, given I had never before been a fan, let alone one of a 'legion' (devotion to Jane Austen notwithstanding!).

I should have been used to it, having grown up in the habit of waiting a week for new episodes of favourite TV shows to air, but this felt different. An interest in something that felt more than simple curiosity or enjoyment.

At first, 12[1] and I crushed over *Heartstopper* together, but she quickly moved on to an anime series, whereas I fell deeper and deeper. I'm so old that I could not name a single gay person at my high school growing up (although of course we were there!); I never heard my parents or people in my community mention homosexuality, let alone all the other sexualities in the queer spectrum. It wasn't so much a case of being 'in the closet', but rather 'What do you mean there is a closet?'.

I experienced none of Charlie's trauma at being outed or bullied, never struggled with my sexuality or identity. Compared to many, the discovery of my sexuality was easy. I moved to a capital city, saw women walking hand in hand, realised liking women was a possibility in life, told everyone I was a lesbian and never looked back.

Yet suddenly, years later, here was this queer love story for young people, and I unexpectedly found myself wishing that had been my high school experience. To have had the chance to ride on the rollercoaster of emotions attached to a teenage romance that involved kissing a girl in the secret corners of the school. To have experienced a crush that made my heart rate rise across the desks of a classroom rather than a dance floor in a club. That my first kiss had been with a girl instead of with a boy.

When I had devoured everything available in the comic chapters, I searched for more.

This required a significant up-skill of my online capabilities that I had been stubbornly refusing to develop since the internet was

---

1. The number refers to the author's child, aged 12 at the time.

created. As a high school teacher avoiding snooping students, I had never used any type of social media; I didn't use Facebook or Instagram or any of the similar platforms. A Google search for my name only ever turned up one thing: a letter to the editor I had once sent to a newspaper to support same-sex marriage.

With my discovery of fanfiction, my exposure to online communities was about to grow exponentially. When 12 first showed me where fans wrote their own *Heartstopper* stories on a site I had never heard of called 'Archive of our Own', there were around 3,000 stories in the *Heartstopper* fandom, and I read almost every single one. At the time of writing this, there are close to 10,000 stories.

I have been reading fanfiction consistently for 3 years. At some point, around 6 months into reading, I decided to have a go at writing my own, something I never imagined I would do. I've since written Nick and Charlie and their friends as students, in pretend relationships, as neighbours, old people, parents, husbands and had them involved in more meet-cutes than I can remember. The stories I read and write are full of warm romantic feelings that are a happy escape from real life. Hopefully, my own stories, filled with fluff, humour and happy endings, have provided a small joyous moment of escape for others in the fandom too.

I waited with anticipation for the Netflix series, desperate for it to be a good adaptation, and it did not disappoint. Series One, and its soundtrack, were on repeat for such a long time that 12, who had since turned 13, complained that I had ruined her 'Spotify Wrapped' that year with *Heartstopper*.

While Episode One of Season One holds a special place in my heart, there are two moments in Episode Three that made me squeal with queer joy. The first is the moment Tara and Darcy kiss on the dance floor surrounded by rainbow lights, out and proud for everyone to see. Nick's face as he watches them, knowing that he wants that too, mirrors my own. My second favourite moment, Nick and Charlie's first kiss in the ballroom, is an almost perfect replica of the comic in every way. I have no idea how they made that scene so wonderful, but I will never get bored of watching the close-ups of their faces, so beautifully portraying their nerves and their courage.

A comment by a reader in one of my stories invited me to join a *Heartstopper* server on Discord, leading to my installing my very first social media app on my phone. I was like an awkward baby giraffe trying to join in on my earliest conversations with the 300-odd strangers from all over the world in that group, but our combined love for *Heartstopper* made me push past my awkwardness and participate, despite my age and the fact that I typed with one forefinger instead of my two thumbs.

I found so many supportive people in one place, discussing sexuality, relationships, recipes, family matters and, most importantly, our *Heartstopper* stories and the multitudes of ways we had developed our own versions of the *Heartstopper* universe. Many of them were my own age and equally surprised by their fascination with *Heartstopper*.

For someone who had always believed online friendships could not be real, I now chat daily with a group of people, most of whom I've never met, nor am I likely to. Some live on the other side of the world, and yet they have become even closer to me than some of my real-life friends. In real life, my friends and I are busy adulting and need to coordinate our schedules to make time to meet. The same constraints don't apply to the people in my phone. They are there whenever I need them, and I would never have found them without *Heartstopper*.

Writing this forced me to think about why *Heartstopper* means so much to me. I still haven't told anyone about my obsession. It feels embarrassing to confess I am a 50-year-old professional with a fixation on a teenage romance. 12 is now 15 and scoffs every time she sees me reading on AO3. Most people who know me would be incredibly surprised if they knew. They will never find out from me, though, because this is a joy for me to cherish on my own. A secret little part of myself that makes me happy and stretches my imagination in ways I had forgotten I was capable of.

I'm proud of the *Heartstopper* stories I have written. I'm happy whenever I'm able to tell someone else I loved a *Heartstopper* story of theirs so much they made me cry or laugh at their beautiful words. My stomach swoops with every update from Alice Oseman. I get 'proud mama' feelings whenever I see the cast of *Heartstopper* doing amazing things in their careers, and I still get a warm feeling inside when I read the original comics. The look on Nick and Charlie's faces when they first spot each other feels like a warm hug. The image of Charlie's feet on tiptoes as he kisses Nick still gives me an instant hit of endorphins.

Even though I haven't explicitly told anyone of my obsession, when a student at school tells me they love the stickers of the *Heartstopper* leaves on my laptop, or that they like the pins on my lanyard, we share a smile of joy for *Heartstopper* together. *I found another one.*

Lety's Story

When I first watched *Heartstopper*, my heart pounded in my chest for a really long time, and I fell in love with their friendship and journey of discovery. I wished I could be their fun, supportive aunt! TV series and movies are something I generally enjoy a lot. One day, I stumbled upon this little show that warmed my heart and left me thinking about it for several days. Eventually, a colleague of mine, a sociology teacher, mentioned the show in the staffroom. She explained that she thought of it as a teaching opportunity and felt it would be a great project to do together as a team.

This conversation renewed my interest in the show, and I decided to watch it again. Soon, I found myself rewatching it over and over, and falling down rabbit holes all over various social media platforms, and this eventually led to my meeting the most amazing group of humans. I had never been part of a fandom before, so bonding with others over a TV show was new for me.

The show and the fans I met online touched my heart in ways I still can't fully comprehend. I found myself diving deeply into everything related to *Heartstopper*; so much so that I bought and read all of Alice's books, followed them on social media and eventually read many other queer books as well. I immersed myself in LGBT+ literature and media, but my first love will always be *Heartstopper* and the boys I adore, Nick and Charlie.

Out of all the characters, I mostly relate to Charlie. Similarly to him, I was not popular at school and had quite low self-esteem.

I believed I found my "Nick" when I met my former partner. I thought he was someone who cared about me, who truly loved me and put me first in his life. He was bright and charming, and he made me believe that I was the love of his life.

We were together for twenty years and had two kids together, only for me to come to terms with the fact that he was more like Ben. Anytime we argued, he was outright mean, and most of the time, he made me feel like I should be grateful for his so-called love. I found over time that he was a consummate liar; for some time, I still thought he didn't lie to me, but after a while, I felt like I couldn't trust anything he said anymore. He even used the words Ben said to Charlie, telling me, "It's not like anyone else will want you." He said so many other hurtful things that my already low self-esteem declined even further. As a result, I've remained single for the past ten years, since we separated, and will most likely stay that way.

I can only hope to truly find my "Nick" one day, but I think it is highly unlikely. I wish I could find someone who tries to understand my sexuality (I am demisexual) and supports me, respects my wishes and boundaries, and who proves themself trustworthy.

When I finally got into the teaching project, I decided to include it in the health and adolescence coursework. This included a PowerPoint presentation with definitions of the different sexualities and gender identities, as well as some of the pride flags associated with them. I also created introductions to the main characters, incorporating content from both the graphic novels and the TV show.

I shared the material with my colleague, who loved what I had prepared and used it in her sociology classes as well. I teach the health and adolescence class to 14- and 15-year-old kids, and it includes reproduction and sexuality in the syllabus, so I started working on the content I wanted to present to the kids. I found that not only can the show be used as an example to teach about sexuality and identity, but also to address topics like peer pressure, consent, and bullying. It is an excellent teaching tool against bullying and discrimination.

The first year I included it, we only had season one of *Heartstopper* on Netflix. I decided to actually watch it at school with the kids. The responses were mixed. Some were surprised, some were silent, and some were uncomfortable or even rude about seeing boys kissing on screen. One girl in particular was very happy, and she came out to me as bi later on. I immediately addressed any unkind behaviour, explaining to them that it was unacceptable, and that they should be respectful and try to understand that everyone loves in a different way. Afterwards, as one of the activities, we made posters with a variety of pride flags and enjoyed discussing their meaning and what they represent in a friendly environment.

I asked my friend Rowan (co-author of this book) if it was okay to share his transition story with the class, and he agreed. My plan was to ask the students to write down little motivational messages on the pride flag posters we'd created, and send them to Rowan as a surprise. They happily agreed, and we filled two posters with messages of love and support. [Author's note: When I received these posters, I was overwhelmed and overjoyed. The messages were so thoughtful and kind, and I will treasure them always.]

The following year, season two was out, and it enabled me to include some information about eating disorders, as that topic is touched on as part of Charlie's journey. I asked the students to watch the show and answer some questions on a study guide I made. They knew a little about eating disorders because that topic is covered early in the year in my class, along with nutrition and diet. As we discussed how it is portrayed in the show, and how the signs of eating disorders are often well hidden and difficult to pick up on, they asked a lot of questions about some of Charlie's behaviour. They showed interest in the topic, and it was great to raise awareness.

Finally, after season three was released, I was able to update the curriculum once more. It is the one I'm most proud of because I created some very interesting short videos revolving around key moments of *Heartstopper*. For example, one of them focussed on Charlie's battle with his eating disorder, and another on the theme of bullying, which is illustrated at various points throughout the show.

A great way to demonstrate the importance of express consent was to compare Charlie's assault by Ben with the first kiss he shared with Nick. I covered peer pressure through Imogen's journey, from the moment she asked Nick out on a date in front of all her friends, to the scene in the park where Nick explains how he feels, and finally Imogen sharing how she felt pressure to have a boyfriend because it's what "cool girls do" while they talk at the hotel during their uni visits.

These videos stimulated discussions and questions of all sorts and also helped my students to reflect more on the topics we covered. Season three also allowed me to dive deeper into gender identity, explaining gender dysphoria through Elle's character and her journey.

Overall, this particular class is the one I'm always the proudest of. For the last three years, it has provided for some of the most rewarding moments in my career, and I intend to continue doing it as long as I'm actively teaching.

Kermit's Story

When I first watched *Heartstopper*, I remember thinking it was absolutely adorable, but when Nick and Charlie were allowed to kiss uninterrupted at the arcade for Charlie's birthday, and when Charlie did his little happy dance after Nick asked him on a double date to the milkshake cafe and nobody ruined the moment for him, I knew the show was different.

After finishing Season 1 for the first time in July 2022, I immediately watched it again so I could enjoy it without feeling anxiety during those happy moments. And then I could not stop watching. I actually thought something was very, very wrong with me because all I could do was watch *Heartstopper*. I couldn't stop crying. I couldn't sleep. I couldn't think about anything except *Heartstopper*. It was all the more strange because, in general, I'm not a TV person, I've never been in a fandom before, and at the time I thought I was straight.

Heartstopper changed literally everything about my life. I couldn't figure out why I couldn't stop thinking about it, and that sent me on an intense journey of self-discovery. I spent hours every day just thinking about the show, turning all the scenes over in my mind. I would go on long walks every day and literally just think about *Heartstopper* the entire time. There was no one event or scene that helped me in my self-discovery – it was just the culmination of all this rumination that allowed things to surface in my mind, I think.

I first watched it at age 41, and it helped me realize that I'm bi and ace. I had suspected I was ace before I watched the show, but I wasn't sure. Something about my intense ruminations over the show allowed past experiences to surface that made me realize that I'm bi, and that realization helped me realize I'm also ace.

I started doing a lot of journaling and reading various things, and through that, I also realized that I'm autistic. My intense hyper-fixation on *Heartstopper* was actually one of the things that made me realize the autistic piece of the puzzle (among many other things).

I also joined the *Heartstopper* fandom and started writing fanfiction, which I barely even knew existed before *Heartstopper*. I first joined Tumblr because I had stumbled across some *Heartstopper* gifs somewhere on the internet, and I could *not* stop watching them. Then I remember Googling, "Is something wrong with me that I can't stop watching *Heartstopper*?" and I found a Reddit thread of other older fans who were having the same intense emotional reaction as I was. On there, I found some links to a few fanfiction stories.

I had no idea what fanfiction was, but I clicked and started reading and was instantly hooked. I thought I would only be a reader, never a writer, but about 9 months into reading, I suddenly started getting ideas for little one-shots[1]. My first fic was a series of short one-shots, one posted each day, to celebrate Pride month in June 2023. I thought that would be it, but as soon as I was done writing those, my mind was crowded with more ideas, and I've never stopped writing since!

---

1. In fanfiction, a one-shot is a story told and published in a single instalment, as opposed to multi-chapter fanfiction stories that can be published over a period of weeks or even months.

Because of *Heartstopper*, I've met some of the best friends I've ever had and found a wonderful community through the fandom. I joined the *Heartstopper* AO3 Discord the day after I published the first one-shot in my Pride month series, and it opened up a beautiful community of fellow writers and readers. I met people in this community who have become some of my closest friends, with whom I talk daily. I relate to them as queer and neurodivergent people in a way I've never really related to anyone before, plus we have our shared love of *Heartstopper*, so I feel that I can talk to them about things I can't share with anyone else in my life.

Heartstopper showed me how important it is to show up in the world as your authentic self. In a sense, I've always shown up in the world as my authentic self, but I didn't fully know who that authentic self really *was* until *Heartstopper*. The show has illustrated for me all of the ways in which I just assumed things about myself (that I was straight, that I was neurotypical) just because that's who society tells us we are, whether or not it's true. This journey gave me the courage to leave my job, move across the country, and make a major change in my career that is more aligned with my purpose.

It also showed me that a different world is possible, one in which people are kind to each other and communicate in a healthy way, as opposed to all the toxic relationships and relationship dynamics we usually see portrayed in the media.

Almost always in TV shows and movies, whether they portray LGBTQIA+ relationships or straight relationships, people act in really emotionally immature, toxic ways. They don't communicate, partners in romantic relationships seem not to like each other very much, they take everything personally, etc. *Heartstopper* shows us that if we communicate with kindness, assume positive intent, and take responsibility for our own emotions, things work much better. We never see healthy communication portrayed like this in the media; all we see is unnecessary, unhealthy drama. And when you don't have a model for how to treat others, it's really hard to act that way yourself.

Alice is also showing us other aspects of how we relate to one another we never get to see portrayed in a healthy way: how to navigate consent conversations, how to support someone dealing with mental illness; the fact that love doesn't cure a mental illness, that codependency isn't romantic, it's deeply problematic; that you don't have to rush into sex if it doesn't feel right to you (especially for teenagers); and that friendships are just as important as romantic relationships.

Heartstopper is showing us that it's possible to treat each other in a more compassionate, kind, loving way, whether we are in a romantic partnership or a friendship. I've always tried to live my life that way, but *Heartstopper* helped me recommit to actively trying to create that change in the world.

Final Thoughts
By Rowan Murphy

Writing this book has been a very enriching journey. I have met many amazing people, and I've been greatly inspired by the stories they shared. Although I have probably mentioned this before, I cannot fully express how surprising and wonderful the response from the fandom has been. I admire the courage it took for so many people to share their most vulnerable and personal experiences with the world.

Fandoms are communities, but the *Heartstopper* fandom is more than that: It is a safe environment, a soft place to land. It is found family, with degrees of connection ranging from distant relations to those that feel like siblings or favourite aunts and uncles. It is home.

Reliving our experiences through the retelling of them has deepened the bonds we formed over our shared love for these fictional characters, who burst into our lives like a bright comet illuminating a night sky and landed with earth-shattering impact. I hope that by sharing these stories, we will show the world how full and amazing life can be when we embrace all parts of ourselves and realise that we deserve happiness, no matter who we are or whom we love. If we have been able to extend the beacon of hope and positivity created by *Heartstopper* to even one additional person, we have achieved our ultimate goal.

The depiction of queer joy and the normalisation of LGBTQIA+ identities in the show and graphic novels have empowered self-discovery without barriers. One thing I have learnt is to approach labels with care, as they can create artificial boundaries that inhibit our ability to change. We shouldn't allow words to box us in. Labels can be very useful in defining and describing parts of our identities, but we grow and evolve, and some parts of us are inherently fluid. For example, someone can go for decades thinking they are homosexual, only to find themself falling in love with a person of a different gender later in life. We are not fixed points on an axis, but moving pieces on a spectrum of human experiences and desires.

Heartstopper has already had a massive impact on my life; I finally feel at home in my own skin, I have rediscovered my love for writing through the world of fanfic, and I've made many new friends. But through this project, I have been inspired and motivated to make some additional, major life changes. Fear has been a dominant force in my life throughout the decades, but now I refuse to dwell in spaces, whether physical or emotional, where I feel unsafe. The rising anti-trans sentiment where I live is a threat to my newfound authentic existence, and I am therefore embarking on an adventure. I am leaving the US to find my place in the world, where I will feel at home.

In the 27 years I have lived in this country, despite my best efforts to assimilate (which I generally excel at), it has never become home; the cultural differences have been insurmountable for me, and I decided years ago that I would eventually leave. Recent social and political developments were merely the proverbial last straw, accelerating my plans. The crucial distinction is that I am not running from something, but rather running towards a future full of potential in pursuit of happiness and fulfilment. I have always been a huge anglophile, and every time I've visited the UK, I have loved every minute. I have many friends there, and my dream is to someday call it home; in the meantime, I plan to spend as much time there as I can.

As I write these closing words, listening to the dulcet tones of Orla Gartland's *Why Am I Like This,* I think I have found my answer: I am like this because I found the strength and courage to break free from the mental prison I had lived in. *Heartstopper* crashed into my life and woke me up, reigniting a desire for self-actualisation, for finding purpose and fulfilment in my life. I think I am finally open to being loved, because I love who I am.

THE END?
By George Hightower

Heartstopper Forever, the movie, is in post-production as I write this. It is scheduled for release next year. It feels bittersweet to think that the end of this enchanting series is on the horizon. Or is it? Whether there will be another season of *Heartstopper* is up to us in a way. *Heartstopper* has sown an ecosystem of friendship and care that has grown beyond entertainment, into practical support. We can harness that positive momentum to advance individually and collectively. **We are the sequel**.

Heartstopper opens us up to a better way of being and affirms our existence with a long exhale. It says: What if happiness is worthy of the spotlight too? What if handholding, softness, and animated leaves can wield as much power as suffering? In the landscape of media and entertainment that often resorts to unnecessary drama and spectacle, *Heartstopper* reminds us that patience and tenderness, represented faithfully, can be revolutionary.

The show's legacy is readily apparent. It has cascaded into our social circles, homes, and classrooms, fortifying us with the courage to pursue the life we want. Its message lives on in the millions of hearts it touches, the communities and relationships it builds, and the future it helps to imagine. By that standard, it has earned its place in the pantheon of LGBTQIA+ history and beyond.

> "The *Heartstopper* characters are like silent companions that are there for me in my everyday life."
>
> Diana

In my attempt to answer the key question, "why are we like this?" I have observed that many of us whose lives have been changed possess shared qualities conducive to that change: We tend to be open, supportive, sensitive, flexible, and willing to be vulnerable and entertain new ideas, as well as having the courage to act on them. Timing also plays a role when we are ready to take a leap of faith to follow our hearts, not necessarily knowing where the path will lead us, but believing that we are heading toward something better. *Heartstopper* beckons us to dream because it first enables us to trust and believe in ourselves, as echoed by Baby Queen's song *We Can Be Anything*.

On a deeper level, the show conveys an ethos that brings us closer to our collective oneness in the face of so much that tries to separate us. After reading all the stories that fans submitted, I have concluded that there is no single answer to the question because each person's story is unique. However, what all the stories share is the magic of *Heartstopper* that cannot be articulated or measured; it's ephemeral, like lightning in a bottle we have opened.

What began as a small story about two boys falling in love became an allegory about what it means to be human. That might be its greatest gift: it reminds us, at the heart of it all, that love is a story worth telling.

If we continue to apply the lessons we have learned from our heart-stopping odyssey together, and remain open to love, then Nick and Charlie's story will live on in us as we follow their footsteps in *Heartstopper* **forever**.

Acknowledgements

This book would not have been possible without the legions of fans who supported this project, especially those who opened their hearts and shared their stories with us. This is a truly special fandom, comprised of kind and compassionate people who aren't afraid to be vulnerable and open with each other.

Red Letter Days, you have challenged us in the very best ways through the editing process and helped us polish this book into a gem that we can be proud of. Galactic Hare, your eagle eye during proofreading has been invaluable. And a huge thanks to Lenny DiChiara for translating our vision for the cover design into this amazing image; we could not have wished for a better outcome. Each of you has been incredibly patient and gracious as we navigated our learning curve.

Rowan deeply appreciates his close-knit friend group of three years (currently dubbed the FOMOsexual Pocket Pals) and everyone who has supported him during his wobbly moments. He also wants to thank Kate, his therapist, for being a veritable cheerleader and always encouraging him.

George would like to also thank all of his friends who supported him during the most difficult times to help him reach the point of being able to write this book.

Glossary

This glossary is by no means all-inclusive. It is intended to provide some insights and contains the terminology used in this book alongside other common LGBTQIA+ terms.

Acronyms

The earliest acronyms I could find to describe the rainbow community are GLB (Gay, Lesbian, Bisexual) and LGB (Lesbian, Gay, Bisexual), used in the early gay rights movements in the 1970s.

The next iteration, which is probably the most well-known, came about in the late 80s and has become synonymous with the community: LGBT (Lesbian, Gay, Bisexual, Transgender); the T was added as transgender individuals gained more visibility.

Around the turn of the millennium, the Q was added for "queer/questioning" to acknowledge those who didn't identify with any of the other four letters.

LGBTQIA+ is the result of adding Intersex and Asexual identities, along with the plus sign to represent the many additional possibilities of sexual and romantic orientation or gender identity, to achieve better inclusivity.

Other iterations include 2S or 2, representing two-spirit persons, U for unsure, QQ to include both queer and questioning, P for polyamorous or pangender, or an O for other. There seem to be countless variations, but generally, LGBTQ+ and LGBTQIA+ appear to be commonly used.

Some people prefer using the term "queer" as an umbrella term to replace the acronyms, as younger generations feel they have reclaimed the term. Due to its offensive history as a slur, older individuals are opposed to its usage.

Sexual Orientation

The constraints of a binary view are often referenced in the context of gender identities, but they apply equally in the understanding of sexual orientations. This spectrum spans from sexual attraction to only the opposite gender (heterosexual, or "straight"), to sexual attraction to people of the same gender only (homosexual, or gay/lesbian), with many variations in between, such as bisexual or pansexual (see definitions below). It also encompasses various levels of sexual attraction, from allosexual (regularly experiencing sexual attraction) to asexual (not experiencing sexual attraction). The terms listed below explain some of these identities, yet there are many more.

Sexual orientation describes a person's romantic or sexual attraction (or both) to others. Sexual orientation is different from gender and gender identity; it's about who a person feels drawn to romantically, emotionally, and sexually. There is a lot of nuance to how people experience these forms of attraction, and some people don't feel like the labels accurately capture their identities. Choosing a label (or deciding not to use one at all) is a deeply personal decision. It is also important to reiterate that our desires and preferences can change and evolve.

The following list is not all-inclusive, but is intended to provide some nuance beyond lesbian, gay, and bisexual, which are the most commonly known sexual orientations. While I have tried to keep the descriptions as brief and simplistic as possible, it is important to acknowledge that there is more to each of these identities. A lot of information is available on the internet, and some resources are listed after the glossary.

Asexual: Often referred to as "ace". A person who experiences little to no sexual attraction to others. It is also an umbrella term for many identities under the asexual spectrum, including:

- **Demisexual:** Individuals who only experience sexual attraction after forming a deep emotional connection with someone.

- **Greysexual/Grey-asexual:** Individuals who experience sexual attraction only rarely or under very specific circumstances.

Allosexual: A term used to describe individuals who regularly experience sexual attraction and desire, in contrast to the asexual spectrum.

Bisexual: Individuals attracted to more than one gender, but not necessarily to the same degree.

Fluid: This describes a person whose sexual orientation changes over time. For example, someone might identify as lesbian at one point and bisexual at another, or be attracted to different genders at different times. Some people describe themselves as fluid to avoid a label that might box them in.

Gay: Men attracted to other men.

Heteronormativity: The assumption of heterosexuality as the default and norm, leading to the marginalisation of LGBTQIA+ individuals.

Heterosexual: Attracted to individuals of the opposite gender. The term "straight" is also commonly used.

Homosexual: Attracted to individuals of the same gender.

Lesbian: Women attracted to other women.

Omnisexual: Individuals attracted to all genders, with gender playing a role in the attraction. In other words, they recognise and are attracted to a person's gender, even if their attraction isn't limited to or determined by gender.

Pansexual: Sexual attraction to people regardless of their gender. The focus is on the individual and the connection they share; gender isn't a determining factor in their attraction. Some pansexual people describe their attraction as gender blind.

Polysexual: Individuals attracted to more than one gender, but not necessarily to all of them. This label acknowledges attraction to a range of genders without encompassing every possibility. For example, a polysexual person might be attracted to men and non-binary people but not women.

Queer: An umbrella term that generally refers to people who are not heterosexual. Originally a slur, this term has been reclaimed by some individuals and groups, sometimes as a way to reject heteronormative and binary thinking. The term queer can include a variety of sexual identities and gender identities that are anything other than straight and cisgender.

Questioning: Individuals who may be unsure of their feelings or hesitant to use a specific label sometimes choose to identify as "questioning". More generally, questioning refers to the period when someone is trying to understand who they are attracted to or what gender they identify with.

Romantic Attraction: The desire to form a romantic relationship and emotional connection with someone. This term focuses on emotional intimacy and bonding, which is separate from sexual attraction and the desire for physical intimacy. For example, a person can be asexual and still experience romantic attraction.

Romantic Orientation: Describes the sex or gender to which a person feels romantic attraction or may have a romantic relationship with. These terms are often used alongside sexual orientation.

- **Aromantic:** Individuals who experience little to no romantic attraction to anyone. When used in conjunction with Asexuality, this is often referred to as aro/ace.

- **Biromantic:** Individuals who experience romantic attraction towards more than one gender. A person can be homosexual and biromantic, meaning they only experience sexual attraction to people of the same gender, but can feel romantic attraction to individuals of another gender.

- **Homoromantic:** Individuals who experience attraction towards people of the same gender

- **Panromantic:** Individuals who experience romantic attraction towards another person regardless of gender.

- **Polyromantic:** Individuals who experience romantic attraction towards many, but not all, gender identities.

Gender Identity

The gender binary has been the basis of heated debate in recent years. Many people reject the concept of a gender spectrum entirely, insisting that the only valid genders are male and female. Within this book, we talked about how deeply ingrained this concept is in modern society, and how problematic the resulting expectations and pressures to conform can be.

The gender spectrum is as rich and varied as the sexuality spectrum, with male and female as fixed points and many identities in between, including nonbinary (gender identity outside of the male/female binary) and agender (little or no personal connection to gender). Some examples are listed below, but this list of terms is not all-inclusive. Our goal was to provide some insights into the variety of gender identities, while outlining some of the most common terminology and identity descriptions. More information is available through several organisations listed in the resources at the end.

Gender Identity describes a person's inherent self-perception as female, male, both, or neither, or any other area on the spectrum. It is separate from and completely unrelated to sexual orientation; gender identity is about who you are, not who you want to be with.

Gender is not the same as sex, which is "assigned" at birth solely based on physical characteristics. A person's gender identity may or may not align with the sex they were assigned at birth. As with everything else, this part of our identity can also change and evolve. Gender is a complex and innate sense of self, comprised of many factors that make up a person's identity.

Agender: Someone who has little or no personal connection with gender.

Assigned Female/Male at Birth (AFAB/AMAB): A term used to describe the sex assigned when a person was born, which is recorded on their birth certificate. It is based on external physical characteristics, usually the genitalia.

Bigender: Someone who identifies with both male and female genders, or even a third gender.

Cisgender, or **cis**: A person whose gender identity matches the gender they were assigned at birth.

Gender Affirming Care: Medical, mental health, and/or non-medical services for transgender, nonbinary and gender-nonconforming people to help align their bodies and lives with their gender identity. This can include name changes, finding the right pronouns, and medical interventions such as puberty blockers, hormones, or surgeries.

Gender Affirmation Surgery: Some individuals elect to undergo surgical procedures to change their physical appearance to more closely resemble how they view their gender identity. These decisions are private and personal, and it is best to avoid asking a transgender person questions about them. A lot of information is available on websites for LGBTQIA+ organisations.

Gender dysphoria: The distress experienced by a person whose gender identity doesn't align with their assigned birth gender. This is a separate concept from a person's gender identity, which is their internal sense of being male, female, both, or neither.

Gender expression: This refers to the external appearance of a person's gender identity as expressed through behaviour, clothing, body characteristics or voice, and which may or may not conform to socially defined behaviours and characteristics typically associated with being either masculine or feminine.

Genderfluid: Someone whose gender identity and/or expression varies over time.

Gender Nonconforming: Someone whose gender identity and/or gender expression does not conform to the cultural or social expectations of gender, particularly in relation to male or female. This can be an umbrella term for many identities.

Genderqueer: Someone whose gender identity and/or expression falls between or outside of male and female.

Hormone Therapy: Also referred to as Gender Affirming Hormone Therapy (GAHT), this treatment involves taking hormones to induce physical changes that align with a person's gender identity. For transgender women, this includes taking oestrogen to promote feminising changes; for transgender men, it means taking testosterone to cause masculinising effects. The decision to use hormone therapy varies from person to person. The changes are gradual, and it usually takes months for them to become noticeable.

Intergender: Someone whose identity is between genders and/or a combination of gender identities and expressions.

Intersex: A term for people born with biological sex characteristics, such as anatomy, chromosomes, or hormones, that do not fit normative definitions for male or female bodies. These variations are natural congenital traits that can become apparent at birth, in puberty, or later in life. Intersex is a socially constructed category that reflects real biological variation, and people who are intersex can have any gender identity.

Nonbinary: A term for people whose gender identity falls outside of the traditional gender binary of male and female. This umbrella term includes people who may identify as both genders or have no gender. Nonbinary individuals may use different pronouns, the most common being they/them. Nonbinary identities are diverse and can be a blend of masculine and feminine, a gender different from both male and female, no gender at all, or a gender that changes over time.

Pangender: Someone whose identity is comprised of all or many gender identities and expressions.

Pronoun: Pronouns are words used as substitutes for nouns and have existed for a very long time. They/them are pronouns used to refer to a single person, and the use of a singular "they" is not a new concept; in fact, it dates back to the 14th century and was common in older English literature. It is a generic third-person singular pronoun to refer to a person whose gender is unknown or irrelevant to the context of the usage.

Puberty Blockers: Medications to temporarily pause the physical changes brought on by puberty through the suppression of the body's sex hormones. They are used to treat conditions that cause puberty to start too early and to treat adolescents with gender dysphoria to allow them time to explore their identity without the added stress of developing secondary sex characteristics. An important point is that the effects are temporary; puberty can restart when the medication is stopped. These medications have been the subject of controversy in several countries but have been used successfully for quite some time with children who started puberty too early (precocious puberty).

Transgender, or **trans:** Someone whose gender identity differs from the one that was assigned to them at birth. Many transgender people identify as either male or female, while others may see transgender as an umbrella term and identify as gender nonconforming or queer. How transgender people choose to express their gender is individualistic, as is their transition.

Transition: The process through which some transgender people change their gender expression to more closely resemble how they view their gender identity. This can include personal, medical, and legal steps, such as using a different name and pronouns; dressing differently; changing one's name and/or sex on legal documents; hormone therapy; or gender affirmation surgery. Some transgender people may not choose to make these changes, or only make a few. The experience is an individual one; there is no right or wrong way to transition.

Other Terms

Ally: An LGBTQ+ ally is someone who isn't part of the community but actively supports and advocates for LGBTQ+ people and their rights. Allies educate themselves on LGBTQ+ issues, speak out against discrimination and bias, and work to create a more inclusive and equitable environment for LGBTQ+ individuals. Being an ally involves more than passive support; it requires active engagement and a commitment to challenging oppression and fostering respect.

Biphobia: Prejudice, fear, hatred, discomfort, or mistrust directed at people who are bisexual, or the identity of bisexuality. It can involve harmful stereotypes, as outlined in this book, and lead to bisexual erasure.

Bisexual erasure: The dismissal and invalidation of bisexuality as an identity, often rooted in the assumption of a sexual binary (that everyone is either heterosexual or homosexual).

Chosen Family/Found Family: People who are not necessarily biologically or legally related, but have formed intentional relationships for mutual support, love, and care. A chosen family is a voluntary association built on deep personal connection and commitment.

Cis-het: This term is a blend of the words cisgender and heterosexual. It is used to refer to a person whose gender identity aligns with their sex assigned at birth, and who is sexually attracted to members of the opposite sex.

Coming Out: Short for "coming out of the closet", this is the process of figuring out and accepting one's sexual orientation and/or gender identity and sharing it with others. Coming out is a personal decision; no one should be forced to disclose their identity. As Coach Singh said to Nick, nobody owes others that information.

Comphet: Short for compulsory heterosexuality, this term describes the societal expectation that heterosexuality is the only valid sexual orientation.

Deadnaming: Referring to a transgender or nonbinary person by their birth name or a former name they no longer use, often known as a "deadname". This is harmful because it invalidates their chosen name and gender identity, causing anxiety and stress, and triggering dysphoria. If it happens accidentally, an apology and correction can go a long way to making the person feel less anxious.

Homophobia: The fear, hatred, discomfort with, or mistrust of lesbian and gay people, those with same-sex attractions or perceived same-sex attractions, resulting in negative attitudes, aversion, harassment, discrimination and violence.

Inclusive Language: Communication that avoids bias, prejudice or stereotypes, using expressions or words that do not exclude particular groups of people, identities, or experiences. Inclusive language recognises human diversity, especially regarding race, ethnicity, gender identity, sexual orientation, age, and disability, by using words and phrases that are respectful, equitable, and create a sense of belonging.

Misgender: Using names, pronouns, or other gendered terms that do not align with the person's gender identity. For example, using "she" when talking about a transgender man, or using gendered language when talking about a nonbinary person.

Transphobia: The rejection of trans identities and refusal to believe they are valid or even real. Transphobia can include fear, aversion, hatred, violence or anger towards people who do not conform to social gender roles. It results in attacks on trans rights, from attempts to remove access to gendered spaces such as bathrooms, to impacting the accessibility of gender affirming care.

Organisations supporting the LGBTQIA+ Community

Rainbow Railroad: Rainbow Railroad is a global not-for-profit organisation that helps at-risk LGBTQI+ people get to safety worldwide. Based in the United States and Canada, this organisation helps LGBTQI+ people facing persecution based on their sexual orientation, gender identity and sex characteristics. A portion of the proceeds from this book will be donated to support their work, which is currently more important than ever.

Human Rights Campaign: The Human Rights Campaign is an American LGBTQ advocacy group. It is the largest LGBTQ political lobbying organisation within the United States. HRC has a great website showing various pride flags and their meanings and resources for terminology.

GLAAD (Gay & Lesbian Alliance Against Defamation): GLAAD is an American non-governmental media monitoring organisation. Originally founded as a protest against defamatory coverage of gay and lesbian demographics and their portrayals in the media and entertainment industries, it has since expanded to queer, bisexual, and transgender people.

The Trevor Project: The Trevor Project, based in the US, is not only an organisation focused on suicide prevention efforts among non-heterosexual youth, but they also provide information and resources to understand LGBTQ+ Youth and how to best support them. They maintain a blog with content for Gay, Lesbian,

Bisexual, Transgender, and Questioning Youth and other LGBTQ Resources.

SAGE (Services & Advocacy for Gay, Lesbian, Bisexual & Transgender Elders): Focuses on improving the lives of LGBTQ+ elders through advocacy, community, and support. They work nationally and globally to protect LGBTQ+ rights, build health and longevity, and preserve the vibrancy of the community as we age.

Transgender Law Center (TLC): A trans-led organisation advocating for self-determination and liberation for transgender and gender-diverse people.

TransActual: A UK-based, trans led and run organisation focussed on working for trans adults in the UK. Their work is broad ranging, with particular focus on healthcare and trans people's legal protections.

National Center for Transgender Equality (NCTE): Advocates for Trans Equality fights for the legal and political rights of transgender people in America, with a focus on changing policies and society to increase understanding and acceptance of transgender people.

interAct, Advocates for Intersex Youth: interACT works to empower intersex youth and advance the rights of all people with innate variations in their physical sex characteristics through advocacy, public engagement and community connection.

OII Europe: Organisation Intersex International Europe (OII Europe) is the umbrella organisation of European human rights-based and intersex-led organisations. They provide a range of informational materials on intersex to read online or for download.

PFLAG: PFLAG is an LGBT advocacy organisation founded and led by friends and family of LGBT people. PFLAG is a national organisation presiding over decentralised local and regional chapters. PFLAG has nearly 400 chapters across the United States, with more than 350,000 members and supporters.

It Gets Better: It Gets Better is a nonprofit organisation with a mission to uplift, empower, and connect lesbian, gay, bisexual, transgender, and queer youth around the globe. It Gets Better has a nice glossary of terms that can be downloaded as a PDF.

All Out: A global not-for-profit organisation that is focused on political advocacy for the human rights of lesbian, gay, bisexual, transgender, queer/questioning, intersex, asexual/aromantic and all others in LGBTQIA+ communities. It was first established in 2010 as a program of Purpose Foundation, later becoming its own legal entity, Purpose Action, and finally All Out Action Fund, Inc. in 2014. All Out has staff members in Brazil, Colombia, Germany, Italy, Mexico, Kenya, Portugal, Spain, and the USA.

Global Action for Trans Equality (GATE): An organisation and think tank on gender identity, sex characteristics and bodily diversity (transgender and intersex) issues.

Human Dignity Trust: A UK-based registered charity that focuses on strategic litigation challenging the criminalisation of homosexuality around the world. Human Dignity Trust's team consists of lawyers, activists, researchers, and communications specialists who work with LGBT organisations, activists, and local attorneys worldwide to defend LGBT rights.

International Lesbian, Gay, Bisexual, Trans and Intersex Association (ILGA): An LGBTQ+ rights organisation that participates in a multitude of agendas within the United Nations, such as creating visibility for LGBTQ+ issues by conducting advocacy and outreach at the Human Rights Council, working with members to help their government improve LGBTI rights, ensuring LGBTI members are not forgotten in international law, and advocating for LBTI women's issues at the Commission on the Status of Women.

International Lesbian, Gay, Bisexual, Transgender, Queer & Intersex Youth and Student Organisation (IGLYO): An international LGBTQI organisation that was created in 1984 as a reaction to the need for better cooperation among regional, local and national LGBTQI youth and student organisations. It advocates on behalf of members to international bodies, institutions and other organisations. IGLYO is a membership-based umbrella organisation representing 95 member organisations in more than 45 countries.

The International Lesbian, Gay, Bisexual, Transgender & Intersex Law Association (ILGLaw, formerly the International Lesbian and Gay Law Association): An international association of gay, lesbian, bisexual, transgender and intersex lawyers. The group also welcomes law professors, judges, law students, paralegals and laypersons, as long as they are committed to LGBTI equality under the law.

Kaleidoscope Trust: A UK-based nonprofit organisation that campaigns for the human rights of LGBT+ people around the world. Its mission is to help create a world where LGBT+ people are free, safe and equal everywhere.

Organisation Intersex International (OII): A global advocacy and support group for people with intersex traits.

Outright International (Outright): An LGBTIQ human rights non-governmental organisation that addresses human rights violations and abuses against lesbian, gay, bisexual, transgender and intersex people. They document human rights discrimination and abuses based on sexual orientation, gender identity, gender expression and sex characteristics on a local, regional, national and international level.

Matthew Shepard Foundation: A US-based organisation focussed on combatting hate crimes against the LGBTQIA+ community. They also provide resources for LGBTQ+ youth.

George House Trust: A UK-based charity providing support, advice and information for people living with HIV.

Mental Health and Crisis Resources

Suicide.org provides global lists for suicide hotlines by state (within the US) and by country (outside of the US).

Lifeline International: An international resource with over 200 LifeLine Centres operated by 37 Members in 29 countries – and growing, working on making more suicide prevention resources available in more places.

Trans Lifeline: Provides trans peer support in the US and Canada, run by and for trans people.

Trevor Lifeline: Part of The Trevor Project's services, their lifeline offers chat, call, and text options for LGBT+ youth to reach out for help.

Befrienders Worldwide: An international network of over 90 help centres spanning the globe. Their members provide emotional support to people who are suicidal or in distress.

Crisis Text Line: USA, UK. A hotline to reach crisis counsellors in the US or the UK (available in England, Scotland, Wales, and Northern Ireland) 24/7 for free, confidential support.

Beat Eating Disorders: A UK-based eating disorder charity that has a national helpline to encourage people to seek help and provides advice for families, so they are better equipped to help their loved ones recover.

Mind: Mind works across all of England and Wales, with head offices in London and Cardiff. They provide information and support for people living with mental health problems, campaign for change, and raise awareness.

OCD UK: A UK-based organisation focussed on children and adults affected by obsessive-compulsive disorder. They provide advice, information, and support services for those affected by OCD. Everyone involved in the organisation has personal experience of OCD, either directly or through a loved one.

YoungMinds: A UK-based organisation that helps young people and their families work through mental health challenges. Their purpose is to stop young people from reaching the point of crisis.

MindOut LGBTQ Mental Health Service: A UK-based Lesbian, Gay, Bisexual, Trans & Queer Mental Health Service run by LGBTQIA+ staff who have experience with mental health. They provide a chat service for individuals aged 18 and up.

Rethink Mental Illness: A charity provider of mental health services in England, providing services and local support groups and working to raise awareness of mental health issues.

Switchboard LGBT+ Helpline: A UK-based national LGBTQIA+ support line, available to discuss anything related to sexuality and gender identity.

RAINN (Rape, Abuse & Incest National Network): Based in the USA, it is the nation's largest anti-sexual violence organisation and operator of the National Sexual Assault Hotline. RAINN's mission is to stop sexual violence by supporting survivors, holding perpetrators accountable, and creating safer communities.

Safeline (Preventing and Surviving Sexual Abuse): A UK-based specialist charity that works to prevent sexual abuse and helps those affected to cope and recover. They provide early intervention/prevention services to help prevent child sexual abuse, and counselling and therapeutic support to survivors of sexual abuse throughout England and Wales.

WPATH (World Professional Association for Transgender Health) and **EPATH (European Professional Association for Transgender Health)** are non-profit, interdisciplinary professional and educational organisations devoted to transgender health. Their website offers a provider search for medical providers, including therapists.

Participant Demographics

Below are some demographic details of all participants who submitted their stories to us, including those not published in this book.

Participant Countries:

USA: 50%
UK: 22%
EU Countries: 13%
Australia: 6%
South American Countries: 4%
Canada: 3%
Asian Countries: 1%
South Africa: 1%

Gender Identities of Participants:

Cisgeder Female: 59%
Cisgender Male: 20%
Non-binary spectrum: 10%
Transgender male: 5%
Prefer not to answer: 3%
Transgender female: 1%
Other: 1%

Participant Age Groups:

15 and under: 6%
16-18: 6%
19-25: 12%
26-30: 15%
31-35: 15%
36-40: 9%
41-45: 12%
46-50: 10%
51-55: 9%
56-60: 3%
61-70: 4%
71+: 1%

Sexual Orientation of Participants:

Due to technical constraints, participants could only select one option. Some participants identified with more than one of these labels, which is not reflected in the numbers.

Bisexual: 41%
Homosexual (gay/lesbian): 21%
Asexual spectrum (Ace, Demi, etc.): 16%
Pansexual: 8%
Heterosexual: 7%
Other: 4%
Prefer not to answer: 3%

About the authors

Rowan Murphy

Rowan is a transgender gay man in his early 50's. He is a certified life coach, passionate about empowering and guiding his clients through personal challenges, with particular focus on identity issues. Rowan grew up in Germany, studied English Literature and French Linguistics at University of Heidelberg, and recently rediscovered a love for writing. Based on his own metamorphic experience, he felt compelled to investigate the alchemy of *Heartstopper* and understand the transformative spark that motivated him and other fans to find more joy, fulfillment, and connection in their lives. By sharing these stories, he hopes to inspire more people to overcome fear, pursue happiness, and live authentically.

George Hightower

George holds a Bachelor's degree in psychology from New York University and St. John's University. He has a Master's degree in counseling psychology from the University of Santa Monica, and the focus of his postgraduate work was on personal development, human potential, and transpersonal psychology. He has devoted his life to helping others, especially those in the LGBT+ community. In addition to participating in demonstrations and advocating for medical resources for Persons With AIDS, he worked on a National Institute of Mental Health sponsored AIDS research project at Memorial Sloane Kettering Cancer Center in New York City. Heartstopper was his catalyst for a profound healing journey from life-altering trauma. George is searching for the commonality in our experiences that answers the fundamental *Heartstopper* question, why are we like this?

www.ingramcontent.com/pod-product-compliance
Lightning Source LLC
Chambersburg PA
CBHW070611030426
42337CB00020B/3760